AF651510

THE CENSUS ADMINISTRATION UNDER THE RAJ AND AFTER

Listed in over half a dozen International Who's Who's Dr. **S.R. Maheshwari** has spent the greater part of his teaching career, spanning thirty-eight years, as Professor of Political Science and Public Administration in the Indian Institute of Public Administration, New Delhi. He has also taught at the University of Rajasthan, St. Stephen's College, Delhi and Agra College.

Educated at Kanpur, Delhi and Philadelphia (USA), he has specialised in civil service systems, administrative reform, development administration and human resource development.

Among the various assignments handled by Prof. Maheshwari are: visiting fellow in France to work on the French higher civil service (1988); lecturing in senior level training programme for civil servants in China (1992); visiting research fellow at the Australian National University (1980) and Institute of Developing Economies, Tokyo (1982-83); visiting professor, University of Guelph, Canada (1987); member of the Administrative Reform Committee, Government of Uttar Pradesh (1973); honorary secretary-treasurer of the Indian Public Administration Association (1975-78); president of the Indian Public Administration Association (1989-90) and member of the executive council of the Indian Institute of Public Administration.

Prof. Maheshwari is the author of more than forty books and 200 papers published in national and overseas journals.

THE CENSUS ADMINISTRATION UNDER THE RAJ AND AFTER

SHRIRAM MAHESHWARI

CONCEPT PUBLISHING COMPANY, NEW DELHI - 110059

All rights reserved. No part of this work may be reproduced, stored in a retrieval system, or transmitted, in any form or by any means, electronic, mechanical, photocopying, recording or otherwise, without the prior written permission of the copyright owner and the publisher.

ISBN 81-7022-585-X

First Published 1996

© Shriram **Maheshwari** (*b.* 1931)

Published and Printed by

Ashok Kumar Mittal
Concept Publishing Company
A/15-16, Commercial Block, Mohan Garden
NEW DELHI - 110059
Phones : 5554042, 5504042

BIMLA

Who has given meaning to my life.

OTHER WORKS BY THE SAME AUTHOR

1. Indian Administration. Orient Longman, 1/24 Asaf Ali Road, New Delhi - 110 002.
2. The Evolution of Indian Administration, Lakshmi Narain Agrawal, Hospital Road, Agra - 3.
3. The General Election in India, Chaitanya Publishers, Allahabad.
4. Public Administration (co-author), Lakshmi Narain Agarwal, Hospital Road, Arga - 3.
5. Government Through Consultation, Indian Institute of Public Administration, New Delhi - 2.
6. The Administrative Reforms Commission, Lakshmi Narain Agarwal, Hospital Road, Agra - 3.
7. Local Government in India, Lakshmi Narain Agarwal, Hospital Road, Agra - 3.
8. The Study of Public Administration (edited), Lakshmi Narain Agarwal, Hospital Road, Agra - 3.
9. The Civil Service in Great Britain, Concept Publishing Company, H-13, Bali Nagar, New Delhi - 15.
10. President's Rule in India, Macmillan Company, Ansari Road, New Delhi.
11. State Government in India, Macmillan Company, Ansari Road, New Delhi.
12. Teaching of Public Administration in India (edited), Indian Institute of Public Administration, New Delhi.
13. Public Administration in India, Management of Change, Bangalore University, Bangalore.
14. Open Government in India, Macmillan Company, Ansari Road, New Delhi.
15. Indian Parliamentary System, Lakshmi Narain Agarwal, Hospital Road, New Delhi.
16. Administrative Reforms in India, Macmillan Company, Ansari Road, New Delhi.
17. Electoral Politics in the National Metropolis, Ritu Publishers, B-1/30, Ashok Vihar, Delhi - 52.
18. Comparative Government and Politics, Lakshmi Narain Agarwal, Hospital Road, Agra - 3.
19. Political Development in India, Concept Publishing Company,

H-13, Bali Nagar, New Delhi - 15.

20. Rural Development in India, Sage Publications, India, Pvt. Ltd., M-32, Main Market, Greater Kailash Part-I, New Delhi.
21. Higher Civil Service in Japan, Allied Publishers, 13/14, Ansari Road, New Delhi.
22. Administrative Reforms (edited), Indian Institute of Public Administration, New Delhi - 2.
23. Lok Prashashan (co-author), (in Hindi), Lakshmi Narain Agarwal, Hospital Road, Agra - 3.
24. Tulnatamak Rajniti (in Hindi), Lakshmi Narain Agarwal, Hospital Road, Agra - 3.
25. Bharat Main Sthaniya Shashan (in Hindi), Lakshmi Narain Agarwal, Hospital Road, Agra - 3.
26. Mandal Commission and Mandalisation, New Delhi, Concept, 1990.
27. The Higher Civil Service in France, New Delhi, Allied Publishers, 1991.
28. Theories and Concepts in Public Administration, New Delhi, Allied Publishers, 1991.
29. Problems and Issues in Administrative Federalism, New Delhi, Allied Publishers, 1992.
30. The Indian Administrative Year Book 1990, New Delhi, Concept Publishing Co., 1992.
31. Education in Public Administration in India, New Delhi, I.I.P.A.
32. Administrative Reforms in India, New Delhi, Jawahar Publishers & Distributors, 62/1 Bersarai, New Delhi - 110 016.
33. Indian Administration: An Historical Account, New Delhi, Jawahar Publishers & Distributors.
34. Administrative Theories, New Delhi, Allied Publishers, 1994.
35. Mandal Commission Revisited, New Delhi, Jawahar Publishers and Distributors.
36. Lok Prashashan, Agra, Lakshmi Narain Agarwal.
37. Indian Administrative System, New Delhi, Jawahar Publishers & Distributors.
38. Public Services in Canada and India (co-authorship), New Delhi, Jawahar Publishers and Distributors.
39. Uchhatar Lok Prakashan (in Hindi), Agra, Lakshmi Narain Agarwal.
40. Bhartiya Prashasan: Iska Vikas (in Hindi), Agra, Lakshmi Narain Agarwal.
41. Uchha Civil Sevayan, Delhi, Vivek Prakashan.
42. Akhil Bhartiya Sevayen, Jaipur, Panchsheel Prakashan.

PREFACE

> You and I are forever at the mercy of the census-taker and the census-maker. The impertinent fellow who goes from house to house is one of the real masters of the statistical situation. The other is the man who organises the results.
>
> — **Walter Lippmann**: 'The Golden Rule and After' *A Preface to Politics, 1914*

Census is one of the oldest activities of the Government of India, having begun in a regular way as early as in 1881. Also, it is India's single largest exercise even though it is undertaken once in ten years. Even when Great Britain discontinued the head counting in 1941 when it was engaged in war, India carried out this exercise with undiminished efficiency. Yet census has remained an unresearched area; those who have been—and are—drawn to it are generally demographers. Though it is the single largest administrative exercise it has not attracted the attention of public administrationists of the country. The present work is thus a modest attempt towards filling a gap in the public administration of the country. As it deals with the census since its beginning in the nineteenth century, it should evoke interest in all the three countries which constituted undivided India, namely, India, Pakistan and Bangladesh.

In my academic life, chance, not planning (or, preplanning, to be more precise), has shaped many decisions. I strayed into Political Science by chance. It was again sheer chance that I discovered myself in the discipline of Public Administration. In my researches too, accident, not design, has played the dominant role. After my retirement from the Indian Institute of Public Administration, I was searching for a topic for my research. It was in the course of this search behaviour that I hit upon the census as an area amply worthy of an in-depth study. I then met Amulya Ratna Nanda, the Census Commissioner, and his response was most encouraging. He readily made available all the facilities in his organisation. M. Vijayanunni, his successor, continued his support. M.K. Jain in the same office was most cooperative in carrying out of research. K. S. Natarajan was equally helpful. The major research for the work was conducted in the National Archives of India. I am deeply thankful to all of them—and many more—who have helped me in various ways in completing the study. A word of caution here is necessary. None except myself is responsible for any inaccuracies that might have crept into the work.

14 January 1996
Makar Sankranti

S.R. MAHESHWARI

CONTENTS

1

INTRODUCTORY

The word 'census' comes from the Latin 'censere', which means 'to assess', 'to rate', 'to estimate'. Census is the numbering of people. The Webster's Dictionary defines it as an official enumeration of the population, with details as to age, sex, occupation, etc. Census has a long history behind it, being primarily used for purpose of taxation. Kautilya's *Arthasastra*, written around 321-296 B.C., laid stress on census taking as a measure of State policy for purpose of taxation. Census is discussed comprehensively in his chapter thirty-five dealing with the duty of the revenue collector. While defining his functions Kautilya writes: 'He shall also keep an account of the number of young and old men that reside in each house, their history (*charitra*), occupation (*ajiva*), income (*aya*) and expenditure (*vyaya*) . . . They (*spies* specially deputed by him) shall also find out the causes of emigration and immigration of persons of migratory habit, the arrival and departure of men and women of condemnable (*anarthya*) character, as well as the movements of (*foreign*) spies.'[1] In ancient Rome, too, census was first conducted for purpose of taxation. Originally, thus, census and taxation were virtually inseparable.

With the passage of time, more benefits of census came to be known. Census yielded accurate information on various facts of people's life and thus became a valuable tool for socio-economic policy-making and planning. In modern times, it has become a periodic exercise, generally undertaken every ten years. A census of the population has been taken every tenth year since 1790 in the United States of America. France introduced census in 1791 and Great Britain in 1811. In Ireland the earliest census was taken in 1813, since then it has been taken simultaneously with that of Great Britain.

Reliable data of India's population in ancient times are not available. Perhaps, this reflected the Indians' cultural disinclination to record and maintain historical facts. Speculative assessment of India's population has nevertheless been attempted, broadly based on socio-economic factors prevailing at a given time and assuming that population size was a function of the stage of civilisation reached. Evidence exists confirming advanced urban civilisation in the Indus Valley around 3000 B.C.—1500 B.C. The Aryan civilisation, which followed later around 1500 B.C. to 600 B.C., was clearly supportive of growing population. According to the *Rigveda*, the population was scanty and was living in small villages. The *Ramayana* refers to a sprawling countryside still uninhabited. But the *Mahabharata* provides impressions of a populous land. Chandragupta Maurya (320 B.C.) had an army of no less than 700,000 men, which leads to a safe surmise that a substantial population alone could have supported such a large army.

Quantitative estimates of India's population in different periods of time have been made by modern scholars. Pran Nath has estimated that around 300 B.C. it was between 100 and 140 million. The figure remained more or less the same around A.D. 1600 during Akbar's reign. In the medieval period (A.D. 500 to 1800) India's population was in a plateau. The social fabric was feudalistic and science and technology were stagnant. Wars were also frequent. These conditions were not conducive to the growth of population. W.H. Moreland estimated India's population at 100 million in A.D. 1600. Kingsley Davis places the figure at 125 million, A. Das Gupta at 135 million, and Jatindra Mohan, too, at 135 million.

Table 1.1 giving estimates of India's population at different times has been prepared by Country Monograph Services of the United Nations Economic and Social Commission for Asia and the Pacific:

TABLE 1.1

Year	Population (million)	Author
300 B.C.	100-140	Pran Nath
A.D. 1600	100	W.H. Moreland
	125	Kingsley Davis
	135	A. Das Gupta
	110	J.M. Datta
	140	John D. Darnand
A.D. 1750	125	Kingsley Davis
A.D. 1800	207	P.C. Mahalanobis and D. Bhattacharya

It is only when one comes to the period of British rule that the use of the term 'census' for population count in India is fully justified. The British came to India for trade, but stayed to rule. This transition passed through three broad phases. The trading role commenced when Queen Elizabeth I granted the Charter to the East India Company in 1600, and continued undiluted till 1765. In that year, in addition to trade, the Company began to perform the ruler's role as well. The trading concern came to an end in 1833 when the Company's commercial role was terminated and it emerged as India's ruler. In 1857, after Indians unsuccessfully revolted against the British rule, direct control of the British Crown was established all over India. The East India Company was wound up, after an existence of 357 years.

Among the first concerns of Great Britain in the role of direct ruler of India was to find out its population. The Government in India was asked by London in July 1856 to organise a census, but the census could not be held on account of the armed uprising of 1857. The matter was taken up by India in the 1860s with the return of peace. Census was taken in the North-Western Provinces (the present U.P.) in January 1865, in the Central Provinces and Berar in November 1866, in Bihar in 1867, and in the Punjab in January 1868. Censuses of the cities of Madras, Bombay and Calcutta were taken in 1863, 1864 and 1866 respectively.

In 1865, the Government of India and the Government in London agreed on the principle that a census should be taken in 1871. As a result, between 1867 and 1872 censuses were conducted in as much of the country as was then practicable. Though these were based on a uniform set of schedules, they were not centrally supervised or compiled. This series of censuses is commonly known as the census of 1872. It was not, however, a synchronous census nor did it cover all the areas of India.

The first regular all-India census was taken in 1881. Since then it has been organised without interruption every tenth year. Not even in 1941 was it suspended in view of the Second World War, though the head count was suspended in Britain itself. India conducted the head count in those troubled times, thanks to the special pleading for its holding by M.W.M. Yeatts, the Census Commissioner for 1941. Neither did popular agitations seek to obstruct census taking. The census of 1921 took place amidst Mahatma Gandhi's non-cooperation movement, but the Mahatma himself made a historic pronouncement in favour of cooperation with the census.[2]

Though the focus of the present work is not on the number of heads in India, Table 1.2 is given to show the country's population ever since the census of 1872.

The actual census operation is virtually casting a net over the entire country, each mesh in the net being a block in the charge of an enumerator. The census system is a combination of the simultaneous (until 1931) and the spread-over-a-period system (since 1941). Each enumerator covers his area and fills in the schedule, keeping it ready till the census night. At the appointed hour, each enumerator goes round checking his list,

TABLE 1.2

Year	Population	
1872	20,61,52,360	
1881	25,38,96,330	
1891	28,43,14,671	
1901	29,43,61,056	
1911	31,51,56,396	
1921	31,89,42,480	
1931	35,28,37,778	
1941	38,89,97,955	
1951	35,68,79,394	(After the creation of Pakistan)
1961	43,92,34,771	
1971	54,79,49,809	
1981	68,33,24,097	
1991	84,63,02,688	

making such additions or omissions as may be necessary. In the case of persons travelling, checks are maintained at railway stations and returns are obtained from hotels, etc. Tramps, *fakirs,* cave dwellers and vagrants are all counted; in the words of an old patwari, 'we must catch every man'.[3] The houseless population has always been counted on the night of 28 February to 1 March—a practice which has remained unchanged since the first census of 1881.

From the very beginning a skeleton plan of census had been outlined consisting of the following parts. First, census of population of India was necessary and was to be undertaken. Second, a district was to be sub-divided into smaller units, coterminous with lower revenue divisions, identifying each village, hamlet and house. Thirdly, no new agency was to be created for holding census but instead, an existing agency with which the people of India were already well familiar was to be used for censusing. Fourth, so much information as could be entered before the actual taking of the census was entered in the census papers. A census was supposed to collect information on age, sex, civil condition, literacy, language, occupation, etc. Specialised information was to be sought by expert bodies especially set up. Finally, the results of the counting were compiled into convenient form. For this, an officer was to be especially appointed and given special instructions.

The ball is set rolling with house numbering. The house-list is required for three main purposes. First, it is wanted to correct the estimate of the number of schedules in each language required in each tehsil or taluk and municipality which are provisionally drawn up on the basis of the last census figures. Secondly, a house-list is required as a basis on which the various tehsils and municipalities may be divided into uniform blocks. In municipalities, the chairman is always made the charge officer. Thirdly, extract from the house-list is copied into the block lists which every enumeration block contains and serves as a chief guide to the enumerators in the preliminary and final census. Thus, the house-list is the basis of the whole census operation, and too much care cannot be bestowed upon its preparation and upon checking and correcting it until it is as accurate as it is possible to make it.

The smallest unit in census administration is the block, containing from 30 to 50 houses, in charge of an enumerator. Its size depends on the number of houses for which the enumerator can reasonably be expected to carry out the final enumeration between 7 p.m. and midnight of 28 February—1 March. There is an advantage in having small blocks if a sufficient number of enumerators is available. Next above the block comes the circle, containing 10 to 15 blocks or above 500 houses, under a supervisor who is responsible for the work of all the enumerators in his circle. The size of a circle is determined by the number of villages for which the supervisor can thoroughly check the preliminary enumeration during the last week or so before the final enumeration. The third and largest census unit is the charge, a group of circles, under a charge superintendent who exercises general supervision over the census operations and tests as large a proportion as possible of the work of his subordinates. A district is divided into charges and circles by the district collector.

The first general census in India was held in 1881. But a beginning had been made by holding head count in individual provinces. This was a sensible device as it provided to the rulers the valuable experience of organising census in an entirely different culture. Wild imaginations were excited by the novelty of a census under the British rule, by the elaborate preparations made for it, and above all, by the mystery of it being conducted at night. At places, there was alarm leading to emigration across the border and concealment of girls. But no violence marked the people's behaviour.

The censusing principle is based on the actual house-to-house enumeration being made on the same day (or to be more correct, night) throughout the country, distinguishing all the people enumerated, originally, into adults and minors, men and women and also according to their castes and professions. In other words, census is information gathering about the people from the people themselves. The information collected was on certain common points and these, in the beginning, were four: age, sex, caste and occupation. In India, returns on age, caste and occupation were glaringly unreliable, so much so that W.C. Plowden said in 1881: 'it is doubtful whether the age statements at the next succeeding census will show any improvement upon the present'.[4] The exact age was seldom known to the respondents themselves.

Catching every person entails a massive organisation. The structure of this organisation is given in Chart 1.

Chart 1

Functionary

Census Commissioner for India
↓
Superintendents of Census Operations
↓
District Officers
↓
Sub Divisional or Tehsil Officer
↓
Revenue Circle, Pargana
↓
Village Patwari

The district is the main unit of administration in India, and the census builds its census chain to fit in with the administrative chain. Both authority and economy counsel such an arrangement. By inducting the district collector, subdivisional officer, tehsildar and patwari into the census work the latter is enabled to bask in the traditional authority of the revenue administration. The arrangement is economical too because these functionaries become links in the census chain without payment. It is also true that the quality of enumeration in rural areas is much better; in contrast, enumeration in urban areas always presents difficulties.

Enumerators have been the linch pin of censusing. The enumerator is a tail-ender in the census hierarchy, and he came from a variety of backgrounds. In the beginning, the Government of India tried the police as the census enumerating agency. But police in India is notorious for its image as an agency of coercion, and strict control over it became necessary. The official memorandum issued at the time of the 1871 census said: 'The police should be strictly prohibited from entering houses without permission. They should call at each door and ask for the information.' This experience was not happy and the police was as a rule kept out of census work. The patwari was the preferred enumerator. In the words of a deputy commissioner (1869) 'the patwaris are the most useful agency for taking a census and it would suffice to employ them'. Even after Independence, patwari continued to be the trusted enumerator in rural India for some time.

India's experience with volunteers for census duty has not been happy. The employment of volunteers resulted in the census work being full of errors as they did not take the enumeration responsibilities seriously. The census of Oudh in 1869 made use of the voluntary agency of landholders, their agents, bailiffs and such like persons. A.O. Hume, in history famous as the founder of the Indian National Congress, was in 1869 the district collector of Etawah and in his report on the census of Etawah, he emphatically condemned the agency of volunteers. He wrote:

> As it was, all the papers were ready and had been fully filled in by patwaris, schoolmasters, etc., and had been thoroughly tested by responsible officials before the date fixed. All the volunteer enumerators had to do was to go round from house to house and see that at the hours fixed the houses really contained the exact numbers entered in their lists, or if not, make the necessary corrections. Yet several of them gave in their papers unverified, some scratched them all over with hieroglyphics, some lost, and most dirtied them. Luckily, we placed no great dependence on them, and the next morning all the doubtful ones were looked up and re-tested or re-drawn.[5]

An indispensable aid in the planning of a census is a calendar or time-table indicating the sequence and estimated duration of each of the component operations of the census. The census calendars are essential. They indicate the dates on which each of the operations, which make up the census, are to be started and completed. They serve as tools to measure the progress of each stage of the census operation.

The census bureaucracy required is huge and sprawling. The lower level field bureaucracy in the 1901 census comprised 9872 tabulators, 122,503 supervisors and 1,325,478 enumerators. In the 1931 census, the charge superintendents were 10,068, supervisors 1,65,093 and enumerators 2,023,516. Ten years later, in the census of 1941, the respective numbers were 14,628, 1,41,152 and 1,056,856. In the census of 1951 (held after the country's partition), their numbers were 9,854, 80,006 and 5,93,518. The 1991 census pressed into service no less than 15 lakhs enumerators and 3 lakh supervisors.

The paper work entailed in census taking is enormous. Right from the beginning in 1881, schedules and forms are printed in different languages. J.A. Baines, the Census Commissioner for India in 1891, gives an account of the scale of preparation made for the 1891 census. As he mentions :

> The standard rules had been sanctioned and circulated so that the local officers could start on the work of translation and printing, and for this 17 languages were selected. The census superintendent, in his turn was issuing his general instructions, and the district level functionaries were mapping out their charges for purposes of enumeration, and estimating the number of schedules required for use in each subdivision specifying the languages and even the character in which each indent should be printed and arranging for their circulation throughout the subdivision from the nearest railway station.

Speaking of the scale and volume of the work involved, Baines mentions in his Report on the 1891 census that 'about 290 tonnes of paper were used for the schedules, and just under a million men and boys were employed as enumerators'.[6] He continues:

> In a country where only about 11 males in the hundred can read and write at all, and the standard of that accomplishment is by no means a high one, the difficulty of finding enough competent men was got over by the adoption of a plan tried with success in 1881, namely, that of entering before hand in the schedules the whole of the domiciled population of the place and merely bringing it up-to-date on the night of enumeration.[7]

Baines rightly concluded: 'The census of India is the heaviest enterprise of the kind that has ever been undertaken, especially as the final enumeration of over 250 millions of people was carried out within four hours'.[8] Since then, the paper work has increased tremendously as have other tasks. The cost of the 1931 census was Rs. 48 million, or Rs. 12 per 1,000 persons enumerated. The cost of the previous census (1921) was Rs. 14 per 1,000 persons.

The census in India was *de facto* but since 1941 it became *de jure*. That is to say, that instead of recording the actual individuals found during the prescribed hours of enumeration through the area censused, the census should record the individuals normally located in every dwelling place in that area together with all nomads who have no fixed dwelling. By adopting *de jure* census it was possible to reduce the number of enumerators by giving to each a bigger area. This change, on the other hand, added force to the demand for payment and further aggravated the disinclination to take on the enumeration work at all.

From the very beginning, public policy had been to appoint as supervisors government officials. This is because much depends on their adequately checking the work done by enumerators. Insistence on supervisors being government officials flows from the thought that they must be amenable to government discipline. Enumerators were usually persons of the class of patwaris or clerks in government offices. The superintendent of census operations, Madras (now Tamil Nadu) wrote in 1910 that the census supervisors were drawn from departments like land revenue, salt and *abkari*, registration, public work, civil courts, forest, survey, settlement, education, local fund, medicine, vaccination and court of wards. For enumerators the necessary qualification was the ability to read and write.

The practice followed for enumeration was this. Almost everywhere in the rural areas the patwaris themselves wrote up the preliminary record for all the blocks in their circles and the enumerators went round and checked it on the night of the census. This system produced records which in most cases were almost perfect except when there was some difficulty in understanding instructions. In towns where the land records staff was not available for census work the results were inferior to those in rural areas.

Census comprises two broad stages—enumeration and compilation. The first might be said to be catching the men, and the second, counting them. The catching is an affair of a system: One has got to make a net to cover the whole country and it is a minor matter how many questions are asked. But in counting, one is in a different field, for here every count we make costs money. It is but logical that the same officer should do both, which would incidentally be convenient as well as economical. One must also note that enumeration is much the more vital stage in the census. Once the enumeration is over and the schedules reach the responsible hands, the census commissioner at the headquarters could control the whole operation and thus ensure authenticity. The enumeration period could be put at 18 months. Yeatts, the Census Commissioner for 1941, wrote:

> I could control the tabulation even if the census superintendent had to be recalled to service elsewhere; I could, for example, have the tabulation done in Delhi under my own eye. But I cannot, and no census commissioner ever could, run the enumeration of a province. It is the enumeration that produces the information that is tabulated, and therefore, the importance of a first-class provincial control at this stage becomes evident.

Yeatts concluded:

> Once again, with a possibly wearisome but I think, necessary iteration, I would impress the fact that the Indian census is not like a European census, conducted by forms which are filled up by householders: it is carried out through a small army of men whose efficiency, diligence, uprightness and standing reflect the quality of their chief, the census superintendent.[9]

In the census of 1872 in the North-Western Provinces, the inequality of the sexes was well marked. The proportion per thousand was 533 males to 467 females: the females rising to 479 among Muslims and falling to 424 among Hindus. Females were thus more numerous among Muslims than Hindus and among the lower castes than higher ones. The disparity was considered to be mainly due to the wide prevalence of female infanticide, which implied not merely active deprivation of life but also neglect and disregard in the rearing of girls.

Rumours were rampant with earlier exercises at population counting. One was that Government wished to find out how many men were aged thirty, who would be fit for the Afghan war; another, that a noted criminal had escaped and the census was a stratagem to catch the offender; third, that the Russians were advancing and the object of the enumerations was to ascertain the numbers that would be opposed to their approach. Suspicions were in general raised by specific enquiries and answers were generally influenced by the suspected motives of Government. Thus, the enquiry for the first time on the number of families was regarded as preliminary to revive the obsolete hearth-tax. The Gujars of Hoshiarpur went so far as to break up their hearths on the day of the census. Recording of sex and age led to the hurried marriage of girls, as it was believed that soldiers were wanted for the Kabul campaign and young wives for the British soldiers. Other rumours were that a search was being made for a lost child of the British Queen or the Imam Mehdi; that Government was about to transfer a part of Madras and Bengal populations to the Punjab; that the rain was not allowed to fall till the census was over, lest it should wash off the house numbers; and that the numbering of people was unlucky and the deaths which followed the preliminary records were due to this cause. Nor was enumeration at those earlier path-finding activities entirely free from societal biases and prejudices. For instance, the birth or death of a female child in certain parts of India was not considered a very significant matter. The Report of 1881 Census had the following to observe: 'The truth is that the great bulk of enumerators have been singularly obtuse in comprehending the fact that the counting of females was a matter of any importance in census work.' The Census Commissioner for India noted, 'To understand how this is, we must take into account the low estimation in which females are held in this country (India) and also the reticence of the people on all matters connected with their female relatives.'[10]

The attitude of the people towards census was one of plain indifference even in the 1901 counting. It was feared that census was to lead to fresh taxation. As the magistrate of Darbhanga (now in Bihar) wrote after the 1901 census:

> The enumeration was recognised as a whim of the Sarkar in which there was no particular harm, even if, to their minds, little good. There were rumours of course—there are few things in this country about which there are not rumours. Naturally, recent events connected them with the war and the plague; that the males were to be sent to fight; that plague was to be introduced to thin out the people where they were too dense or in another variation, to adjust the balance between white and brown, in consequence of the losses of the former in battle, were all reports that were brought to notice.[11]

The educated, however, regarded both the census and the suspicions with amusement. A curious illustration is supplied by an original comedy entitled 'Census' which was performed at Lahore for several nights in succession to crowded houses by a travelling company of Parsis. The piece, played with considerable comic power, was immensely enjoyed by the audience.

With the passage of time, references to public reaction showed a definite decline and it may be assumed that suspicion died a natural death and the operations were regarded by the masses at the worst as a whim of the Government. Famines and epidemics and political agitation continued occasionally to affect census operations but no serious sustained obstruction was presented.

The Indian census is sometimes described as 'amateur', on account of its dependence on voluntary effort drafted for census work. This was the tenor of the debates in the Central Legislative Assembly when it finally passed the Census Act, 1941. M.W.M. Yeatts felt chagrinned by such remark and called it 'unfortunate'. In his Note of 23 November 1939, he observed:

> It is unfortunate that there should have been such play made on the alleged 'amateur' nature of the Indian Census, both by unofficial members and the Government spokesmen. Actually, I doubt if there is better enumeration anywhere in the world

> than in the villages of our better provinces, and it is, for example, much superior to anything produced in the majority of the USA States. It cannot be too strongly emphasised that no elaborate super structure of theoretical treatment can make up for doubtful original enumeration and, as an administrative feat, the Indian Census, far from being 'amateur', is a major performance and recognised as such outside this country. It is a pity that Government spokesmen accepted a term of which the last has not been heard. The unfortunate census commissioner can be quite sure that this word 'amateur' will be thrown up frequently in the future.[12]

Among the prerequisites of the success of census is the closest cooperation and consultation between the Centre and the Provinces. The basic idea of the census is that at the enumeration stage, the people with local knowledge and responsibility get together and arrange all such appointments so as to produce the maximum of convenience along with efficiency. The census legislation deliberately and properly reposed the power of appointments as census officers in the provincial governments. After all is said and done, the fact remains that, to quote Yeatts, 'no census is better than the people of the country and its level is determined by them'.[13]

Indian census enjoyed a rare international reputation, evidenced by the fact that it used to be consulted on this matter by many countries such as Ceylon (Sri Lanka), Burma (Myanmar), Malaya, etc. This meant a growing contact of Indian census with other countries. These contacts were of interest to India itself as an opportunity to influence the lines of enquiry in these countries. Especially considering that all these countries contained some Indian population, such contacts were welcome. Around 1945, China, considering how best to take a census, consulted India. India was the obvious country to consult, Britain and the United States being far less relevant to Chinese conditions of life and administration. In the international eyes, India has always been perceived as an advanced country in matters of censusing.

REFERENCES

1. R. Shamasastry: *Kautilya's Arthasastra,* Mysore, Wesleyan Press, 1929, 3rd ed., p. 159.
2. See *Census of India*, Vol. V — Bengal and Sikkim, Part III—Administrative Volume by W.H. Thompson, Superintendent of Census Operations, Bengal, 1923, p. 28.

3. Government of India's Press Release, 13 February 1939.
4. The Census Report for 1881, p. 467.
5. The Report on the Census of Oudh, Vol. I — General Report, 1869, p. 20.
6. 1891 Census of India, Part I, General Report, p. 283.
7. *Ibid.*
8. *Ibid.*, p. 287.
9. Government of India — *Home-Public* F45/27/39.
10. The Census Report for 1881, p. 54.
11. Report on the Census of Bengal, 1901, Administrative Volume, pp. 37-38.
12. Government of India — F 45/12/38-Public, p. 13.
13. Government of India — *Home-Public* F 45/11/41.

2

GENESIS OF CENSUS IN INDIA

The idea of taking the census of India's population had been in the minds of the colonial rulers for a long time. As long ago as 1856, the Government of India began considering the means by which a general census of the country's population might be taken in 1861. Evidence exists of census activity in British India from even earlier times. For example, in the senior province, Madras, there is on record a computation mentioned by the Court of Directors in 1687, and between 1800 and 1872 the province saw more census attempts than one per decade. Characteristically, the famous Sir Thomas Munro turns out to have been pioneer in this line also and the enumeration in 1822 was carried out on a form devised by him for a census taking in 1802. Between 1813 and 1850, a three-yearly count was carried out along with the determination of the land revenue for the year, and in 1850 a five-yearly sequence began which was absorbed in 1872 into the all-India series.

It was, however, in 1856 in a despatch of the East India Company that the proposal for a general census all over India and its underlying principles was first laid down. The despatch said:

> The practice of taking a census of the population every ten years prevails not only in Great Britain but also in the United States of America, and in some of the countries on the continent of Europe, and we see no reason why the enumeration of the people should take place more frequently in India. But we attach much importance to the manner in which the work is accomplished, and are very desirous that the census should be made upon a system and at the same period for the entire country under our administration. The next general census of our Indian territories may be taken in 1861 to correspond with the next census of Great Britain, and thence forward at intervals of ten years.[1]

The Government of India was consequently considering the holding of the census in 1861, but the 'mutiny' —or the first war of Indian independence—broke out in 1857. The subject was naturally laid aside, but only temporarily. On the restoration of peace and tranquillity in the country, the discussion of the question was resumed and the Government of India arrived at the conclusion that it would not be prudent to undertake a general enumeration of the people so soon after the violent disturbance by which a great portion of India had recently been agitated and from which it was not quite free in all parts even yet. Could there, then, be a partial census in some parts of India? The view taken was that such a partial census would carry 'small value'. Therefore, it was recommended to the Secretary of State that the undertaking might be postponed. He concurred with this view.

The next initiative came from Bombay. In 1863 the Bombay Legislative Council passed a Bill for taking a census of that Presidency. The Government of India signified its assent to the proposal, at the same time drawing attention to the correspondence that had taken place with the London Government on the subject. The London Government, however, disallowed the census proposed by Bombay Province but at the same time requested the Government of India to consider whether it would be expedient to pass a law for taking a general census of the population of India.

The Government of Bengal, too, revived the proposal for a general census.[2] It urged that the considerations which led to the postponement of the census of 1861 no longer existed, and that the want of anything like even an approximate knowledge of the population was acutely felt in every Department of the Government. The Government of India concurred with the proposal and submitted it to the London Government for final clearance, with the condition that when the time approached, the measure would, if necessary, be suspended, as it was in 1859. The Secretary of State for India, Sir Charles Wood, fell in line with the recommendation. Meanwhile, a census of the population of the North-Western Provinces (present U.P.) was taken in January 1865 and that of the Central Provinces in November 1886.[3]

Armed with the London Government's approval, the Government of India embarked on a process of consultation with the provincial governments. Some provinces were opposed to the plan of enumerating the population 'of all-India at the same time'. The suggestion was that a census of each province should be taken separately and that not till every province had been separately subjected to the process and all had become accustomed to it by experience, should a simultaneous census for all-India be made. The North-Western Provinces wanted to spread the census over two years.

The Government of India appreciated the objections against simultaneous census in 1871, and the final decision accommodated the provincial concerns. The census could be held in the same week or month. The two-year length of the census, as demanded by the North-Western Provinces, was however, termed 'simply mischievous'. The Government of India's decision was:

> The Government of India does not think it absolutely necessary to have the census taken throughout the Empire on one and the same night, and that in Bengal, where no previous census has been taken, permission has been given to protract the census, if necessary, during the whole season; but the Government still wishes to have the imperial census as far synchronous as possible, and hopes that His Honour (*i.e.,* the Lieutenant-Governor of North-Western Provinces) will be able to fix some date in November for the whole North-Western Provinces. If there should happen to be any particular administrative advantages likely to accrue, no great objection would be raised to the census of some few districts being taken a few days before, and a few others some days after, the general census; but so far as may be practicable, this should be avoidable.[4]

The final decision was, thus, in favour of a simultaneous census for the entire province. The year chosen was 1871, and the day, the first of January. It was clarified: 'All that was intended is that the census should be made upon system and at the same time', *i.e.* some time in 1871, the time to be determined in each province by the local authorities. No object would be served by taking the census all over India in one night, but there was a great object in getting a census of all provinces 'at the same period' for a particular year. The Viceroy concluded: 'The view would meet the somewhat shadowy difficulties urged above.'[5]

The general census of 1871 was preceded by isolated census exercises in individual provinces. A census was held in the North-Western Provinces (present U.P.) in 1865. The province of the Punjab had also organised a census. The experience gathered, the forms used and the procedures adopted were of enormous value in the all-India census planned for 1871. Forms were developed for general adoption throughout India as it was desirable to secure uniformity for the purpose of facilitating comparison of the statistics of one part of India with that of another. The Secretary of State of India meanwhile desired that 'the Local (*i.e.* provincial) Governments should use every effort to familiarise the minds of the people—who might be likely to regard with suspicion a measure, the purport of which they do not fully understand—with the idea of a census to be taken sooner or later in the province or district in which they may be residing'. Provincial Governments were consequently invited to express their opinions on the census. 'The consensus was in favour of holding a census but not all provinces concurred with the plan of simultaneous census taking. One related view was that it was more important to get trustworthy provincial returns'[6] whether these were severally taken on the same date or even in the same year was quite immaterial. It was important that the census of each district and probably of each entire province, should be on the same day; but for the whole Empire, it did not really matter whether the census was a year or two earlier, or a year or two later.

The Missionary Initiative

Meanwhile, a demand for census emanated from an altogether unexpected quarter. On 10 January 1866, John Murdoch, who was educational agent to the Christian Vernacular Educational Society, a missionary organisation, wrote to the Viceroy of India highlighting the need for an 'educational census of India as well as of a general census in the country'. He wrote: 'With some diffidence I beg also to allude to the want of, what has been so often felt, a general census of India'. Murdoch referred to the 'existing practice in the Government of India of publishing commercial statistics, which was of great value. The utility of commercial statistics and of educational statistics (if collected) will much increase by a tolerably correct account of the population.' He observed: 'Without it [the census], the relative consumption per head of each article cannot be calculated. A census would also be useful for many other purposes, *e.g.* to ascertain the comparative amount of crime in the different divisions of India'. 'A census in a simple form might be taken without much trouble or expense. In most parts of India the Government organisation is so complete that information can be obtained with little difficulty. Perhaps in some cases the aid of the police would be available'. Murdoch regarded the year 1866 as a 'fitting time' for the census. India was already in such a state of transition that, as in France, a census could be taken quinquennially with advantage. He discounted all fear of violence and disorder accompanying a general census. In the Punjab, he pointed out, a census was twice taken without any evil consequences. 'The people are now so accustomed to what they consider our vagaries, that a general census, quietly taken, should excite little notice.'

The Government's reaction to this proposal was, however, hardly heartening. It gave a laconic reply: 'The Governor-General-in-Council is unable to entertain the proposal for a general census in the present year'.[7]

As said earlier, individual provinces were going ahead and holding census in their respective areas. March was thought the best month for the exercise. It was proposed that the night of numbering should be a moonlit night. The following heads were suggested for collecting information:

I (a) Number of enclosures
  (b) Number of houses
II (a) Men
  (b) Boys (12 years of age and under)
  (c) Women
  (d) Girls (12 years of age and under)
III (a) Hindus
  (b) Mohamedans.

Preparation for the All-India Census of 1881

The final decision having been taken in 1867 to hold an all-India census in 1871, between 1867 and 1872 censuses were taken in as much of the country as practicable. The Government of Berar carried out its census in 1867, the Punjab in 1868, the North-Western Provinces in 1865 and Oudh in 1869. This series of censuses in commonly known as the census of 1871-72 or simply 1872. In what follows is described the manner of head-counting organised in the Punjab, the North-Western Provinces. and Oudh.

Census of the Punjab, 1855 and 1868

The Punjab had its first ever census in 1855, and the second in 1868. Neither of these censuses, on account of their shortfalls and gaps, can strictly be called scientific. In 1855, no preliminary record was prepared, and the entire enumeration was completed on the night of the census (1 January 1855) itself. Neither in 1855 nor in 1868 was any attempt made to record particulars separately for each person enumerated. On both occasions, the enumerator merely ascertained from the head of the house how many children, youths and adults of each sex were sleeping under his roof, whether as members of the family or as visitors.

Census of the North-Western Provinces, 1865

The North-Western Provinces has a long history of censusing. The first attempt at census in the province was made in 1852—five years before the uprising of 1857. A few enumerations were held even earlier, though these were more or less conjectural: in these population estimating exercises the actual population of a small area used to be counted, and on the data thus ascertained, the number of the remaining inhabitants was estimated.

The Census of 1852 was the first regular house-to-house counting of all the people in the Province at one fixed time—namely the night of 31 December 1852. It was the intention of the Government to repeat this exercise at ten-yearly intervals. But then came the uprising of 1857, a destructive famine and pestilence. In 1863 it was decided to make a fresh enumeration of the people. In 1865 W.C. Plowden was entrusted with the responsibility of holding the provincial census and writing the report. Plowden's report brought him reputation as an excellent census administrator. The report was rated as being 'of unusual value and interest' and won him encomiums from all quarters, including the highest. Lieutenant-Governor Thomason, commending his work to the Government of India wrote:

> The Lieutenant-Governor cordially thanks and commends Mr. Plowden for the work he has done, and His Honour trusts that His Excellency (*i.e.* the Governor-General) will also acknowledge his services and concede to him a substantial token of his satisfaction at the manner in which he has carried out the duties entrusted to him.[8]

For purposes of census, the existing revenue territorial divisions were adopted, the lowest unit being the block. A block containing an average of a hundred houses, was entrusted to an enumerator who carried out at leisure the preliminary census of his tract. As the preliminary census was taken beforehand, ample time was left for supervision and check. The preliminary returns were carefully tested on the spot by supervisors, each supervisor having under him from ten to twenty enumerators. The returns were then subjected to a second check by government officials.

Errors having thus been eliminated as far as possible, the returns were redistributed to the enumerators. On the census night, *i.e.* 10 January 1865, each enumerator compared the entries in his return with the actual facts. The returns were finally collated and compared in the offices first of the tehsildar and afterwards of the district collector by whom they were furnished upward, namely, to the Board of Revenue, which was the agency responsible for conducting the census. The conduct of the census in the North-Western Provinces under the overall charge of the Board of Revenue was a time-honoured practice. The first attempt at census in 1853 too was put under immediate supervision of the Board of Revenue. These formed the ground work of the census report.

The preliminary enumeration was completed in the early winter months of 1864 and the double testing—first by supervisors and next by the district functionaries—was over by the end of 1864. The returns were again checked and altered to tally with facts as existing on the night of 10 January 1865. In 1865, the population of the North-Western Provinces stood at 30,110,615, with nearly 26 million of them Hindus and 4 million Muslims. The enumerating and supervisory personnel came from the career hierarchies of the province.

From the outset, the legendary institution of the revenue administration, the bottom-level functionary being the patwari, was being utilised. The partwari, the all-too familiar figure in rural India, was mobilised as an enumerator and the higher revenue functionaries for supervisory and administrative duties. The Census Report of the North-Western Provinces for the year 1865 has the following to say:

> The machinery for the enumeration is ready at hand, and not untried in statistical investigations. In the village accountants (patwaris) is to be found an agency for collecting information acquainted with the circumstances and the residents of the several villages and accustomed to enquiries of a similar nature.[9]

Census has always observe the principle of areal base of organisation ('organisation by place' according to Luther Gulick). For the purpose of census, the North-Western Provinces were territorially divided, the lowest unit being the village. Every village, every hamlet, every urban locality (mohalla) had an enumerator assigned to it. In rural areas the patwari was deployed for head counting. In urban areas, the *mohalladars* or other respectable inhabitants were made enumerators. The numbering of each enclosure or *ahata* in the block was the preliminary step. Simultaneously, also were entered the names of heads of each family excluding strangers, travellers and casual visitors.

These returns were then tested by the tehsildar. Provision was made for re-testing also which, as already mentioned, was spread over the whole cold season of 1864. On account of the rigorous testing, as the Report on the Census of the North-Western Provinces (1865) claimed 'in no single instance' was a faulty return found.[10]

Holding of the census on the single night of 10 January 1865 naturally required a very large establishment. Tehsildars had already prepared the list of all enumerators. All were at their posts at the end of the first week of January. From 8 to 15 January, no one employed for census work was allowed to leave. The final operation of counting was completed during the night of 10 January 1865. The enumeration schedules were immediately submitted to the tehsil where they were scrutinised. From here the papers were submitted to the sudder office 'previous to the preparation of the returns now submitted'.[11]

The census of 1865 went ahead without any marked popular resistance, much less hostility to head-counting. The machinery of enumeration had already been tested in 1853 and thus gained experience. Nor was the census an absolute novelty and thus excited little suspicion in the people. The Report on the census asserted:

> The patwaris, who formed our chief agency, are a much more intelligent body of men than formerly; and the people have not now the slightest suspicion regarding the motives of Government in ordering the census to be taken, and consequently show no disposition to conceal facts: and I have, therefore, every reason to think the work was carried out with the greatest amount of accuracy which it was possible to obtain.[12]

Census of Oudh, 1860 and 1869

Oudh was annexed to the British Empire in India in 1856, and an immediate need was to assess its population. In 1860 the Government of India asked the Oudh Government to do this. The latter in turn asked its divisional commissioners to furnish estimates of population of their respective divisions. The number of houses in each district was first calculated, by zamindars and patwaris and sometimes by thanedars of police. The number of persons to each house was reckoned at 4.5. In this way, the total population of Oudh was computed in 1860 at 8,71,075. This manner of assessing the total population could not, however, strictly be called 'census'.

In April 1866 the Oudh Government asked Bengal and the North-Western Provinces for their census reports. Bengal supplied to it the papers detailing the measures adopted for taking a census of Calcutta but the North-Western Provinces census report had not appeared by then. The Oudh Government considered a proposal in 1866 to hold a census of its population, keeping in view the basic principle that 'the method of enumeration, returns etc. should be uniform with those of the North-Western Provinces for the sake of present comparison and future combination.'[13] The idea of a provincial census was, however, temporarily shelved on the ground that 'the question of making a census in other provinces is under the consideration of Government of India'.[14]

In the city of Lucknow, a census was carried out in 1866, with the city police as the enumeration agency. The *zamindars* (*i.e.,* the landholders) rendered assistance in the census. They even provided the little wooden boards or tickets to be hung outside each enclosure and house for the purpose of numbering it. Other *zamindars* furnished enumerators gratis. The *patwari* was the preferred enumerator. At certain places, the enumerators were paid as well. Preceding the launch of the census, the district collector held a darbar of *talukdars* (large landowners) and zamindars to explain the object of the census.[15]

In July 1867, Oudh wrote to the Government of India proposing to take a census of the province in January 1869, arguing that the experience gained would tell powerfully on the completeness and accuracy of the general census. A grant of Rs. 6,000 was asked for, which was granted. The proposed census was divided into four parts, namely: (1) to prepare *a pargana*-wise statement of each district, showing the number of *mauzas* (a further territorial division of the district); hamlets and detached single houses; (2) to enter in the census papers so much information as could be entered before the actual taking of the census; (3) to take the census; and (4) to compile the results into a convenient form. 'For this duty an officer will be especially appointed, who will receive separate instructions.'

The operational responsibility of the census work was borne by the revenue agency of the district. The settlement officer or deputy commissioner was entrusted with part one of the work, which was to be submitted in English first to the commissioner of the division. After the necessary scrutiny in the commissioner's office, it was forwarded to the provincial level officer appointed to compile the results of the census (that is, the provincial census chief). To carry out the second and third parts, returns in Hindi or Urdu were prepared for every village. This return, which was crucial, gave information on the age, sex, caste and occupation of every person enumerated.

All enclosures and houses in the province were numbered and enumerators were appointed, who filled up the return for every house in the ten or eleven weeks between the issue of the circular and the end of October. Information was collected on name of the individual, caste, occupation, and the number of his servants and guests, with their caste and occupation. November, December and January were devoted to the supervision of the preliminary work, which was performed under the immediate superintendence of the higher officials of the district, the police and the settlement department. The census was to be originally taken on 27 January 1869, but was postponed to 1 February 1869. A total of 21,552 enumerators were employed on the night of 31 January—1 February.

Being the first exercise of its kind, the Oudh Census of 1869 was not without its quota of rumours. A vague sense of alarm prevailed among the people at least in some districts such as Sultanpur, Faizabad, Pratapgarh, etc. In Faizabad, many men endeavoured to conceal some members of their families, fled from their houses on the night of 1 February and slept in the fields or went into the neighbouring province. Ayodhya in Faizabad saw crowds of people flocking over the river Gomti to avoid being communicative. The lower castes especially tried concealment and for some weeks immediately preceding the census night, a considerable migration took place. The rumour regarding the forcible abstraction of women for the use of European soldiers led to wholesale concealment of the young unmarried women. In Bahraich district, which was particularly gripped by a rumour that fine unmarried females were wanted for the European army, several unmarried women made engagements at once to escape such a conscription.

A similar rumour prevailed in certain parts of the Central Provinces also. 'There was a story that the British Government wanted wives for its soldiers and would take any girls who might be unmarried at the time of the census. Accordingly all parents made the utmost exertions to find husbands for their daughters, and when they had married them off they quietly awaited the result. The Census Report of Oudh, 1869 makes a mention about some, nay many villages especially in Sultanpur and Pratapgarh districts, the census returns for which hardly contained any girls at all'.[16] The numbers of the girls were singularly disproportionate to the number of boys throughout Oudh. 'The result I now arrive at from these facts is that there has been a strong tendency every where to enter girls in the returns as women'.[17]

Let it be remembered that people at this time were absolutely new to the census culture. Their imaginations were naturally fanned by the utter novelty of the exercise. Among the lower classes, dread and suspicion struggled with instinctive reverence for authority and perhaps confidence in the intentions of the rulers.[18] Among the upper classes, a similar feeling prevailed at first, but as they gradually found themselves personally enlisted in the work of the census, mistrust gave way, and in the case of the non-official instructors and enumerators was succeeded by a feeling of pride at being entrusted with a share of participation in the State's responsibility.

To sum up, the prevalent rumours were:

1. The British Government in India was going to impose a poll tax.
2. The Government was about to take one member of every family as a recruit for the army.
3. One male from every house was to be compelled to emigrate or to work without pay on the roads.
4. Women were wanted as wives for the European soldiers.
5. Every fourth man was to be taken to build an enormous fort.
6. Indians were wanted to colonise a distant settlement.
7. Every fourth Indian was to be recruited to the army.

The Report on the Census of Oudh (1869) narrates a strange rumour, namely that the country of the English had suddenly become very warm and Queen Victoria had sent orders to the Governor-General in India to send to England at once two virgins from each village that they might fan her night and day and keep her cool; and the census was only a subterfuge on the part of the authorities to enable them to be put on board vessels ready to receive them.

Rumours thus did prevail. Yet the demeanour of the people was on the whole quiet and submissive during the whole of the long winter period during which the preliminary countings were going on as well as on the night of the census. As the Report on the Census of Oudh, 1869 observes, the people at large did not assist in any way; neither were they disposed to be communicative. But they made no attempt to obstruct or interfere with the census operation. Even ticketing the house aroused little apprehension. To quote from the Report:

> Everybody's house was to be ticketed and so all felt safe. The danger was felt rather to be in the house left unticketed. This feeling induced the common people everywhere to take great care of the little wooden tickets, and to prevent the children from playing with them. In some districts the numbers were not recorded on these wooden tickets, but were painted on the walls of the houses in coloured chalk; in those places the people were careful to keep the colours bright so that the number might be plainly visible, and they made it as conspicuous as possible by smearing the surrounding parts of the walls very smoothly with cowdung.[19]

Petty cases of corruption were not entirely non-existent among enumerators at this stage. At a few places, the enumerators were found collecting a copper coin from every house visited by them. Some were exacting a fee of three pie per house as diet money. A few took a few annas from the people saying that the red ochre and oil used in numbering the houses had to be paid for. One man falsely represented himself to be an enumerator, and went about on the night of the census collecting fees in the name of Government; he was sentenced to two years' rigorous imprisonment. The Census Report on Oudh concludes: 'It is probable that small fees were often levied by the ground-level functionaries while performing census tasks'.[20]

Consisting of 12 districts, the Province of Oudh employed a total of 21,552 enumerators, which gives an average of 1,796 persons per district. There was nearly one enumerator per village.

The Census Report for Oudh for 1869 gives an account of the actual process of enumeration.

> On the night of 1 February (1869), the census was taken in every town and village throughout the province. Persons of all classes were pressed into Government service for this one night. In addition to the paid enumerators, the village patwaris, the whole of the subordinate district and settlement establishments, and in some districts also the police were employed. Then talukdars, and their agents and bailiffs, zamindars great and small, mir mahalladars in towns, sarbaratikars of estates under court of wards, kanungos and their private moharirs, and in short almost everybody who could read and write were required to give their services for the occasion. The orders had been that the enumerators were to see everybody whom they counted, except of course the *purdahnishin* (veiled) women, but I fancy these orders were not carried out. It would have been hardly possible to do so. The plan generally followed appears to have been for the head of the house to sit at the door of his house, frequently with a light burning, till it came to the turn of his family to be counted. He then himself gave the information required to the enumerator. Even following this plan the enumeration must in many large village have lasted the entire night. All persons were enumerated in the place where they were on the night of the census, whether they ordinarily resided there or not. [21]

These census exercises, which approximated in different degrees the modern concept of a census, were characterised by progress in coverage. They made whatever use they could of the existing administrative or other agencies, a principle which to a greater or less degree has always characterised the Indian census.

From the census angle, Bengal was on an especially weak wicket. It had no administrative machinery sufficient for making a complete census of the province. 'In every department of the administration, the fact meets one at every time that in Bengal, the Government has no means of doing anything or learning anything about the people of the country.'[22]

What has been discussed in the foregoing constitutes at best the preparation for an all-India census, held in 1881. These countings suffered from shortcomings and limitations but at the same time provided experience of an exercise in which the State comes into direct touch with every soul living within its boundary, whether young or old, male or female. These were based on a uniform set of schedules. But they were not synchronous. Nor were they centrally supervised and compiled.

When census in India was originally proposed a suggestion was made to hold it synchronously with that of the United Kingdom. This was to emphasise the 'imperial' character of the operations. In Britain the census, as is known, is taken in April every ten years. But in India April marks the advent of hot season, making it unsuitable for the inspection of the preliminary record and other preparatory work for the census. Moreover, winter is the typical time in India for official tours, and when the officials are on tours they could as well inspect the preliminary census records. One may add that it is to this inspection that the accuracy of the enumeration was mainly due. India, therefore, did not adopt the time-table of Britain for census. Taking into account the climatic conditions, the month of February was fixed, as being equally away from extremes in both winter and summer. The month of February is a settled fact for census taking in India ever since.

An important principle of census is that it must be synchronous, which means the entire population in India must be counted on the same fixed day (or night). This ensures accuracy. Economic reasons were no less urgent. To control public expenditure on kerosene oil, lanterns etc., a full moon night was preferred. The time of night made a ready appeal, for people generally tend to keep indoors then. But this raised a problem. The night of the full moon is the occasion when India's principal religious gatherings at shrines, temples and bathing places are held. This meant that very considerable portion of the population would be away from home on that night. Therefore, the census had to be held a few days before or after the full moon night. It was always a matter of uncertainty how long before hand it was the custom to start on such excursions, but as a rule there was a tendency to return with greater expedition than marked the journey out. It was found, accordingly, that what with the number of festivals that were purely local in their attractions, and the facilities available for visiting the places of wider renown by rail, the third day after the auspicious occurrence would generally find the bulk of the pilgrims back home. It was on this consideration that the census night was fixed both in 1881 and in 1891.

As the census date was to be fixed according to the lunar calendar, only a close correspondence could be obtained in the dates of the decennial census. Thus, the first general census of India was held on 17 February 1881, and the second census on the night of 26 February 1891.

Full moon night was selected to enable the enumerator, the backbone of the census operations, to go round his beat economically. In the rural area, his beat includes a comparatively large tract. The enumerator's duties, one must note, are much vaster than the responsibilities of his counterpart in the West. In a European country the enumerator merely collects by day the census schedule which has been prepared for him by the householder himself, who is most likely to be highly literate. In India on the other hand the population to be enumerated contained not more than about six in the hundred who could read and write. This being the level of illiteracy, the whole of the census record had to be prepared by the enumeration agency.

As it was impossible to provide enough enumerators of the necessary qualifications to do the entire enumeration in the course of a single night, an innovation was made. First, the enumerator filled up the schedules of his beat with the required information for all the habitual residents therein, before the census. Then, on the appointed night, he brought this up to date with a second round. In this round, he struck out all who had died or were found absent, and entered all found on the premises who were not there when the preliminary visit was paid, such as guests, travellers and the newly born. As he was bound to visit all the outlying parts of his beat, wherever casual sojourners were likely to be found, efficient inspection became necessary.

A basic feature of census is that it should graft itself on to an existing organisation already moving among and thus familiar to the people, thus causing minimum disturbance or inconvenience. It is not only economical but also judicious. Physical head counting was a novelty and a mystery in India. The mystery would be reduced, if not removed entirely, when it was put through agencies already familiar to the masses. This agency, obviously, was the revenue one.

REFERENCES

1. *Home—Public*, 22 May 1869, No. 79-90.
2. *Home—Public*, June 1865, No. 36.
3. *Ibid.*
4. *Home—Public*, 22 May 1869, No. 79-90.
5. *Ibid.*
6. *Home—Public*, 22 January 1866, Nos. 48-51.
7. *Ibid.*
8. *Home—Public*, 1874, Proceedings, February 1874, No. 58.
9. *General Report on the Census of the North-Western Provinces*, Allahabad, Government Press, 1867, p. 3.
10. *Ibid.*, p. 4.
11. *Ibid.*
12. *Ibid.*
13. Quoted in *Census of Oudh*, Vol. I, General Report, 1869, p. 3.
14. *Ibid.*
15. See *Ibid.*, p. 9.
16. *Ibid.*, p. 12.
17. *Ibid.*
18. *Ibid.*, p. 13.
19. *Ibid.*
20. *Ibid.*, p. 17.
21. *Ibid.*, p. 13.
22. *Home—Public-A*, 28 January 1877, Nos. 38-43.

3

THE PLOWDEN COMMITTEE FOR A GENERAL CENSUS IN INDIA

In 1877 a census committee consisting of W.C. Plowden (chairman), H. Beverley and W.R. Cornish was appointed to consider the suggestion for a general census in India in 1881.[1] The Plowden Committee submitted its 26-page Report in 1878. Its major recommendations are summarised below:

1. The Committee formulated the broad outline of the organisation for census:

   We recommend that there should be one controlling officer who should supervise and direct the enumeration in the different provinces, it being clearly understood that the responsibility of the local (that is, provincial) governments as regards the enumeration of the people shall not thereby be weakened. This officer should, in fact, be the adviser of each local administration (provincial government) in this matter, and should be responsible for the compilation of the tables in which is exhibited the information collected at the census. Under this officer, who might be designated the Census Commissioner, a deputy should be employed in each province, under whose supervision the census would be taken, and who would manage the provincial office where the abstracts for each province would be compiled. It might in some few cases be necessary, and undoubtedly would be so in Bengal, to have branch offices for compilation where there is any difficulty in procuring, at the headquarters of the province, clerks who could work up the returns given in characters other than those in general use at the headquarters. Both the Census Commissioner and his deputies should be employed some time previous to the date of the census. The chief controlling officer would have to see that the instructions preliminary to the enumeration were uniform and explicit and would have to make such modifications in them as might be required to meet the necessities of particular provinces. He would be responsible for exactitude of definition in regard to the terms to be employed, and, in those cases where identical definitions could not be made use of, would have to arrange that the information obtained, if not the same absolutely throughout the empire, should at all events be sufficiently akin in the different provinces to lead to no confusion in the compilation and subsequent comparisons.

2. One identical time was to be fixed for conducting the census in the whole of British India. The enumeration throughout the country was to take place on one and the same day.
3. 1 April 1881, which was the date when Britain was holding its census, was not suitable for India. The Committee noted:

The difficulties in the way of fixing so late a date are those relating to season. To secure accuracy and careful listing of the entries in the schedules, it is absolutely necessary that the supervising establishment, including the district officials, should be out and about the best part of the day immediately succeeding the enumeration as well as the night or day of the census, to say nothing of the exposure necessitated during the time when the schedules are being filled up, which will cover nearly a month. It is only by a careful personal scrutiny of a certain number of entries in the schedules that these can be properly tested. The intense heat in the day-time so late as April would make such a scrutiny, attended as it must be by rapid movement from one village to another, and probably involving a ride of 20 to 30 miles in a broiling sun a most laborious undertaking. Putting out of sight all ideas of exposure, the mere fact that it would not be possible to get through so much work in March and April as in a cooler season of the year, particularly in the more southerly provinces, makes it desirable to adhere to time which in practice, throughout the country, has been found best adopted for the work. This, as a rule, is the middle of the cold weather, or rather past the mid-cold weather season. . .

The Committee continued:

Without, therefore, fixing any definite date, and having in view the advantages accruing from the use of a moonlight night for such a purpose as an enumeration, the Committee recommends the early part of February 1881, within two or three days of the full moon, as the date best suited for a synchronous census of British India.

4. It was impossible to rely on the inhabitants to fill up their own returns as in England. The schedules would have to be filled up by other than the householders' agency and this would have to be done prior to the census, so that on the day fixed for the enumeration, the entries recorded a few days previously might be examined and corrected so as to correspond with the facts on the day of enumeration.
5. Not more than 300 persons, or 60 houses were to be allotted to one enumerator, and a supervisor was to look after every ten enumerators.
6. The agency undertaking enumeration and supervision was not to be a paid one. The objection of expense was alone insurmountable. Nor was it necessary. In rural areas, the patwari or his equivalent was able to deal with the population.* The Committee pointed out a third reason also in favour of non-payment. An introduction of payment to the enumerating staff would create suspicion in the people as to the motives underlying census, which could defeat its object. This was in contrast to what Britain's Registrar-General recommended. He supported the employment of paid enumeration agency which gave the census authorities 'more control over them' and even led to 'greater accuracy'. In towns, unquestionably, there would be instances when paid enumerators had to be employed. But even in these cases the number would be small. The Committee warned against the use of the police for census work: 'We deprecate the general employment of the police considering that such action is open to misconception and may result in some cases in oppression or extortion.'
7. The Committee favoured a special legislation to back up the decennial census, the motive being to secure more Government control over both the enumerators and the enumerated. 'For want of legal authority in the census, the people did not cooperate with the enumerators, pretending to be asleep and not to hear the

---

* See his letter to the Under Secretary of State for India dated 10 January 1877, *Home—Public* b, Nos. 76-78.

enumerator to open their door and bring lights. . . All was darkness, and the police dare not resort to force.'

The main Plowden Report supported a single executive for census administration. One member of the Committee, W.R. Cornish, himself a provincial census chief at the time of 1871 census-taking, supported, instead, a plural executive of two or three members on grounds of existing practice in Great Britain, workload as well as health.[2] Cornish appended a minute of dissent and argued in favour of a multi-member body to conduct the census giving the example of England. He observed that in England and Wales, Scotland and Ireland it was the rule for the Registrars General of those provinces to be associated with joint commissioners for conducting a census. When these small-population countries had multi-member census bodies, India, in view of its much larger population and changed socio-economic conditions, hardly needed any elaborate justification. Cornish commented:

> If the necessity for such an arrangement has been felt in countries where the people are comparatively few, and able and willing to help in giving the detailed information desired of them, how much greater must be the need of a division of labour in regard to the gathering together of the statistics of nearly 200 millions of people of diverse races, nationalities, religions, languages and social customs, and who for the most part are unable to give any assistance in their own numbering and classification.

He appreciated all the advantages resulting from a single central authority but 'in my view a commission of three members would do the work proposed by the (Plowden) Census Committee much more effectively than one individual. He emphasised: 'I am further of opinion that the proposed duties are so heavy that one officer could not conduct them either to his own satisfaction or to the advantage of the State.'

Cornish further argued on the ground of physical health and fitness also.

> In recommending a census commissioner for the whole Empire, no provision is made for a possible break-down in health of this official, who would have to travel over the length and breadth of the country, and to be responsible for the uniform preparation of the census results. This is not an idle objection. The difficulty actually occurred in Madras, where the officer selected in 1871

> for the duty of compiling the census results, and who was familiar with all the details of the work, fell ill and died in the midst of his task to the great inconvenience of Government and of everybody concerned. All the knowledge and experience acquired by the late Mr. Gover in connection with the organisation of establishments and tabulation of results perished with him. . . My own labours and anxieties in connection with the completion of the work were more than doubled by the fact that all the threads of the tangled skein had to be picked up *de novo*. What has actually occurred in Madras may happen again in regard to the more important interests of the whole Indian Empire, if the vast labour and responsibility of the next census tabulation be made to devolve on the continuance of health and life of one individual.

Cornish went on to observe that with three commissioners, (one of whom might be appropriately represented by the Department of Agriculture, Statistics and Commerce), the danger of a break-down owing to individual failure of health or life would be lessened and a division of the labour of local inspection and control could be effected, so as to permit of the work being thoroughly done.

> I infer that the officers of such a commission would be appointed in time to enable them to discuss and settle all the preliminary arrangements of a census and that the two members, other than the officer of the Statistical Department, would then decide the inspection work of the several provinces, and that all would subsequently work together in the arrangement of the report and tabulated results.

He concluded his minute of dissent by saying: 'On these grounds it has seemed to me that a census commission would not only be unobjectionable, but more advantageous to the Government than the appointment of one Imperial Commissioner with individual authority and responsibility.' A multi-member commission form of organisation for census administration would ensure uniformity of precept and practice and was also to be more economical. 'In my view, a commission of three members would do the work proposed by the Census Committee. I am further of opinion that the proposed duties are so heavy that one officer could not conduct them either to his own satisfaction, or to the advantage of the State'. Cornish's recommendation notwithstanding, India does not have a census commission. It has a single chief executive, the Census Commissioner for India, to administer the census.

The Plowden Committee Report is easily the most memorable document on censusing in India, articulating as it does the administrative framework of head-counting in the country. Members of the Committee were all census administrators and their recommendations were based on both knowledge and experience. It is remarkable that the administration of the census in present-day India is based on the recommendations made by the Plowden Committee more than a hundred years ago. The report is rare and is not easily available today. These reasons warrant its reproduction in the Appendix I.

REFERENCES

1. All the quotations cited in this chapter are from the Report of the Officers appointed to consider the suggestions for a General Census in India in 1881 (W.C. Plowden), 1878.
2. The minute of dissent by W.R. Cornish was published in Home Department, 1878, Public, Proceedings March, Nos. 76-78, Arrangements made for taking Census of India in 1881.

4

CENSUS ADMINISTRATION
What it Involves

The census administration in India comprises the following successive steps:

(1) Division of the province (state) into blocks, the basic units of enumeration and administration.
(2) Preparation of lists of houses and families, and numbering of houses.
(3) Selection of enumerating agency.
(4) Preparation of preliminary record of the population.
(5) The census itself, or the correction of the preliminary record to square it with facts as they stood on the appointed day.
(6) Abstracting of the entries in the census schedules.
(7) Tabulation in detail of the abstracted figures.
(8) Detailed tabulation of the final census tables from these figures.

Basic Unit of Census Administration

The first step in census is to split the district into blocks of such size that a single person can conveniently visit all people living within any one of them on the census night. This principle is not always easy or simple in application. In the hilly tracts, where habitations are remote, it suffices to allot to each enumerator as many of the scattered hamlets and isolated homesteads as he is able to deal with. Leaving aside these exceptions, on the whole the area to be enumerated is divided off into blocks, and a single enumerator made responsible for the enumeration of all persons found within the block on the night of the census. A block is the basic unit of enumeration and supervision.

Preparation of House-List

The next step is to make rough sketch maps of the towns, villages and hamlets, to list the houses in each block and the families in each house, and to paint on the walls of the houses their serial numbers.

The subsequent operations in the house-list preparation include: (1) listing the houses and families to serve as a check-register and index; (2) a preliminary record of census entries, to be made shortly before the census night; (3) the final census at which the preliminary record is squared with the facts as they stand on the night of the census. The first two operations are conducted somewhat leisurely, but the third operation must be performed over the whole country within a single night. It is obvious that the accuracy of the final returns inevitably depends on the care with which the first two steps are performed and upon the capability of the staff employed for the final surveys.

Selection of Agency

It is the district collector who selects the enumerating agency. For rural enumeration, the choice has always fallen on the revenue agency, which is scattered all over the country and is intimately familiar with the rural life. An enumerator's qualification was that he should be 'able to read and write'. The net was cast wide. The Report of the Punjab Census of 1881 notes that 'every soul who had the requisite qualifications was pressed into the service'.[1] The enumerators included all government servants under the district collector together with many lent by other departments, pensioners, candidates for employment, petition-writers, stamp-vendors, holders of licences of sorts—that is 'all who had anything to hope for or to fear from Government were called upon to assist'. Assisting them were village accountants (patwaris), shopkeepers, priests, pandits, maulvis, small landowners, senior pupils of the upper schools etc. The enumerators were preferably locals of the place to be enumerated. The supervisory agency included honorary magistrates, rural notables, assignees of land revenue, merchants, etc.

The phrase 'able to read and write', though simple on its face, was difficult to define precisely in the Indian context. An indication of this is given by the circumstances prevailing in the Punjab in 1881.

> In that province there are seven 'characters current of which only three could be said to possess much certainty in their cursive form while the ordinary clerk can seldom read any of them except

> the Persian, and occasionally the Devnagri or Gurmukhi. The others are confined either to the trading classes or to very limited areas. This category also includes the village shopkeeper who is able to 'read and write' but is often unable to read tomorrow what he wrote today while what has been written by one is deciphered by another much as General Cunningham would decipher a rock inscription of the time of Asoka'.[2]

In the Punjab, the census staff involved in counting in 1881 included 1,758 superintendents, 6,399 supervisors and 52,983 enumerators —or 61,140 in all. Of this number, 45,082 were non-officials, of whom only 431 received payment. What the rest got in return for the work, which was 'of an irksome and uninteresting nature', was the printed letter of thanks and the goodwill of the authorities.

Preparation of Preliminary Record

Having selected the enumerating staff and put them through a short training of practical instruction, the preparation of the preliminary record begins. The enumerator fills in census entries in the schedule before the appointed day by visiting all houses in his beat. On the census night, he again goes on his round to finally check the recorded information by taking note of subsequent births, deaths and movements of the people. The preliminary record might, in f.ct, be called the census itself, for the village population is essentially a stationary one and not many alterations are generally made in the census entries on the night of the census. Thus, the value of the census results substantially depends on the care and accuracy with which the preliminary record is filled in.

The exercise at this stage had its own problems and pitfalls. The entry on caste always presented a headache to the census authorities. A widespread habit was noticed among 'inferior' castes to extenuate their present status by claiming an origin of fabulous glory. It required tact, patience and perseverence on the part of the enumerators and their supervisors to get at the facts. Cases occurred when the statements made appeared implausible. The Report of the Punjab Census of 1881 observes:

> When a lusty male in the prime of manhood tells you that he is 15 years old, or a tottering elder that his winters number '20 or 30', it is necessary to exercise your own judgment in the matter. So, when an oilman says that he is a Mughal or a Rajput he may be so in reality, and it is most unsafe to assume that

> because he is an oilman he, therefore, cannot be telling the truth. But if he is one of a community of Telis (the ordinary oilman caste) and marries among Telis, and is and always has been known to his neighbours as a Teli, his assertion is but vain-glorying and must be rejected. And this is the chief reason why I think that the preliminary record, which is the very backbone of the census, should be prepared as far as possible by the village accountants who live among the people, and know every man, woman and child in the village.[3]

The completion of the preliminary record is followed by an interval which is utilised for making arrangements for the enumeration of the floating population such as dispensary patients, travellers, etc.

The Census

The census night is the most exciting time for the census, involving as it does the door-to-door visit of the enumerators throughout the country within the span of a few hours. The census of the Punjab in 1881 describes what happened on the appointed night. A couple of days before, supervisors visited their blocks to assure themselves that all the enumerators were at their posts with the completely tested record in readiness, and distributed the red ink which had to be used for alterations and additions made on the census night. Proclamations were issued requesting the people as far as possible to stay at home after nightfall, not to go to bed till the enumerator had visited them, and till then to keep a lamp burning. During the day time the nomad grazing camps of the western plains were visited, and the census was taken in some of the more mountainous tracts where the snow and the difficult nature of the terrain made a night visitation impossible. But the great mass of the population was enumerated by moonlight. Evening brought the husbandmen and cowherds home from the field and pastures; and as soon as night fell and the lamps were lit, the enumerators, accompanied by the village headmen and by men carrying torches, started on their rounds. As a rule they found the head of the family waiting at the door with a lamp in his hand to receive them. They read out to him the entries in the schedules, cut out such persons as had died or gone away, entered those who had been born or come to the house in the interval, and passed on to the next house.[4]

Compilation of the Figures

Subsequent to the actual enumeration, the figures need to be abstracted and tabulated, the entries classified and the whole rendered to the form in which they are presented in the final census reports. The answer to every question that is asked by the enumerator has to be tabulated, which costs money and effort.

The phase of tabulation begins after the schedules have been filled in. In the earlier days, tabulation was done in the following manner: The details were transferred to slips of paper varying in colours to indicate communities. Each slip bore a symbol indicating the sex and a mark within the symbol showed whether a person was unmarried, married or widowed. Thus, a triple classification was secured by the very act of recording. The figures of enumeration reached a high standard of accuracy, so close was the mesh which was laid for the country. One of the great desiderata of the time, however, with its curiously blind acceptance of figures was to avoid the crediting of figures with more accuracy than they really could bear. For example, when one is counting millions of heads, the last two digits could hardly be treated as significant.

The process of tabulation and abstraction is laborious in the extreme and to a large extent purely mechanical. The process is thus described in the Report of the Punjab Census of 1881:

> The work was done by a picked staff of 1,000 village accountants (patwaris) who were taken from their districts and collected in ten divisional offices established at centres along the line of rail. Their duties were confined to abstracting the figures for each different entry which appeared in the enumerators' schedules, and tabulating them separately for each of the 53,000 blocks into which the Province was divided. The wearisome monotony of making four long ticks and then crossing them by a fifth day after day and all day long, was beyond description; the men were kept away from their homes and families, were living in cities instead of in villages, and were held to their work with unaccustomed strictness; and when they were at length released, their joy found vent in paeans of song which were published in the native newspapers.[5]

The final stage is the compilation of the final census tables from the figures tabulated in detail. The final shape would classify the innumerable entries according to religion, language, birthplace, caste and occupation.

Single Night Theory of Enumeration

For accuracy, the total population of a country as enumerated must relate to a fixed predetermined point of time. An early and important point for consideration in the census, therefore, was its timing, or the 'census moment'. Implicit in it was the question of the extent to which uniformity of timing in censusing in the entire country could be enforced.

In other words, between the two modes of head counting—the simultaneous (or synchronous) and the gradual (or spread-over) one—India had to make a final choice. The Government of India supported the one-day theory. Waterfield in his 'Suggestions for the Next Census of India' observed: 'A census should be taken in 1881, throughout India, as nearly as possible on the same day.' He elaborated: 'In most census there would not apparently have been any difficulty in arranging for greater uniformity of time. In general it would seem that the object to be gained by uniformity of time in a census is not unattainable in India'.

Opposition to the one-day theory, however, came from the North-Western Provinces (present U.P.) and Bengal. Bengal argued that a simultaneous census would cost 'a very great deal' and would not be so satisfactory as a gradual one. The absence of an adequate local-level administrative agency in Bengal perhaps prompted its reservations regarding a simultaneous census. It had no ground level organisation whatsoever except, of course, the police. A high-ranking civil servant of Bengal suggested the appointment of a 'special deputy magistrate', whose sole duty was to be 'to control and organise the machinery required for the census'. There was to be full work for a single officer for at least a year in collecting the necessary information and settling and arranging all the details. The census was to be taken thana-wise. Each thana was to be divided into circles; each circle was to be under the charge of a supervisor, the whole being supervised by the 'special deputy magistrate'. The precise nature of the agency available for the 'deputy magistrate' in each village was not spelled out.

Equally opposed to the one-night theory, the Government of North-Western Provinces favoured the spreading of the census over two years. It wrote to the Central Government:

> . . . a leading feature in the past history of taking census, wherever

> it had been attempted in India, is the extreme suspicion and dread of mischief which, endangered by ignorance and superstition, have seized the minds of the people, especially on the first introduction of the measure. It is almost incredible what wild and absurd tales have become current, and been implicitly believed striking terror into the whole mass of the population. The feeling does not disappear until their minds have become used to the practice by its repeated performance. . . . There are large provinces throughout the empire in (which) census has not hitherto been tried, and where, no doubt, the experiment will be open to the same difficulties and risks which have been experienced elsewhere.[6]

The letter continued:

> There is also something novel for India in the notion of a universal enumeration on a single day. It is impossible to say how this new idea and the approach of the day over the whole empire might strike the national mind, or what wild reports of our intentions it might not excite.

The provincial Government concluded: 'Such being the case and there being no special practical advantage in the census being absolutely synchronous . . . it would be better not to appoint one and the same date, but rather to leave a range, say, of a couple of years, within which, according to the opportunities and circumstances of each district, the census might be carried out.'[7]

The Government of India still subscribed to one-day census, but accepted the Bengal viewpoint. Ultimately the decision taken was to permit Bengal to depart from the principle of simultaneous census in the case of certain of its districts and for them a modified system of taking the census was adopted. The Government at that time respected local difficulties and tried to be flexible and accommodative in its decision-making.

In other words, the census of 1871 was not simultaneous. Nor did it claim all-India coverage. The dates of the enumeration in 1871 were as follows:

Ajmer	1 May 1872
Bengal and Assam	Chiefly in January 1872 but the enumeration was going on at various places from November

	1871 to May 1872
Bombay	21 February 1872
Punjab	
Oudh	No counting was done
Berar	
British Burma	15 August 1872

This is why the census of 1871 is not regarded as the first general census in India—this credit goes to the enumeration of 1881. Head-counting was done on a single night until 1931. The one-night theory of enumeration was, however, abandoned in the 1941 census and for good reasons. The one-night census necessitated the recruitment of a large number of enumerators: the number employed for the 1931 census was of the order of 2 million. 'These features meant that in many areas shop-keepers and outsiders of all kinds had to be pressed into service as enumerators and the net had to go far wider than village officers, school masters and persons of similar standing and responsibility. Hence the possible entry of error or through less suitable personnel'.[8] M.W.M. Yeatts, Census Commissioner of India for 1941, commented on the discontinuance of one-night enumeration thus: 'Once away from the old practice, there is no longer any need to hunt for a night graced by a full moon, and undisturbed by large festivals (to discover any day which did not carry somewhere in India some element of disturbance of this sort was impossible always)'. Yeatts continued: 'And, finally it will make it possible to relate India's census to the same date in every decade presuming a common census season is retained. The statistical convenience of this is obvious'. Yeatts concluded that all considerations led to the first requirement: the one-night theory ought to go. And the census of 1941 saw it going. The census of 1941 introduced many changes and marks a watershed in the administration of population counting in India. It, in short, heralds the present system.

The abandonment of the one-night theory claimed several additional advantages and had none of the shortcomings earlier feared. The one-night theory was convulsive and less natural. In Yeatts' words, 'in the past the one-night system meant that even after the preliminary record, every enumerator, supervisor etc. had to be on the move again on the single night and as part of a rush to put in provisional totals at the earliest possible moment, tehsil offices worked at pressure over some days getting the results out and the district offices similarly for a day or two compiling the district total'. He observed, 'I have removed all this now. The record will be taken. There will be no rush to put in provisional totals: these will be prepared with reasonable expedition but there will be no telegraphing etc.'[9] The enumeration being spread over a number of days permitted the formation of larger blocks than hitherto. For the increase in the size of the block placed no strain on the enumerator. The consequent reduction in the total number of blocks meant a corresponding reduction in the number of enumerators, and this was conducive to a more selective recruitment. A larger block economises enumeration slips. Over a period of days—half on either side of the central census date—the enumerator devotes more time to the census work with greater equanimity and does the counting of his entire circle single-handed during this period.

Till 1931, the census in India was, so to say, *de facto* rather than *de jure*. That is to say, the census aimed at a return of all persons actually found in the country at a given moment. It was, however, becoming less and less feasible to make a census completely synchronous. It was also being realised that a *de jure* census was likely to be much more suitable for India than a *de facto* census. A *de facto* census is efficient only in smaller countries of much greater social, climatic and geographical homogeneity. The substitution of a *de jure* for a *de facto* census enables the enumeration to be spread over a long period (as in the USA) so that the climatic variations may be accommodated. The unhealthy dependence on voluntary organisations may also be eliminated.

Simultaneous population counting was discontinued in 1941: the enumeration since then is spread round the reference date. But the idea has a longer history. It was a divisional commissioner posted in Orissa who first suggested what later became the accepted practice in census. As early as in 1870, E.W. Molony of the ICS objected to the holding of a simultaneous enumeration on a single night. He recommended that counting be spread over a period of time. 'The returns might all bear reference to a single day or night but will have to be gradually collected.'[10] Even when the single-night theory dominated the census, departures were allowed. In other words, the simultaneous census for the whole of India always respected some exceptions. In 1871 the exceptions were more numerous. The mountainous or difficult tracts were exempted from the one-day count. Similarly, while census agency was generally unpaid, payment was also occasionally given, of course, on an austerity scale.

Information Gathering

Census taking is information gathering about the people from the people themselves at a pre-fixed moment of time. The range of information to be collected inevitably depends on the stage of development of the given society no less than the broad orientation and administrative capabilities of the State. When the British consolidated their rule in India and introduced political stability in the country they needed to know what the population of the newly conquered colony was. A knowledge about the country's population is basic for any planned activity.

The items on which information is sought in the census have constantly been undergoing revision and refinement. The census form adopted in the 1865 census of the North-Western Provinces was the basis for the all-India census of 1881. Originally, information on age and education was not collected: these two items were added in 1871. The census of 1871 asked most of the standard questions one expects in a census—age, sex, religion, caste, country of birth, occupation, literacy and infirmities. Marital status was not asked on the presumption that marriage in India was universal among adults and the result of an enquiry on it was not worth the effort involved. The caste return was always elaborate even though its utility was questioned by some civil servants. At the earliest stages of census taking in the 1870s and 1880s, the details on which information was sought were kept to the minimum, simple and free from any elements of uncertainty or ambiguity. Bengal, while observing that it did not possess an administrative machinery adequate in size and strength at the lower levels to take up the task of census, wanted the minimum possible information to be collected — not much more than 'a simple enumeration of adults and children'.[11] But this suggestion had no sponsors. In the beginning forms seeking information were of a very simple character. The first general census elicited information on the name, religion, race and occupation of the males and the number, religion and race of females. Finding out names of females was not favoured for fear that this might be 'vexatious annoyance or impertinence on the part of an ignorant or malicious enumeration'.[12]

The schedule for the 1871 census was brief, seeking information on only six items. These were age, sex, religion or caste, race or tribe, occupation and infirmities. The census of February 1881, known as the first general census of India, required somewhat more information and in greater detail, on ten items. These were: age, sex, civil or conjugal condition, religion, caste, birthplace, mother tongue, degree of education, occupation and infirmities. One may thus see that in 1881 four entirely new matters of inquiry were introduced and the information on some others was sought in much greater detail.

Items on 'age' and 'caste' posed considerable problems to the census authorities. The exact age was seldom known even to the local people themselves. Besides, the more minute the inquiry and record made, the more suspicion was created in the public mind and the greater were the attempts to render false returns. Equally unsatisfactory was the item on 'caste'. General ignorance of this subject prevailed among the people themselves. The same caste was often known by different names at different places and the tendency existed to confuse caste with occupation, especially in the lower classes. W.C. Plowden, who wrote the 1872 census report on the North-Western Provinces, observed, 'The caste statistics are the most unsatisfactory part of the return'.[13] This is the refrain in the subsequent census reports also. Plowden recommended abandoning the attempts to distinguish castes in any future census, but the column retained principally on two grounds. First, in India a person could not always be identified by his name alone without his caste. Secondly, in the absence of caste particulars, the social and economic problems of the people could not be classified for social reform measures.

In 1881, items on conjugal state and language were added to the schedule while 'birthplace' became an independent query. Thereafter, there was little alteration in the schedule of questions. For the census from 1901 to 1921, the schedule of questions was identical, save that the question on Muslim sect was asked for the first time in 1921.

In 1881, men and women were classified only under the two categories of those who had an occupation, and those who had no occupation, though nothing was said about their means of livelihood. In the census of 1891, it was intended to distinguish between workers and dependants but adequate provision was not made for the distinction in the schedule. In the census of 1901, three columns were provided in the census schedule to record the dependants and the occupation on which they depended. But since this gave room for misunderstanding, in the census of 1931 the basis of classification was changed and four columns were provided:

(1) earner or dependant
(2) principal occupation of earners
(3) subsidiary occupation
(4) industry in which employed

Especially in the agricultural communities members of the family, including women and even children assist the principal earner in his work, and therefore, this further classification was justified. Although this change may have been for the future, it has made comparison of various censuses difficult. The 1931 schedule resembled its 1921 predecessor but with certain modifications. The definition of a census 'house' was altered in order to produce a more objective approach to the real habitation connoted by the term. Age, which in the past censuses had considered only completed years, switched over to the nearest birthday. Mother tongue was stated instead of the looser 'language ordinarily spoken in the household': while through a new, separate column, classification was made of everyone as earner or dependant and then a division of occupations into principal or subsidiary, with the provision that only an earner could have a principal occupation. On the other hand, a special industrial census was carried out in 1911 and 1921 by means of a separate return. This was abandoned in 1931 for political and other reasons and a new column incorporated in the general schedule to provide for information of this kind. Other changes were the identification of sect for Hindus and Jains as well as for Christians and Muslims. The treatment of caste was also modified. Provincial superintendents of census were informed that it was not necessary generally to tabulate figures of castes for which the provincial government did not regard such tabulation as important. In 1921, the minimum for the tabulation of caste population was raised from two per thousand to four per thousand. A separate schedule was also introduced for educated unemployed; but the result was disappointing. The general attitude to it by the people in Madras, whom it affected, was 'You don't propose to give me a job. I am not bound to answer it. Why should I?'

The 1931 census sought information on sixteen items. These were:

1. Name
2. Religion and sect
3. Male or Female
4. Married, Unmarried or Widowed
5. Age
6. Race, Tribe or Caste
7. Earner or Dependant
8. Principal Occupation
9. Subsidiary Occupation
10. Industry in which employed
11. Birth District (or country)
12. Mother tongue
13. Other languages in common use
14. Whether literate (*i.e.* able to write and read a letter)
15. Whether able to read and write English
16. Insane, totally blind, deaf, mute or leper

In the 1941 census the following 22 questions were framed:

1. Name
2. Sex
3. Race, Tribe or Caste
4. Religion
5. Married, Unmarried, Widowed or Divorced
6. Age
7. Number of children born to a married woman
8. Her age at birth of first child
9. Are you wholly or partly dependant on anyone else
10. If so, means of livelihood of person on whom dependant
11. Do you employ (a) paid assistants, (b) members of household
12. Are you in employment now
13. (Only to those who reply in negative to question 12). Are you in search of employment?
    To those who reply in the affirmative the further question will be put—How long have you been in search of it?
14. Means of livelihood in order of importance
15. (Only to be asked in regard to means of livelihood of a person shown as partly dependant against or any subsidiary means of livelihood returned by other person against question 14) Does this means of livelihood exist throughout the year. If not, for what part of the year?
16. If you are employed by someone else what is his business?
17. Were you born in this district? If not in what district?
18. Mother tongue
19. Other Indian languages in common use
20. Can you both read and write? If so, what script do you write? Can you read?
21. How far have you read?
    Give any examination passed?
22. Are you literate in English?

A census must seek some fundamental information, and these ordinarily are items regarding age, sex, and civil state. Occupation or means of livelihood is a massive item, necessitating the abstraction of a large number of tables. The caste table was the most expensive and difficult of all and a record of individual caste was, in the opinion of M.W.M. Yeatts, no longer worth the money spent upon it.[14] A note prepared by Yeatts in November 1939 shows that the caste tabulation in 1931 was heavily curtailed, while the sorting of caste was detailed in the 1921 census. There was no sorting of caste in 1941. The list of questions asked, he said, must not be permitted to grow too long.

In a census, items on which information was collected must not to be too numerous nor of trivial nature. The questions should be so framed that they were susceptible of answers by the husband or father. The overall guiding principle in questions was to be that they were such as would easily pass the filter of the enumerator's understanding. If he was able to understand the questions he puts then he would be able, or at any rate he will be more likely to extract a satisfactory and intelligible answer. Census administration must guard against two pitfalls. The first was the temptation to seek detail for detail's sake. This is a great temptation into which statisticians and census bureaucracy too often fall. The second variable is the manageability of the census. The census must be within the limit of manageability from the point of view of cost as well dimensions. It must, therefore, guard itself against admitting all details. No use, in other words, is served merely by asking a question. Even a single additional question means answers given by crores of people, which would necessarily involve enormous expansion of tabulation staff. The answers have got to be tabulated. Tabulation necessarily costs money. Enumeration costs much the same whether one asks three questions or two: the essential cost is in the organisation; the cost of tables, on the other hand, differs widely. For example, the means of livelihood table, regularly occupies a third of the tables published. The point to be made is that questions considered to be essential alone should be asked in the census.

REFERENCES

1. Report of the Census of Punjab, p. 9.
2. *Ibid.*, p. 8.
3. *Ibid.*, p. 3.
4. *Ibid.*, p. 10.
5. *Ibid.*, p. 12.
6. Officiating Secretary to the Government of the North-Western Provinces, C.A. Elliott's letter to Secretary to the Government of India, A.O. Hume, No. 1673A dated 13 December 1870. *Home—Public*, 4 February 1871, No. 115-116 C.
7. *Ibid.*
8. *Census of India*, 1941, Vol. I, India, Part II, Administrative Report, Simla, Government of India Press, 1941, p. 11.
9. M.W.M. Yeatts' note dated 11 November 1940 to Secretary to the Government of

India, Home Department.

10. *Home—Public*, 1870, Nos. 54-56.
11. Bengal's letter to the Government of India dated 6 June, 1870. See *Ibid.*
12. See Registrar General, Lower Provinces, H. Beverley's letter to the Secretary to the Government of Bengal. *Home—Public-A*, 28 January, 1877, Nos. 38-43.
13. *Home—Public*, 1874, Nos. 58-59, February 1874.
14. Yeatts' note dated 2 February, 1939. *Home—Public* F1/1/39-Public.

5

THE FIRST GENERAL CENSUS, 1881

The first all-India census was preceded by isolated census exercises in individual provinces. The experiences gathered, the forms used and the procedures adopted in them were of use in the all-India census. Forms were developed for general adoption throughout India as it was desirable to secure uniformity for the purpose of facilitating comparison of the statistics of one part of India with that of another.

The first general census was taken on 17 February 1881 and in six months' time, that is in August 1881, provisional population was made known. In Bengal (which included present-day Bengal, Bihar, Orissa and Chotanagpur) work for the census of 1881 began with a Government circular on 6 February 1880. The circular read:

> The census is to be taken everywhere on the same day, save in a few exceptional tracts, regarding which special instructions will be given. It is thus essential that all the preliminary arrangements should be very carefully made, and that every district officer should form a clear conception of the task before him, and have all the necessary machinery in complete working order at the earliest possible date.[1]

The circular made it clear that 'There can be no better test of administrative ability than the manner in which a district officer carries through an operation of this kind.' Today, the census does not figure that important an item in the district collector's administrative life. Priorities have changed.

This census, which was of a path-breaking nature, compiled information on a limited number of items. The society of the time was largely unlettered, with literacy percentage standing at less than seven. People were not conversant with matters which in the west require no great elaborate effort to understand. Age, for instance, was a matter of guessing in India. As W.C. Plowden, the Census Commissioner for India in 1881, observed: 'The most imperfect of these returns are those giving the ages; that dealing with castes, and the statement of occupations'. He even went to the extent of saying that it was doubtful whether the age statements at the next succeeding census would show any improvement upon the present.[2]

Censusing date and time required some careful thought in India. The month of April, when census in Great Britain is taken, did not suit India, as the hot season, which is not suitable for head counting, sets in by this time. The date of the full moon was deliberately chosen. It was considered essential that the enumerator should have moon light to guide him round his beat, which included, in the rural tracts, a comparatively large area. In India, the population to be enumerated contained no more than about 6 in the 100 who could read and write so that the whole of the census record had to be prepared by a special agency.

As there were not enough literate people of the necessary qualifications to count the heads in the course of a single night, some special arrangement became a situational necessity. The census was per force to be divided into two parts. First, the enumerator himself filled up the schedules of his beat with the required information for all the habitual residents therein, before the actual census. Then, on the appointed night, he brought this up to date with a second round, during which he struck out all who were found absent, and entered all found on the premises who were not there when the preliminary visit was paid, such as travellers, guests and the newly born.

For enumeration work in the jungle tribes, the village officials were better able to find the people out than any stranger deputed for the purpose. In certain hill tracts there were no local educated men to serve as enumerators for the final census. The difficulty was met by importing competent men from the plains on modest payment. A beginning was made by taking a preliminary list of villages, houses and heads of families, and then by making, during the fortnight preceding the general census, a careful preliminary enumeration of all the hill tribes according to families and residence. This was the basis of the census but on the day appointed for the general census heads of families was instructed to note the numbers of adults and children sleeping in their houses on the night in question. This was done by giving them sticks on which notches were cut for the numbers in the house on the subject. For instance, sticks a foot long and unbarked served for male, and peeled sticks for female adults while sticks six inches long would serve for children wherever possible, these sticks were collected the next morning, and any difference between the numbers as shown by the sticks and the numbers given in the preliminary enumeration lists was inquired into and the return prepared accordingly.[3]

Census, covering the entire country, is necessarily an expensive event and economy of expenditure is an absolute necessity. The selection of the fullmoon night was a sure measure of economy : it saved the cost of lighting. Yet, this night itself could not be fixed for the census for sociological reasons. In India it is the full moon night when all the principal religious festivals at shrines, temples and bathing places are held, so that a very considerable portion of the population remained absent on that night from the native place. It was, besides, a matter of uncertainty how long beforehand it was the custom to start on such excursion, which constituted one of the chief pleasures, as well as the main ceremonial observance, in the life of the masses, but, as a rule, a tendency was to return home with greater expedition than marked the journey out. It was found, accordingly, that the third day after the auspicious occurrence would generally find the bulk of the pilgrims back in the villages. It was on this consideration that the census night was fixed in 1881 as well as in 1891. As a result of this and many other measures, the cost of the Indian census was kept very low. The cost of the 1881 census, including the tabulation, was Rs. 24,79,730-15-5 (Rupees 24,79,730 annas 15 and pies 5). It, in addition, maintained an office in London costing £482, 3s, 9d. In all, the Indian census cost Rs. 24,85,517 which came to Rs. 11-15 anna per 1,000 persons.[4] The Census Report for 1881 notes:

> The great economy with which this great work has been effected will be evident, if we take this rate and apply it to the figures for the population in England and Wales, according to the Census of 1881. At this rate the cost for England and Wales would have been £26,000, and taking the value of money in India as against England to be as six to one the total cost for the census of the population of England and Wales, and for compiling the report and returns, would be £156,000, a sum very largely below what the real cost of the English census has been.[5]

The first general census was taken on 17 February 1881 and the provisional population, compiled in six months' time, was 208,202,050. The report was published in 1883 in three volumes.

The first chapter of the Census Report of 1881 was missing and I could not lay my hands on it. The second chapter dealt with religions, describing some of the popular practices and beliefs of the people. The third chapter discussed the sexes. The proportions borne by males to the females throughout India, with the exception of Travancore (present-day Kerala) was in marked contrast with those noticeable in European countries. Males exceeded the females. This coexisted with very early marriages. A greater difference marked the ages of husband and wife than was found in England and France. The excess of males was less marked among the Muslims, where the difference in age between the husband and wife was less marked. The Census Report observed:

> The great and abnormal excess of males over females is attributable to the social habits of the people, which, inducing very early marriages, the difference in age between husbands and wives being always relatively greater than in Europe, tend to permit a wider play to the physiological law which are traced in the influence of the ages of the parents on the sexes of their progeny.[6]

Female infanticide was noticed in India. The Census Report noted a certain amount of concealment of females between the ages 5 to 14. In other words, concealment was most marked in early ages when females became marriageable.

Chapter 4 of the Census Report was entitled 'The Civil Condition of the People' and dealt with matters such as the fecundity of different religions, the social position of women, the treatment of widows, the size of families, etc. A bride was a very valuable possession and both force and purchase were put in action to obtain her'.[7] Chapter 5 discussed ages of the population. It mentioned: 'The inaccuracy of the whole population in respect of returns of their ages comes out in a marked manner in the figures with which I am about to deal'.[8]

Chapter 6 discussed the rates of mortality and the mean duration of life. Indian population contained a large proportion of children as well as a small number of old persons. In other words, India was a land of an exceptionally high birth-rate and a correspondingly high death rates. The enumeration of females in India was less perfect. Chapter 7 was devoted to statistics of language. The report observes:

The language which is returned as numbering most speakers is Hindustani or Urdu. It embraces more than 82,000,000 (out of the enumerated population of nearly 20 crores) and is spoken throughout the whole of (India). Its numbers are over-stated and it is quite clear from the returns that Hindi, which is a distinctly separate language from Hindustani, the latter being a compound of Hindi, Persian, Arabic and Turki has not been separately distinguished for any provinces except Ajmer, Bombay, Central India, Hyderabad and Madras.

The Report continued:

'The largest number, speaking Hindustani in any province, is given in the North-West Province and Oudh, 43,221,705, and is in this province probably that most of the error occasioned by the omission of Hindi from the returns, and its inclusion in Hindustani has been caused'.[9] 'My impression is that quite half of the persons shown as speaking Hindustani might strictly be described as speaking Hindi'.[10] Other chapters deal with birth-place, literacy, the insane, blind, deaf and lepers and urban and rural population. From the point of view of religions, the Hindus were ahead of Muslims in the matter of education. The Census Report of 1881 observes: 'Whereas in 1,000 persons of all religions the illiterates are 898, among 1,000 Hindus the illiterates are 881 only; for every 67 men of all religions who can read and write, the Hindus can show 79, and for every 34 scholars of the whole populations they can show 38'.[11]

The Report explains:

The facile and receptive Hindu has from the earliest times lent himself to all such new learning as seemed to promise him advancement or profit; he has ever been an eager student both of his own and of exotic learning; in the times of the Mughal Empire, though most of those posts, whose splendour caught the eye and filled the imagination, were appropriated by the ruling race, the humbler, but perhaps hardly less lucrative, appointments in the general administration were held by Hindus, whose capacity for business fitted them for the administration of details which were beneath the notice or beyond the patience of their masters. . . When the Mohammedan Empire fell before the growing power of the

> British, the Hindu changed the direction without abating the earnestness of his studies, and while the Mohammedan, proud and bigoted cherishing the memory of a ruined greatness and the traditions of a faded splendour held sullenly aloof from the conquering race, and partly from dislike, partly from pride, refused to acquire their language or to countenance their measures, the pliant Hindu redoubled his exertions and soon succeeded in obtaining almost exclusive possession of all posts in the country that were open to natives. Since that time the Hindu has taken full advantage of the facilities which the British rulers provided for the education of the native subjects, the more intelligent classes among Hindus applied themselves to the study of English. The better classes among the Muhammedans began to wake up from their lethargy and some advance was made in the spread of learning among them. Among the lower classes, however, this 'renaissance' has had little or no effect, and their ignorance is as complete as ever.[12]

The next important Chapter is 10, which deals with castes. The first general census identified 273 castes in all. Chapter 13 and 14 relate to occupations of the people and their mobility. The last chapter is entitled 'Concluding Remarks'.

The account given in the Census Report for Oudh for 1869 of the actual process of enumeration of population holds broadly true in the case of head counting of 1881 for all-India.[13] Head-counting was not an ordinary experience for the people whose memories of the suppression of the 1857 Indian uprising against the British were still fresh. Indeed, wild imaginations were excited by the novelty of a census under English rule, by the elaborate preparations made for it, and above all, by the mystery of its being conducted at night.

The 1881 census did not pass off entirely without a measure of popular suspicion towards the exercise. While the bearing of the people was generally submissive, the wildest possible rumours were in places circulated. A census, by its very definition, involves, on an elaborate scale, the record of personal matters respecting every soul in the country, of whatever sex or age and yet bereft of any definite result clearly perceptible by the local mind. At some places tribal demonstrations occurred. Objection was taken to the numbering of the houses and of the people and to the record of their names. The fact that the final enumeration was carried out at nightlent colour to some deep-seated conspiracies by the Government. In Santhal Pargana, terror gripped the people necessitating dispensing with the final noctural enumeration. At some places, troops were called out to maintain order. Yet on the whole, censusing was peaceful. The Census Report for 1881 in Bengal observed: 'There was... scarcely any occasion to make use of the penal clauses of the (Census) Act (becoming a law in November 1880).'[14]

Wherever feelings of fear .persisted, this soon gave way as the wheels of census began moving. As the local aristocratic families found themselves personally enlisted in the work of the census, mistrust vanished, and in the case of the non-official instructors and enumerators was succeeded by a feeling of pride at being entrusted with a share in the conduct of so important a matter.

Mildly amusing stories were associated with these early days of censusing. Enumerations were sometimes visited by small acts of fraud by enumerators. There were reports of a copper coin being collected by the enumerators from every house visited by them. The enumerators were poor men, temporarily placed in a position which gave them a little authority and they endeavoured to use it to their advantage.

The census of 1881, faced its own problems in information-gathering. The occupation of the British-born females were so inaccurately returned that these were not tabulated. Similarly, the married women were frequently returned as following the occupations of their husbands. In one province, one lady was returned as 'Member of Council' and in another case as 'Government advocate'. These certainly constitute the curiosities of census literature. It was the duty of the State to supply the red ochre and oil used in numbering the house and burning the lamp on the enumeration night. Small fees were often illegally extracted by the ground level functionaries while performing these tasks.

It must be noted that the administrative machinery for census had been more or less finalised in the nineteenth century exercises in individual provinces. The whole country was parcelled out into enumerator's blocks. Blocks were grouped together under a supervisor as his circle. Two or more circles were placed under a superintendent as his charge. The emphasis throughout was that no village or house was to be left out nor any getting reiterated enumeration.

The district officer's first task was preparation of the village registers. He then set out to demarcate the district into charges, circles and blocks. Having done the demarcation, his next task was to appoint officers to have charge of each. Simultaneously with the appointment of supervisors and enumerators began the preparation of house lists and the numbering of houses. The Report of the 1881 Census of Bengal says about the grass-roots level functionary :

> But for the willing cooperation which was almost everywhere rendered gratuitously by the more intelligent inhabitants of the districts, the charge to Government for paid enumerators would have been a very heavy one. As it happened, the number of paid census officers was extremely small ; and in point of fact it may be said that enumerators were paid only where their service was of a special character such as the enumeration of the boat population on big rivers and the lake. In rural areas the enumerators were the patwaris or, in some cases, intelligent villagers of influence and position. A better class of persons was police, sometimes even independent gentlemen of position and intelligence.[15]

The Census Report of 1881, compiled by W.C. Plowden, was published in 1883. It commented on the various provincial reports with a very discerning eye. Plowden put the Census Report on Berar prepared by Kitts on the top. The evaluation is worth reproducing:

> The best of the reports . . . is that for Berar by Mr. Kitts. It is approached very closely if not equalled in excellence, by Mr. Baines' Report for Bombay. And, it must be remembered, in comparing the quality of the two reports that the population of Berar is not a fifth that of Bombay. Mr. Coplestone's report for Burma is a valuable work, and has the additional merit of having been produced and printed within less than a year of the date of the Census. The report for the Punjab is a mine of useful information, and is written in a most attractive style. Mr. Mc Iver, who was entrusted in November 1882 with the completion of Madras work, has been expeditious in producing a very good report for that province. But he has been unable from the shortness of time allowed him, to go as fully into details as he would doubtless have done had he been in charge of the work from the first.[16]

Nor was the first Census Commissioner unmindful of the shoddy work put in by some provincial deputy. One civil servant by the name of Driberg, who was in charge of the Assam census, was especially named in the Census Report for his careless work. Plowden wrote: 'Mr. Driberg was the only officer of whom I had any reason to complain.'[17] About his census crew, he had the following to observe:

> All the provincial deputy superintendents have, with one exception, exerted themselves to discharge the irksome and laborious work entrusted to them (exception being Driberg). I have specially to note the good work done by Mr. Baines in Bombay, Mr. Ibbetson in the Punjab, Mr. Kitts in Berar, Mr. McIver in Madras, Messrs Bourdillon and White, in Bengal and the North-Western Provinces, have also deserved praise for the manner in which they have discharged their onerous duties. Mr. Drysdale, the Deputy Superintendent of the Central Provinces, laboured untiringly at his work, and was, I regret to say, reduced to such a state of health that he was obliged to take short leave home. Mr. Stokes had charge of the Madras Census from its commencement till November 1882, and though his departure from the prescribed system of abstracting caused considerable delay in the compilation of the Madras figures, his work has otherwise been excellently done. He, too, devoted himself so entirely to his duties that his health suffered and he was obliged to take leave to England.[18]

Census entailed such unremittingly hard work that it damaged the health of many. The first Census Commissioner for India, W.C. Plowden impaired his eyesight because of excessive reading. He writes: 'In my own report I feel there are many shortcomings and defects, as continued observation of heavy figured statements has so weakened my sight that I have been unable during the later progress of the work to exercise as much personal supervision in respect of the actual tabulation of the figures as I should have wished'.[19]

REFERENCES

1. *Report of the Census of Bengal 1881*, Part I, Calcutta, Bengal Secretariat Press, 1883, p. 461.
2. *The Census Report for 1881*, p. 467.
3. Home Department—Public, March 1880, No. 157-187.
4. *Ibid.*
5. *Ibid.*, p. 471.
6. *Ibid.*, p. 52.
7. *Ibid.*, p. 85.
8. *Ibid.*, p. 114.
9. *Ibid.*, p. 196.
10. *Ibid.*, p. 196-7.

11. *Ibid.*, p. 223.
12. *Ibid.*, p. 234.
13. *The Census Report for Oudh 1869*, p. 13.
14. Report, p.8.
15. *Ibid.*, p. 5.
16. The 1881 India Census Report, London, HMSO, 1883, p. 472.
17. *Ibid.*
18. *Ibid.*
19. *Ibid.*, p. 479.

6

THE CENSUS COMMISSIONER FOR INDIA

The census organisation of India is headed by a single executive, the Census Commissioner for India. He is generally appointed on the recommendation of his predecessor and chosen much in advance in order that the general scheme of operations may be matured well in time, which, ideally, is nearly three years before the decennial census is held. The Census Commissioner is a statutory authority, his appointment being mandated in the Census Act. The Census Act is the enabling Act for the entire census operation, and provides the legal basis of the decennial census. Even the first census of 1881 had followed the enactment of the Census Act, which had the purpose of defining legally enforceable obligations and responsibilities on census functionaries as well as on the people.[1] It was believed from the beginning that the success of the census hinged on the cooperation of both the enumerators and the enumerated, for which a legal enactment was essential. But the Census Act was temporary, and as such lapsed once the census was over. The Census Commissioner's function is described in it in merely twenty words—'to supervise the taking of the census throughout the area in which the census is intended to be taken'. The Act says that 'Central Government may appoint a Census Commissioner to supervise the taking of the Census'. The law is silent on the occupational background of the functionary or his professional qualification. In short, legally speaking, anyone, even from outside the career bureaucracy, may be appointed as Census Commissioner.

The office of the Census Commissioner was first visualised by the Plowden Committee in 1877. The Committee said:

> We recommend that there should be one controlling officer who should supervise and direct the enumeration in the different

> provinces... Under this officer, who might be designated the Census Commissioner, a deputy should be employed in each province, under whose supervision the census would be taken, and who would manage the provincial office where the abstracts from each province would be compiled.[2]

The Census Commissioner had to assemble and galvanise into action what was decidedly the single biggest organisation, with its penetration into every nook and corner of the country. British India had a unitary form of government until the passage of the Government of India Act, 1935. The central constitutional writ ran all over the country, the lower level government being of the status of only local government. The census authority and arrangements did not undergo any change with independent India's transition into federalism. Though the census was—and is—a central responsibility, the whole burden of head counting has always virtually fallen on the provincial shoulders. The Census Commissioner had, therefore, to remain in close and continuous contact with the provinces, particularly with the provincial census chiefs. He extensively toured the provinces and kept the census machinery in a state of animation. The deployment of provincial civil service officers for census work was calculated to promote a greater degree of active association of the provincial government with the census. This entailed its own advantages.

The Census Commissioner has been appointed from the premier generalist service, earlier the Indian Civil Service (ICS) and later its successor, the Indian Administrative Service (IAS). The first Census Commissioner for India, which was his full designation, was William Chicheley Plowden, who was a product of the patronage mode of recruitment, having spent the mandatory three years at the Haileybury College (1850-52). Plowden's credentials were formidable. He had his association with the census work from the earliest times. He had earlier prepared the census reports of the North-Western Provinces held in 1872 and 1865. In 1878, he was appointed the chairman of the committee to prepare a blueprint of census organisation in India.

Plowden's successor, J.A. Baines, was drawn from the Indian Civil Service. The reservation of this office for the members of the ICS or the IAS is provided in the rules governing cadre management. But the incumbent was selected by the Government of India with more than normal care and attention. Besides possessing qualities of efficiency, he had to be tactful, good in judgment, resourceful and a good leader of men proven in field postings who could quickly build rapport with other departments and personnel most of whom were outside his own hierarchy and thus beyond his customary control. Additionally, the person fit for the job was directly familiar with the census work in the past. Baines, for instance, was the census superintendent for Bombay in the earlier counting before he was made the Census Commissioner for India in 1891. Relevant direct experience was nearly always taken into account when appointing senior and middle level positions in the census hierarchy. It was safe to generalise and take the view that a Census Commissioner was drawn from that small group of ICS officers, who had served as provincial in-charge of census in the past.

This practice would continue to be a powerful consideration in the selection in future also. In other words, the Census Commissioner for the year 2001 is nearly certainly located somewhere among the state directors (the new designation for the superintendents) of census operations of 1991. In practice, the universe of final selection turns out to be even smaller, for the incumbent generally comes from bigger states of the Union or according to seniority. The only exception to this norm was R.A. Gopalaswamy, who became Census Commissioner for the 1951 census without possessing any previous experience in the line. At the other extreme falls the case of Ashok Mitra, the Census Commissioner for 1961. Before taking charge of the Census Commissioner from 1958 till 1968, he was the census superintendent of West Bengal in 1951-58, the sub-divisional charge officer in 1941, and had functioned as an enumerator in 1931. Most Census Commissioners may not claim such a long chain of relevant experience, but posting as director (or earlier superintendent) of census operations is an ideal preparation for the Census Commissioner's job.

The Census Commissioner for India, as already mentioned, was appointed by the Government of India out of nominations received from the Indian Civil Service and was selected out of members with twenty to twenty-three years of service. A convention also developed that the Census Commissioner was appointed on the recommendation of his predecessor. J.H. Hutton, the Census Commissioner in 1931, gave the following recommendation for the appointment of his successor: 'The best man by far for the 1941 census would be Yeatts. Failing him, either A.E. Pirties (Bengal) or W.H. Shoobest (C.P.), between whom there is not much to choose'.[3] Yeatts at the time was a deputy secretary in the Central Department of Education, Health and Land. He had earlier handled the census operations in Madras as provincial chief.

Administrative and other qualifications in the appointment of the Census Commissioner were invariably even more crucial. The Census Commissioner had to have evinced conclusively proven qualities of administrative success and leadership. He possessed the quality of getting along with persons with varying backgrounds. He was, equally, a person of literary taste, preferably having experience of similar work in the past. His responsibilities were heavy and onerous, entailing long hours and periods of continuous work. As his job was the ideal case study of 'all work and no play', the physical attributes of the incumbent received special consideration. The selected person was to be of robust health who could cope with hard work of more than twelve hours for long periods without respite. Successive Census Commissioners recommended not only physically sound health as an important consideration but also a long vacation to the selected officer before embarking on his census responsibilities. To give an example, M.W.M. Yeatts availed of twenty months leave before taking up the post of Census Commissioner in 1939.[4] The terms offered for the post were pay in the regular time scale of the ICS plus Rs. 500 as monthly special pay exclusive of over-seas allowance. J.H. Hutton, when appointed to the post, possessed experience of twenty years' service while Yeatts had nineteen years' seniority.

Time is the essence of a Census Commissioner's work. Everything in his job is linked up in a date succession. Nothing, therefore, should be done to upset or unsettle the time sequence. The Census Commissioner was to be appointed long before the census. Hutton, put on the job in October 1929, later complained that this was not early enough. For the census of 1941, Hutton considered that the appointment should have begun about April 1938: the Census Commissioner designate being placed on special duty in the secretariat to study and examine preliminary questions for about three months before proceeding on long leave to return and start the detailed work.

The post of the Census Commissioner was and has been the highest statistical post in India, even in the world, and yet it was always manned by a generalist administrator, drawn either from the Haileybury College or the Indian Civil Service or the Indian Administrative Service. This continues to be the practice even though India presently has a separate Indian Statistical Service. This merits a discussion. Little doubt exists as regards the statistical contents of the job. But the job demands, more than anything else, the proven capability to lead complex organisations and motivate and direct large number of personnel, drawn as they necessarily are from various professions as well as departments of the provincial governments. All these call for a high level of administrative capabilities in the apex level functionary. Nor should one forget that the Census Commissioner had necessarily to enlist the support and cooperation of numerous functionaries working in different departments of both the levels of government as well as non-officials. In the administrative culture of India, an officer carrying the label of Indian Civil Service commanded a level of acceptance and respectability unavailable to other services. To conclude, the Census Commissioner continues to be drawn from the cadre of Indian Administrative Service, and this is most likely to be the position in future also.

Being the nation's chief head counter, the responsibilities of the Census Commissioner are both administrative and statistical, the first part predominating in the initial, pre-census taking phase and the second, namely, statistical part, being the major task after the heads have been counted. His administrative responsibilities are vast, complex and varied, covering selection of provincial chiefs of census, giving them administrative support, fixing the census date and assembling and activating the vast census organisation, to name the major ones. A civil servant, who has occupied the office of the Census Commissioner for India, defines his job as follows:

> In my career of nearly thirty years I had had long tenures in the field, each of which I enjoyed immensely. I 'did' two districts. I held charge of sub-divisions. I was earlier survey settlement officer. Of all the assignments I have held so far, my job in the Census— I had three stints, as Census Commissioner, as Director of Census in the state and as District Census Officer— had been by far the most satisfying. . . The census post is a seductive post: once you are in it you fall deeper and deeper in love with it. When I was first sounded for the post of the Census Commissioner of India, it appeared as a challenge to me—the first ever challenge in my career of holding the census. . . It is unfortunate that the Census Commissioner's job is not rated very high among the civil servants these days as the limelight, today, is on the economic ministries. The Census Commissioner's is a very special post— a very special one at that.

Varied was the quality mix needed in the Census Commissioner. In addition to proven administrative competence, he was to possess communication skill and persuasive ability of higher order and for this he needed to be endowed with an extra-ordinary amount of patience, perseverance and tact. He was expected to quickly and successfully build up rapport with others. As census was an all-India event, he had necessarily to interact with Chief Secretaries and others in the provinces.

He had necessarily to interact with consumers of his product, including the academics and government departments. Today, he has to closely liaise with bodies like the Planning Commission. He has necessarily to tour the country extensively and visit each state for personal discussions.

The office of the Census Commissioner, all told, demands unusual stamina and wide range of competence and was not meant for the average run of officers. R.F. Muddie, the Home Member in 1937, thus explained the nature of work of the Census Commissioner for India: 'The Census Commissioner's post is a particularly exacting one and calls for exceptional qualities—not only high administrative and organising ability, but special knowledge of a subject beyond the experience of most officers and sufficient literay skill to present the results of the census is a form which will make them appreciated by anthropologists, sociologists and statiscians throughout the world'. Yet, sadly, it was not rated very attractive and was not particularly sought after in the civil service during the colonial times. This is confirmed by the fact that not many nominations were received for the post.

The officers possessing the length of service required for filling the post generally reached the point in their career when they began to officiate as divisional commissioners in the provinces or in such other appointments as carried a higher rate of pay. The consequence was that the post of Census Commissioner was not financially attractive. The special allowance of Rs. 500 per month fixed by the Government was not perceived to be adequate compensation. It was also seen that those who functioned in the census hierarchy were left in the cold when it came to selection for prestigious or plum postings in the Government, which created a perception that the Census Commissioner's post was virtually a dead alley.

Matters have not improved even after independence. The top-level posts of cabinet secretary and secretaries to Government have generally eluded the census hierarchy; the only exception being A. Mitra. No Census Commissioner has so far won any State decoration in recognition of his censusing work. His only reward is that his name appears on the census report and his name is fondly remembered long after the names of the administrative heavy-weights of the day have been forgotten. Plowden, Baines, Hutton, Yeatts, etc., have carved out for themselves a permanent place in census history. So is Ashok Mitra and others in independent India.

Though, conventionally, the Census Commissioner was chosen from among the officers who worked as superintendent of census operations in a province in the previous census, it was not a consistently observed practice. Hutton, the Census Commissioner in 1931, who had no previous experience, remarked in his Administration Report: 'An experience of census as a provincial superintendent at preceding census should probably carry more weight in making the selection than it did on this occasion. It is a consideration of very great importance.' R.A. Gopalaswami, Registrar-General and Census Commissioner of the 1951 Census, also had no previous census experience. Gopalaswami was appointed in place of Yeatts, who had been appointed as the Registrar-General and who passed away before resuming duty after his leave.

There was no Census Commissioner for the 1871-72 Census. The list below gives the names of Census Commissioners thereafter:

1881	W. Plowden
1891	J.A. Baines
1901	H.H. Risely till September 1902
	E.A. Gait from September 1902
1911	E.A. Gait
1921	J.T. Martin
1931	J.H. Hutton
1941	M.W.M. Yeatts
1951	M.W.M. Yeatts up to 2 July 1949
	R.A. Gopalaswami from November 1949
1961	A. Mitra
1971	A. Chandra Sekhar
	(R.B. Chari in between)
1981	T. Padmanabhan
	(V.S. Varma in between)
1991	A.R. Nanda
	(Vijaya Unni in between)

On some occasions, the Census Commissioner was either transferred out or was assigned additional duties during his tenure in the post. W.C. Plowden, who was chairman of the Census Committee of 1877 as well as the Census Commissioner for 1881 counting, later complained of delayed appointment in this post which adversely affected his performance. He also criticised the Government action in transferring him out while the enumeration was taking place, as a result of which the arrangements for abstracting and compiling the figures and statistics collected at the census were not as satisfactory as they might have been. Again in 1901, E.A. Gait, who succeeded H.H. Risely before the completion of the All India Census Report, remarked:

> The office of the Census Commissioner for India was held by Mr. H.H. Risely, C.I.E., from its creation in October 1899 until September 1902 when unfortunately his immediate connection with the operation came to an end. Mr. W.S. Mayer, C.I.E., took charge of the office temporarily in addition to his duties as Editor of the *Gazetteer* and I succeeded him as Census Commissioner on 23 January 1903. In spite of the pressure of other work Risely has himself completed the chapter on caste and portions of four chapters.

In the census of 1911, Gait himself had a worse experience. He writes:

> I have held the office of the Census Commissioner for India from the commencement of the operations to the end, but since 11 April 1912, when I was appointed to a more responsible post, I have been able to devote to census work only such time as could be snatched from other engrossing duties. This has not only delayed the issue of the report, and the report fails to discuss certain questions as fully as I had originally intended. . . Work of this kind demands a degree of concentration.

Ex-Officio Secretariat Status

During the Raj, the Census Commissioner had no *ex-officio* status in the Government. As a result, he had to submit to the Government numerous matters for approval, which necessarily took a long time. This was particularly frustrating especially when time was of the essence. The low offcial status accorded to the Census Commissioner adversely affected his performance. This situation particularly irked M.W.M. Yeatts, who sought upgrading of the post. Yeatts argued that census was one of the major performances of the Government of India but its head, the Census Commissioner, with 'the spending of half a crore of rupees in his hands' was rated in the official warrant of precedence along with, for example, the Director of Geological Survey, Ordnance Factories, etc. He referred to his predecessor J.H. Hutton and said: 'I know that Dr. Hutton—a man singularly free from personal reactions—felt that a system which rates him below the chief commissioner of the Andaman and Nicobar Islands, a resident of the second class or the revenue commissioner, Sind and Orissa, did less than justice to the importance of the post and to some extent detracted from the authority he could carry, particularly in the (princely) states'. In his 'Comments' on one or two points regarding the administration of the all-India census, made on 5 August 1938, Yeatts recommended: 'My personal opinion is that the post should be rated with those of the members of the central board of revenue, *i.e.* in item 29.'[5] The suggestion was examined and 'a decision has been reached that no change in the warrant of precedence is possible and that Mr. Yeatts should be informed accordingly on his return from leave.'[6]

Yeatts strongly pleaded for the status of an additional joint secretary to be conferred on the Census Commissioner to maximise his effectiveness. Without such a rank, he was forced to go to the Government even for trivial matters, which was frustrating as well as totally unnecessary. Soon after his nomination as the Census Commissioner for India, he wrote in a note to the Home Department in the Government of India: 'I remember having difficulties in Madras over having to refer minor matters for sanction up to Government and remember rightly, the Census Commissioner had at times to get similar sanctions from the Government of India. I would ask the Home Department to arrange now for this sort of thing to be avoided.' He watched helplessly time being consumed by clerks indulging in uninformative notings. His specific suggestion was: 'One course would be to make the Census Commissioner an additional joint secretary to the Government of India. This would prevent the Home Department being used as a kind of post office for minor references'[7]. The recommendation did not gain acceptance but to mollify the Census Commissioner, he was delegated wider financial powers and made head of Department. C.J.W. Lillie in the Home Department wrote:

> To declare the Census Commissioner as *ex-officio* joint secretary to the Government of India in the Home Department would amount to giving him all the extensive powers enjoyed by the departments of the Government of India and there does not appear to be sufficient justification for agreeing to such a course. The only example of the arrangement of this kind is that of the Members of the Central Board of Revenue (CBR). The circumstances present in that case are, however, special. In the first place, the Board is part and parcel of the Finance Department and the members work directly under the control of the Finance Member. Moreover, a convention has been established—strictly followed in practice—that un-official approval of the Finance Department proper is obtained by the Members before conveying

> sanctions to proposals which are beyond the financial powers formally delegated to the Board. In practice, therefore, the powers of the Departments of the Government of India are not exercised even by the Members of the C.B.R.[8]

But the wheel was moving in the direction of Yeatts' thinking, even though during the whole period of the British Raj, the country's chief head counter had held the substantive post of a deputy secretary in the Government of India. Yeatts was a deputy secretary when he was first picked for this post. But it was nearly agreed to upgrade the post and make it professionally attractive. In May 1949 the work relating to vital statistics was transferred from the Ministry of Health to the office of the Census Commissioner for India. The designation 'Census Commissioner' was consequently changed to 'Registrar-General and *ex-officio* Census Commissioner for India'. Yeatts was the first to hold the post. This event marks the end of the phoenix organisation, and a permanent one came into existence.

Independence has seen two major changes in the office of the Census Commissioner. First, the job has been combined with that of the Registrar-General of Births and Deaths and thus the post has become a permanent one. Secondly, the functionary now enjoys an *ex-officio* secretariat status of a joint secretary. One should thus note that for both these developments, the spade-work had been done during the Raj.

The newly appointed Census Commissioner spares no time and effort in closely studying the reports and notes left by his predecessor. A notable feature of the census organisation is that the outgoing Census Commissioner prepares a very comprehensive, detailed report, called Report on Administration, for the internal consumption of the census bureaucracy including his successor. The state level superintendents of census operations also prepare a volume on administration recapturing meaningful lessons, warnings and concerns for the benefit of their successors and the census organisation. The central census organisation maintains extensive records on census, which are available to the newly appointed Census Commissioner. The new incumbent undertakes tours of the country, visits all parts and talks to knowledgeable persons from all walks of life. All these are part of his preparation for the job.

As said earlier, an administrative volume used to be published by the Census Commissioner for the use of his successor. This was first done at the time of the 1891 census. In the beginning the papers and other material prepared and collected by the Census Commissioner were stored in boxes and placed in the Education Department for the use of the next Census Commissioner. E.A. Gait, the Census Commissioner in 1911, however, did not prepare his Report on Administration; instead, the series of volumes already prepared by him were to serve the purpose. He also prepared a collection of important letters for use of his successor. In addition, he prepared a brief note dealing with various points 'which have occurred to me while writing my report and containing suggestions for removing difficulties and misunderstandings which came to notice in the course of the operations'.[9]

Preparation for census work began with the despatch of circulars covering all items of the census drill to the state level superintendents of census operations. The ball was taken forward, and the provincial government wrote about the census work to district collectors/field organisations. The district collector activated himself and appointed charge officers and other lower level census functionaries were appointed. In other words, it was through succession of circulars that the census organisation was mobilised and animated. These circulars played the role of training of the field census personnel, generously supplemented by personal discussions and conferences also. For enumerators and supervisors, training was organised in two-three rounds, where nuts and bolts were explained and doubts removed.

A convention developed quite early in the census history to offcially and formally thank the Census Commissioner for the work rendered by him as the Census Commissioner. Expression of the Government of India's appreciation of the Census Report was made at the closing down of his census commissioner's office. E.A. Gait, the census chief in 1911, was, for instance, noted for the 'interesting and valuable report which 'the Governor General in Council has read with much pleasure'.

Advance Planning

Advance planning is a prerequisite of successful census administration and the necessary ignition and fuelling is provided by the census chief. In 1991 it began four years before the date of census: this is normally the time when the ball is set rolling. A host of activities await attention and action. Draft questionnaires are developed taking into consideration the past experiences, the requirements of the country to be served by the census data and the recommendations of various bodies like the United Nations etc. These questionnaires are discussed in the Data Users' Conference, where important ministries of the Central Government, the Planning Commission, the state governments, universities, demographic and population institutes, individual experts, etc., are invited. The Census Commissioner is assisted by an Advisory Committee, which is appointed by the Central Government to advise on technical aspects of the census. The questionnaires are vetted by this Committee. Pre-testing of questionnaires in selected areas takes place, and feedback is analysed by the Advisory Committee. There is again a pre-testing to ensure that the questions asked yield precisely the desired response at all places; and no ambiguity is discerned.

REFERENCES

1. *The Census Act*, 1881.
2. Report of the Plowden Committee to consider the Suggestion for a General Census in India in 1881, para 32.
3. *Home—Public*, F 45/4/39-Public.
4. *Ibid.*
5. *Home—Public*, File 45/20/38-Public.
6. *Ibid.*
7. *Ibid.*
8. *Ibid.*
9. See E.A. Gait's note published in Proceedings of the Government of India in the Department of Education for the Month of January 1914, Calcutta, Superintendent, Government Printing, 1914, Notes-Census-A, March 1914, p. 1.

7

FIELD ORGANISATION

In the census organisation, the critical component is the field which comprises the province, the district, the charge, the circle and the block. Each is discussed in the following.

The Superintendent of Census Operations

Census has been a central responsibility ever since the first all-India census of 1881, but the burden of conducting it has always fallen on the provincial (now, state) shoulders. The role and responsibility of the provincial chief of the census organisation thus becomes of critical importance in head counting.

The person who headed the census operations in a province originally bore the designation of 'deputy', which was soon changed to superintendent of census operations. He was an employee of the provincial government and was paid an additional monthly allowance. A person having a minimum of ten years standing in the Indian Civil Service and of the rank of under-secretary was preferred for the job. This functionary was first appointed in 1881. Earlier censuses were generally the responsibility of the Board of Revenue and someone from the Settlement Department was deputed to compile the final census report. An ICS member belonging to the province was preferred as he knew his province and its people intimately—an advantage denied to officials deputed from a distance.

The actual conduct of the census being the responsibility of the province, the job of the superintendent of census operations was onerous and difficult. Care was, therefore, taken to select the appropriate person. He was to be a person of proven administrative competence, a good manager of men and no less important, of robust health. The census superintendent had to build up from virtually nothing and also to resolve overlap between departments of the Government. In addition, he developed his own organisation, of a certain standard. He was to be a person with taste and aptitude for the work and one 'who will agree not to ask for furlough till it (the census) is over'. 'Census is so highly specialised and so completely concentrated in one individual that changes in the superintendent in the course of a census mean far more in the way of dislocation than they do, for example, where a deputy secretary to the Government has to take a couple of months' leave'. Thus wrote Yeatts in his note of 20 June 1938.[1] Dr. J.H. Hutton, the Census Commissioner for India in 1931, emphasised the need for utmost care in the selection of the functionary. As census provides the basis for policy-making on vital matters, it was of the 'greatest importance' that the enumeration was carried out fairly and objectively. The person selected for the post was, therefore, to be absolutely impartial.

His physical fitness was another important criterion for selection. The duties of a census superintendent were extremely strenuous and were likely to cause a breakdown in a person of poor physique. The Census Commissioner for India in 1941 personally experienced many of his provincial chiefs succumbing to illness on account of excessive work load.[2] He wrote after the enumeration of population in 1941 was over: 'I must emphasise here the extreme arduousness of a census superintendent's life. Four of my superintendents had actually to go to hospital and one of them is still there; three others were seriously run down and it must be realised that the pressure of the phoenix system is excessive.'[3]

The functionary needed to be selected much in advance so that he could prepare himself for the job. He was encouraged to go on long leave to refresh himself for the strenuous responsibility of the census chief. 'Drive' was also an important consideration in selecting a census superintendent and 'comparative youth was, therefore, a recommendation rather than a handicap.' Once appointed, the census superintendent was not to be changed, interfered with, or taken away for other duties until his work was finished. Interruption was extremely detrimental to census efficiency.

The intellectual ability of the officers to be selected was, perhaps, an even more important consideration than their bodily health, since the cost of the census was largely determined by the speed with which the provincial units completed their operations. The correspondence issued from the superintendent of census was assumed to have the authority of the Government. He virtually acted as an under secretary to

Government. In the Punjab he was a junior officer, probably a second class joint magistrate, ordinarily in receipt of Rs. 900 per month. A practice grew up of giving the functionary a fixed deputation allowance pay of Rs. 400 per month in view of the special and onerous work involved. He was expected to commence his work nearly a year before the actual enumeration and the census work used to be completed within a period of eighteen months.

It was the Plowden Committee (1877) which first recommended the appointment of 'deputy' under the Census Commissioner: 'a deputy should be employed in each province, under whose supervision the census would be taken, and who would manage the provincial office where the abstracts for each province would be compiled'.[4] This deputy was to be drawn from among the provincial officers themselves, the advantage being that he was well acquainted with the geographical features of the province and possessed direct knowledge of the inhabitants themselves. The appointment of the deputy was to be vested in the provincial government. What ultimately emerged was the designation of superintendent of census operations borne on the cadre of the Indian Civil Service.

The census superintendent's job was broadly twofold—administrative and technical. Under the overall control of the Census Commissioner he conducted the census in his province (now state), and to this end undertook numerous decisions of both administrative and technical nature. He had to find accommodation for his sprawling staff, recruit personnel, impart them training and keep these efficient and trim for the job. He arranged for printing and distribution of stationery. He planned and executed the operation of the census within his jurisdiction and saw through abstraction work too. He was, thus, actively involved in the whole process of head counting in his province.

The profile of an ideal census superintendent was thus portrayed by Yeatts in 1941:

> The Indian Civil Service plays many parts and one of the most strenuous, difficult and important is that of a superintendent of census operations. Selection is not made on grounds of statistical interest or attainment but on a general basis of administrative ability and this and drive are really vital. It is a platitude, indeed a truism, that a force is required to overcome inertia and the circumstances of a census superintendent's life place him up against the inertia of a decade, which has to be removed within a year. To produce a force of this dimension in such a time implies heavy expenditure of energy and that is why for a census

> superintendent one requires men of, to continue the physical analogy, high potential.[5]

A census was unimaginable without the involvement of the lower units of government. Among pre-requisites of the success of census was the closest cooperation between the centre and the provinces. The basic idea of the census was that at the enumeration stage, the people with local knowledge and responsibility got together and arranged all such appointments so as to produce the maximum of convenience along with efficiency. Very properly, therefore, the census organisation reposed the power of appointments of census officers in the provincial governments.

The selection of provincial census superintendent was not always easy nor smooth. There did occur an odd case when the Census Commissioner desired a certain officer from a particular service to be appointed as provincial census chief but the provincial government turned down the request and deputed another officer. Yeatts wanted a particular European officer to be appointed the census superintendent in the communally turbulent Punjab but he was overruled. He then wanted any officer of the ICS belonging to the Punjab cadre, but Punjab placed at his service an officer belonging to the provincial civil service, to his great disappointment. Yeatts ruefully wrote: 'This will add inevitably greatly to my difficulties'.[6]

A similar thing occurred in Bombay. While Yeatts wanted to have Streatfield as the census superintendent there, he was given another officer of a deputy collector's rank, Dracup. Yeatts placed his disappointment on record:

> I am bound, however, to put on record that failing Mr. Streatfield, I would have preferred, if I had to have a deputy collector, a man below 40 to one over 50, who incidentally will prove much the most expensive of all the provincial officers. This must, I think, be the first occasion on which the same impression on me is that Bombay has served its own purposes rather than the best interests of the census when it suggested an officer within reach of retirement. It is odd that when it complains of a difficulty for experienced performers, I have the impression that they are saying good-bye to Dracup without regret.[7]

He continued: 'Bombay in fact have had it both ways: it pushes off the man it wants and it gets the Government of India to take the responsibility of appointing him. All this points to the desirability at future censuses of getting the enumeration responsibility more correctly located *i.e.* on the provinces. Once this is done they will see that a good man is put on to it or will put the whole force of the provincial government behind it— or both'. Yeatts concluded: 'I quite realise that the central government is in a weak position inasmuch as it cannot compel a province to release a particular individual, and as the Bombay case shows, is in the unfortunate position of having to pay the piper without really being able to call the tune.'[8]

Yeatts realised with dismay that provinces like the Punjab were not realising the key significance of the provincial census chief executive. Emphasising the importance of the census superintendent in the task of census taking, he observed in a note to the Home Department:

> Given personality, ability and standing, a Census Superintendent can put across one of the most difficult administrative jobs under the Government of India. Lacking these qualifications, he will become the instrument of his own routine. In a province, where no violent or difficult issues arise, this is serious enough but in a province such as the Punjab or Bengal where they do and in an acute form, it is infinitely more so. We are not even told who the provincial civil service officer contemplated is, but it is impossible to imagine a Muhammadan, Hindu or Sikh member of the provincial civil service carrying the requisite weight and even a European P.C.S. officer will not do so. I observed this at the last census in Bombay, where the first superintendent was an Anglo-Indian officer of the P.C.S. who, despite his considerable abilities, cracked up before the end.

Yeatts preferred an ICS officer for the post of census superintendent because of the virtues of independence and impartiality associated with that Service. For the 1941 census, he desired a British member of the ICS to be appointed as census superintendent in the Punjab, but he was overruled, and one Muslim officer of the PCS was posted. Commenting on the matter, Yeatts observed:

> The Government of the Punjab and the Central Government itself made a mistake in disregarding Dr. Hutton's recommendation and my own that, given the obvious possibility of acute communal tension over the census in the Punjab, a British officer should be appointed for this census. . . In such cases, public confidence is of the highest importance and nothing should be omitted which

> could lead to raise or maintain it. I believe that with a British officer in this post the developments of the last days of February would have been avoided or at any rate been much less pronounced.

For the independence and objectivity demanded by census work, the choice had to fall on the higher civil services such as the ICS, since the PCS had a reputation of being amenable to local pressure and influence.

Yeatts, with his vast experience of census work, was strong in his views on the centrality of the census superintendent in the census operation. He wrote:

> Personally I can think of no post more important to the Punjab and to India in the next two or three years than the census superintendent. The appointment of these officers does not lie with me, nor I suppose technically is my acquiescence required, but as the officer who has been entrusted with the census of India and included in it of the Punjab, I am bound to declare that if an appointment of this sort (that is, from the PCS cadre) is made I consider myself absolved from responsibility for any defective, suspect or heavily criticised enumeration and tables which may flow from it.

Yeatts cited the example of Orissa which, despite its small size, entrusted its census to a British officer of the ICS. He observed:

> There is a history behind this with considerable relevance to Punjab conditions and possibilities. At the time of the last census (1931), the Ganjam District was the focus of the most passionate propaganda and invective between Oriyas and Telugus, each of whom looked to the census figures to support its case for or against the inclusion of particular areas in the new Oriya province. My own particular knowledge of the district and of its language was of special value here as it happened, but my action in securing a European officer for the main months of the enumeration stage was what really settled the issue. That officer was Mr. R.C.S. Bell whom Orissa has now chosen as its Superintendent, and there is no doubt that the steps taken then to put the quality and control of the enumeration into the special charge of an officer, against whom no possibilities of bias could be urged, was the initial base on which the subsequent

delimitation of the province in that area and its general acceptance by the people concerned rested.[9]

Viewing the vulnerability of enumeration stage, Yeatts preferred an ICS officer because he was above local influences and pressure. He contended:

> A census enumeration must be like Caesar's wife. I am not sure that Government is aware of the nature of the pressure often brought to bear on the census officers by interested parties or bodies which think him likely subject for pressure. The appointment of an ICS officer, if it does nothing else, raises by his standing in itself the level of the enumeration and diminishes opportunities for pressure.

With the introduction of separate electorates, allocation of seats in the legislature began to reflect the numerical strength of different religions and thus religion acquired an acute importance, particularly in areas where the community balance was delicate. As Yeatts wrote:

> A P.C.S. officer is under the thumb of the provincial government to an extent no I.C.S. officer is and it is my considered opinion that in the present circumstances and those of the next few years, no enumeration conducted under a Punjab P.C.S. officer could escape heavy criticism and suspicion quite apart from whether he would be able to control and discipline the enumerating forces under him to attain and retain the absolutely objective outlook which a census in any place, but particularly in the Punjab of today, demands.

The functions of the census superintendent still remain unchanged but independence has witnessed several changes in the nature of the functionary. His nomenclature has undergone a change. He is no longer an officer of the provincial government: though still taken from among local officers, he is on deputation to the Central Government and is thus an employee of the latter. His rank has also gone up one step since the days of the *Raj*, from under secretary to deputy secretary in the Central Government. This seems to be in keeping with the trend in independent India, where higher level functionaries perform jobs which were earlier performed by officers of lower rank.

Deputy Superintendent of Census Operations

From the earliest days, a practice grew of appointing a deputy superintendent of census operations say, for five or six months. His task was to supervise the abstraction and tabulation of the census data and to tour the offices under his charge. The jurisdiction of the superintendent of census operations extended to the entire province. The deputy superintendent looked after one of its territorial divisions. Like his boss, he was a full-time officer and headed the sorting office. U.P. had eight such sorting offices in 1931. The functionary had to undertake extensive tours to ensure efficient holding of the census.

Originally, a member of the Indian Civil Service was to be appointed to the post. But the Government of India discouraged the demand for members of the elitist service, considering that a native officer of the Subordinate Executive Service was adequate. Explaining its stand, the Government of India commented: 'The Civil Service in Bengal is . . . not maintained to provide an officer for this duty of the deputy superintendent of census operations, and it is the wish of the Secretary of State and of the Government of India that a member of the Indian Civil Service should not be employed in a post which is not reserved by statute, unless there is no other agency equally fit to hold it.'[10] Competent officers were easily available in the provincial civil service (then called the subordinate executive services), the Government of India pointed out. While, therefore, sanctioning the creation of the post, the central government left the actual appointment into the hands of the Lieutenant-Governor of Bengal, the precise choice to be restricted to the 'native officers' in the PCS.

Joint Census Heads in Provinces

In 1921, each province had its own superintendent of census, including those which had joint cadres, such as Bombay and Sind, and Bihar and Orissa. But during the wartime, because of the strain on the cadres in the provinces, the joint areas were supervised by a single officer.

Yeatts, with his experience of the 1931 census in Madras, strongly advocated the principle of one census superintendent for one province. In his view, the census superintendent carried the very difficult and delicate business of getting the provincial government and all its officers, not to mention municipal and other local authorities, to fall in with a general scheme, which made heavy and continuous demands on them in an activity which was time-bound to an unusual degree. Also, local knowledge was of great importance, as well as local acquaintanceships, standings, etc.

It was also unlikely, he said, that a census superintendent operating in more than one province would be able to exercise the same influence in both, and in the census particularly these inequalities in speed or efficiency would lead to disproportionate delay and expense. Moreover, every province, especially the new ones, would have ideas of their own, which, if met by the superintendents, might contribute substantially to improve their general attitude towards the census.

Finally, it was most desirable that, although census is a central activity the constituent unit should be encouraged to maintain and develop a provincial consciousness, as it were, in this regard. This was one of the strongest assets a census superintendent could have. Even in 1931, a certain attitude of detachment was observable, and if a province had only a portion of a superintendent, his attitude was not unlikely to increase this detachment. Hutton had already indicated serious deficiencies in the Sind census and had remarked that the presence of a census superintendent might do much to mend the bad reputation of the province. Orissa presented problems of peculiar difficulty in enumeration because of the very large extent occupied by tribes and the absence of communications over much of its areas. With a joint superintendent, these areas would receive inadequate attention.

District Level Census

In the district, the district collector was the overall in-charge of the census, even though this was his additional responsibility. For this, he was designated as principal census officer (PCO). The distinct collector's role census-taking was of central importance under the Raj. But in independent India it is but one of his multifarious responsibilities. Also, not all collectors today possess direct experience of census administration; some do not 'do' the census at all. The PCO was assisted by the district census officer, additional district census officer, sub-divisional census officers and charge superintendents. The district census officer was the additional district magistrate and the additional district census officer was from the statistics department. They were paid special allowances for their additional census responsibilities. The sub-divisional officers were made the sub-divisional census officers. The tehsildar was the charge superintendent for rural areas and the municipal commissioner for urban areas. The charge superintendent was assisted by the assistant or additional charge officer.

For purpose of census taking, the traditional revenue district was divided into 'charges'. A tehsil was a 'charge', put under a charge superintendent who was the tehsildar. The work of a charge officer was largely administrative. Indeed, the tehsildar was the pivot of the whole census structure in the tehsil. He was made the channel for the distribution of all instructions and forms to all within his charge. In 1941, additional charge superintendents were appointed for some special tracts.

Each charge was further divided, according to its size, into a number of circles, each under a supervisor, who preferably was a European in the beginning — 'a European subordinate in one of the public offices, a native clerk on a salary of no less than Rs. 70 or a master in a Government or private school'. A few supervisors were non-officials but the work required some clerical experience and voluntarism was not encouraged.[11]

The charge officer appointed the supervisors and the enumerators. A supervisor, who was the first line supervisor, was to be diligent and imbued with a sense of responsibility, and with firmness and tact in controlling his squad. There was one supervisor for 3-5 enumerators.

Each circle was further divided into blocks. The block was the smallest census unit, containing 30 to 50 houses, in charge of an enumerator. Fifty houses constituted a block as an enumerator could reasonably be expected to carry out the final enumeration of this number between 7.00 p.m. and midnight of 1 March. If the houses were physically close together, he could do 50 in the time; if they were scattered the number was reduced. There was an advantage in having small blocks if a sufficient number of enumerator was available.

The lower level functionaries in the census hierarchy have always been, at best, reluctant workers. Even during the Raj, the majority of enumerators did their utmost to avoid selection. Petitions of appeal were common while many enumerators had to be cajoled, even bullied before commencing work. In certain cases, the prosecution of certain individuals for refusing to work as enumerators proved necessary. M.W.M. Yeatts, the Census Commissioner for India in 1941, wrote: 'If the census is to continue, it seems clear that the basis on which enumerators and supervisors are appointed urgently needs revision'.[12] Indeed, reliance on the provincial government functionaries, who as a rule provided the backbone of the whole census organisation, was becoming progressively uncertain. The problem has become, if anything, more serious since 1947. The district collector is already too busy— at any rate, census claims no priority in his work plan. He may not spare sufficient time even to discuss matters personally with the director (or chief) of census operations, especially if the latter is from the 'promotees' rank and he himself of a higher breed, namely is a direct recruit. The tehsildar, as the charge officer (his new nomenclature), takes scant interest in training. In fact, the burden of training falls virtually on the shoulders of the personnel belonging to the state level directorate of census operations. The story is no different in the case of supervisors and enumerators. It has become growingly difficult to take work from the supervisors and enumerators without unpleasantness or the threat of invoking the Census Act.

The enumeration agencies available for census taking have historically included zamindars (land holders), police, patwaris, municipal bodies and volunteers. Who was best fitted for census taking was a topic of debate for a long time. For Bengal, which had no ground level machinery for census whatsoever, the appointment of 'special deputy magistrate' was suggested for conducting the census. The census was to be taken *thanadari*: 'that each thana (police station) should be divided into so many circles; and that each circle should be under the charge of a supervisor, and the whole supervised by the special deputy magistrate'. The precise nature of the agency available in each village was not spelled out by the 'deputy magistrate'.

A proposal to entrust census work to the zamindars was made as early as in 1870. Their agents could be entrusted with the duty of enumeration in the villages:

> Such agency exists in every village but will be of little use unless stimulated by a small fee. This fee should be one rupee for each man employed as an enumerator; Rs. 12 per man should be allowed for supervisors. These should be persons who are independent of the zamindars. A supervisor's duty should be to teach the enumerators their work, patrol their villages while the census is in progress, to examine the returns and report to the collector any inaccuracies which may come to their knowledge.[13]

Even in 1871 the enumerators were selected from the village revenue officers while the assistance of school masters, police and vaccinators was obtained as occasion required. In large towns the census was generally entrusted to the municipal authorities, special enumerators being employed if the ordinary municipal agency was insufficient.

In Bengal, where the village agency was traditionally defective, complimentary letters were addressed to one or two of the principal inhabitants of the place, requesting them to undertake the task of enumeration. A somewhat similar plan was adopted with good effect in other provinces. Provided that a sufficient check was maintained to ensure accuracy, there was no doubt of the great advantage of thus enlisting the services of the influential inhabitants, whose participation in the operation was regarded by the people as an earnest of the good faith of the Government, and thus tended materially to allay suspicion.

The Report of the 1881 Census of Bengal notes in this in context:

> But for the willing cooperation, which was almost everywhere rendered gratuitously by the more intelligent inhabitants of the districts, the charge to Government for paid enumerators would have been a very heavy one. As it happened, the number of paid census officers was extremely small; and in point of fact it may be said that enumerators were paid only where their service was of a special character such as the enumeration of the boat population on big rivers and the lake.

In relatively few cases was it found necessary to pay the enumerators, as the servants of the Government took the work in the ordinary discharge of their duties (receiving only the regulated travelling allowance), and the chief residents accepted their selection for it as a compliment. Landholders were required to give a certain amount of assistance personally or through their agents, pay being granted only where specially good work was performed. In cantonments and in municipalities the task was undertaken by the local authorities, whether civil, military or municipal. In large institutions the census was effected by the superintendent of the building. In the case of Europeans and of any 'natives' who desired it, the papers were left at the house to be filled by the head of the family, as in England. Dr. Cornish even referred to the necessity of employing special persons to enumerate the 'lower' castes, on account of the prejudices of the Brahmin village officers. Exceptional measures were also necessary for recording the wild and wandering tribes.

As enumerators were to be drawn on a temporary basis from the revenue staff, they had to be imparted training for their new assignment. They also needed to be supervised. Like the enumerators, the supervisors were to be unpaid workers taken from the local rural communities possessing a level of education. One supervisor was to be appointed to every ten enumerators, but on the day of enumeration, the supervising staff was to be increased in strength.

Census by its very nature entails extra responsibility. This raises a question whether those associated with census work needed to be sanctioned a financial incentive for carrying out this extra duty. Extra payment for such work was becoming more frequent, and when a case involving grant of bonus to an officer. closely connected with census responsibility, came up, the Government of India passed an order enunciating the general principle governing such imbursements. The order said:

> On broad grounds of general policy the Government of India is opposed to the practice of making extra money grants to covenanted civil servants of good official position on account of any special work they may execute. It is true that at various times special pecuniary rewards have been given for extra work done by an officer, when that work was well done in addition to the regular and legitimate duties of his appointment, and was not akin to them. Occasions may from time to time arise where such rewards may be given unobjectionably and even where they may be expedient and desirable, and cases of this kind have arisen in some provinces in connection with the compilation of district gazetteers.
>
> But His Excellency-in-Council considers that when an officer is relieved of his regular work to perform some special duty not involving additional personal expense and responsibility, he has no claim to enhanced remuneration, since the salary attached to the substantive appointment of every covenanted civilian is supposed adequately to pay for his whole working time, and it clearly rests with the Government to direct him to employ that time in the manner it considers most advantageous for the interests of the State.
>
> Holding these views the Governor-General-in-Council wishes it to be clearly understood that generally speaking he does not view with favour the practice which seems to be growing up of giving money presents to officers of covenanted civil service. His Excellency-in-Council doubts whether such a practice is calculated to enhance the reputation of a service admitted to be one of the noblest in the world, and there is reason to think that many of the leading members of the service also consider the perception of such rewards derogatory to its character. The Government of India is, therefore, inclined to discourage the practice thinking that where a proper spirit prevails officers of the service would do better to look to the approval of the

Government, and the increased prospects of promotion created by that approval, rather than to pecuniary rewards.[14]

Such was the spirit governing governmental behaviour under the Raj. In contrast, Government in Independent India evinces little hesitation in squandering the tax-payers' hard-earned money in covering its employees with all kinds of perks and allowances on one pretext or the other!

REFERENCES

1. *Home—Public*, F. 45/21/37.
2. *Home—Public*, F.No. 45/26/41-Public.
3. *Ibid.*
4. Report by officers appointed to consider the suggestions for a General Census in India in 1881, para 32.
5. *Ibid.*
6. *Home—Public*, F-45/17/36-Public.
7. Yeatts' note to Home Department, *ibid.*, Part II.
8. Yeatts' note dated 27 January 1940, *ibid.*, p. 158.
9. *Home—Public*, F. 45/26/41-Public.
10. Letter from Secretary to the Government of India to the Secretary to the Government of Bengal dated 20 February 1891. *Home Census, Proceedings*—March 1891, Nos. 3 to 7.
11. Census of India, 1901: India—Administrative Volume with Appendices. Chapter on 'Notes by Census Commissioner on Arrangements in Individual Provinces and States', p.75, Calcutta, Superintendent of Government Printing, 1903.
12. Census of India, 1941, Vol. I, Part II — Administration Report, 1942, p. 72.
13. Officiating Collector of Pubnah's Communication to C.E. Lance, Commissioner of the Rajshahye Division (No. p. 998, dated 22 February 1870). *Home—Public*, Proceedings, 11 July 1871.
14. Government of India's Letter No. 273 dated 27 June 1873, *Home—Public*, 1870, No. 114, Proceedings July.

8

THE SECOND WORLD WAR AND THE CENSUS

Preparations for the decennial census of India, due in 1941, started in 1939 with the appointment of the Census Commissioner for India, M.W.M. Yeatts, a member of the Indian Civil Service. But the Second World War broke out in September 1939 and India, a colony under the British, got directly involved into it.

In September 1939 itself, both Bombay and the Punjab wrote to the Government of India suggesting that the census be postponed.[1] The Government of India considered the matter but could not come to any final decision. The war had just begun, and it was difficult to foresee how long it would last.[2] If peace was re-established at an early date, there would be no difficulty in carrying through the programme already chalked out. But if the war was to be a long drawn affair, it was obviously difficult, if not impossible, to continue the census operation to a successful termination.[3] The course of the war needed to be watched for some more time before taking a final decision. Also Yeatts, the Census Commissioner designate, was away in Great Britain on leave and was to return in mid-November. An interim decision was, accordingly, taken reconfirming the holding of the census according to the normal schedule. 'The Government of India is, for the present at any rate, proceeding on the assumption that the census will take place in 1941 as previously decided.'[4]

But the war necessitated economy in expenditure. Accordingly, the Home Department of the Government of India undertook an internal exercise to trim down the expenditure on census. The Central Government also asked the provincial governments 'to seek every means of reducing the cost compatible with efficiency'. The normal cost of the census was approximately Rs. 50 lakhs— of which Rs. 18 lakhs was to fall in 1940-41 and Rs. 30 lakhs in 1941-42. The war had already necessitated additional taxation, and the census exercise would have accentuated the severity of the fresh taxation.

In addition to the financial liability, other weighty factors also disfavoured the holding of the census. The war demanded singular concentration of effort, and Britain had itself decided to postpone its census for this reason. Secondly, the provincial officials, especially the district level functionaries, who necessarily bear the brunt of census work, would be distracted from attending to the exigencies of the war, more so when Gandhiji's civil disobedience movement was also to cause social and political unrest in the country. As against this, the arguments in favour of census were also obvious: it would maintain the decennial series unbroken and besides, would demonstrate to the world the high level of importance colonial India attached to census. Equally pressing was another view. Indian census proceeds on momentum and the acceptance by provinces and the people of a long standing tradition. As Yeatts warned, 'momentum in administration as elsewhere is a precious thing which should never lightly be broken and we should think very carefully, therefore, before we disturb this acceptance. At present the work is going on and can be carried out to a successful conclusion.'

The Finance Department of the Government, when consulted on the matter, was inclined to think that from many points of view the balance of advantage definitely lay in favour of postponement of the census until normal conditions re-established themselves.[5] At the same time, it favoured an early decision of the Government even without waiting for Yeatts' return from leave. The Home Department discussed the view of the Finance Department at its highest level but decided to wait for Yeatts' return in the middle of November 1939, though the Department itself appeared to be not much sanguine about the census. It concluded, 'Though it is extremely desirable that the continuity of census should be maintained, a postponement is inevitable in the end. We have been told that we must expect a three-year war; and it would be unduly optimistic to expect that it would be all over by February or March 1941, *i.e.* in 18 months time.'

However, a vigorous exercise was initiated around this time to effect the maximum possible economy in the census. This took two forms. A proposal was mooted to have a non-synchronous census which would reduce the cost 'very greatly' by allowing use of less number of the provincial revenue personnel in carrying out the census. Secondly, economy could be secured by reduction in the contents of the schedule.

When Yeatts joined duty as the Census Commissioner for India, his first task was to procure a firm decision on whether census was to be held according to schedule or postponed. Crudely speaking, census work falls into two broad areas, as briefly discussed earlier—enumeration and abstraction (tabulation and compilation). To repeat, enumeration covers the whole country and every person in it. As far as enumeration is concerned, it matters little if one question is asked or fifty: it is the system which costs, and the dimensions of that system must remain broadly unaltered. In India enumeration is honorary, nearly unpaid, a factor which sets Indian census apart from every other census in the world. The enumeration cost of the 1931 census was about 10 per cent of the total cost. Tabulation and compilation, on the other hand, stand on a different footing. Here, a direct relation exists between the number and complexity of tables to be put out and the cost involved, even though the cost per table has not been precisely estimated in India. Cost per table depends on the sorting speed prescribed for the different tables, their intricacies and printing cost (printing cost being in direct proportion to bulk).

The first task in census is enumeration. Tabulation begins later and on points decided by the Government. The items on which information is sought need not become unmanageable. Neither does wisdom lie in reducing the number of items below a certain minimum. The basic principle here is this: unless one asks, one cannot have the answers to sort. The cost of enumeration and the cost of tabulation totally differ. Even a single additional question—and answer given by over 375 million of people, the latest estimate of the 1941 figure—would entail enormous expansion of the tabulation staff. In one case, the cost is that of a system and is not affected appreciably by the number of questions put; in the other, the cost is directly proportional to the amount of information it is decreed to be tabulated. What is being conveyed here is that enumeration and tabulation can be regarded as two distinct and separate activities. The first is fundamental and an essential preliminary to the second but tabulation and compilation need not necessarily follow immediately on enumeration. Enumeration is a netting of the population, as it were. The subsequent treatment of the netted bird is a separate matter and it can be safely caged for a considerable period before it could be used for the ultimate purpose for which it was obtained.[6]

Yeatts strongly argued in support of continuing the census. His ten-page note on the matter is a model of clarity of thought, rigour of logic and forcefulness of style. The note took full care of the financial burden involved in census and suggested economy in expenditure, thus securing a reduction of Rs.5 lakhs on compilation. If occupational tables were to be dispensed with, a further Rs.8 lakhs could be saved, but this was to be the last resort. Yeatts concluded his magnificent note summing up:

> Our view being that the census should go on and that we will do our best to conduct it on the most economical basis. After all, they (Finance Department) incur expenses of crores within the twinkling of an eye and they should not demur to half a crore spread over four financial years for a purpose which continues a tradition in which India has had a most honourable place since 1872. The lack of continuity, so undesirable for other reasons, has among its other adverse effects the production of a tendency to look on the census as a new activity to be judged like other new proposals. Actually, it is a continuing function of any government, and in India is far older than many of the departmental activities accepted now as permanences. Personally, I think a proper approach is from this stand point; let us promise all possible economy but do not abandon essentials or promise what is not possible.[7]

He, at the same time, firmly added: 'I have personally no desire to conduct a truncated census.'[8]

The Home Secretary, to whom Yeatts addressed his note, was impressed by his bifurcation of the census activities into enumeration and tabulation and opted for a truncated proposal favouring enumeration of the population, leaving the question of tabulation to be settled later, the enumeration cost being roughly Rs.15 lakhs only. The Home Department sent this revised proposal restricting the census to enumeration part, with a budget of Rs.15 lakhs. The Finance Department persisted with its disapproval, observing that 'the census should be postponed till 1946 or until normal conditions are re-established'. The Home Member ultimately discussed the case with his counterpart in Finance. The decision taken was to refer the matter to the Viceroy's Executive Council; and if the Council's decision was to postpone the census, the case was to go to the Secretary of State for India in London to ascertain his views before the decision was finally announced. But a discussion in the Executive Council required the Viceroy's permission. A summary on the question of the census of 1941 was prepared by the Home Department to which Finance also agreed, and was circulated, with the Viceroy's approval, among the members of the Executive Council in January 1940. Before the Council could meet, the Finance Department withdrew its objection to the proposal. The Home Department, however, wanted to have the case circulated for opinion. The decision reached was that the census was to continue but remain restricted to only enumeration, the decision regarding tabulation to be postponed until October or November 1941 when the question regarding finances was to be settled with the Finance Department.

The decision was also taken that the outside world was not to be informed about the truncated and provisional census. The provinces were told that census would be held on schedule. The census for 1941 was, thus, held in India, which is remarkable if one were to remember that the mother country (Great Britain) did not hold it in view of the on-going war. The tabulation scheme, however, was drastically curtailed. Information was collected on several items but it was not tabulated and printed.

The census of 1941 was conducted under unusual conditions of the war. The census operations for such a large population and areas as that of India are, in the best of times, a difficult and complicated exercise. But in 1941 the circumstances were rendered much more difficult. The war supervened when the plans were in an advanced stage and the whole scheme of census had to be reconsidered. It was remarkable that despite this handicap, the census operations were completed in accordance with the time schedule. The Government of India complimented the census chief on 30 March 1943 for successfully carrying out his census responsibilities. The Resolution, which was published in the Extra-ordinary Gazette of India, said: 'The Governor General in Council desires to place on record his appreciation of the conduct of (census) operations by Mr. M.W.M. Yeatts, C.I.E., I.C.S., the Census Commissioner for India, and of the assistance and cooperation rendered to him in that task by a large staff of officials and non-officials without whose ungrudging, and, in most cases, unpaid, services it would not have been possible to bring the operations to a successful issue at a comparatively cheap cost.'[9]

The census for 1941 relied predominantly on patwaris and persons employed or amenable to administrative control. This meant a far smaller proportion of outside and unreliable 'conscripts' such as had to be used under the old practice. This in itself added to the strength of the system.

REFERENCES

1. Home DO No. 45/27/39-Public dated 15 September 1939. File 45/27/39. Public 1939.
2. *Ibid.*
3. *Ibid.*

4. *Ibid.*
5. *Home—Public,* File 45/27/39 1939, p. 13.
6. *Ibid.*
7. *Ibid.*
8. His note dated 28 June 1939 to the Joint Secretary in the Home Department.
9. Extra-Ordinary Gazette of India, 31 March, 1943.

9

THE CENSUS AND CASTE

To most readers of the census reports, especially those outside the government, their primary interest lies in the information provided on 'caste', the single most peculiar social institution of India. Census reports were the first systematised documents which contained a wealth of information about caste and thus have played a pioneering role in its study. One is reminded that J.H. Hutton, who authored *Caste in India*, first published in 1946 and acclaimed as an authoritative work, was the Census Commissioner in 1931.

Hardly has an item taxed the compiler of the census report more than caste. The question of caste is most complex and getting correct returns on it very difficult. Indeed, W.C. Plowden found it so confusing that he recommended its total abolition from the census returns. In his Census Report of the North-Western Provinces, 1872 he observed: 'I hope on another occasion no attempt will be made to obtain information as to the castes and tribes of the population.'[1] The colonial rulers knew so little about castes that they thought it wise to record minute details. As a result, the classification of castes became, in the eyes of census bureaucracy, over-elaborate, profitless and hardly reliable. 'The shades of difference between *jogee* (योगी) and *shadhoo*, (साधु) *junghum* (झंगम) and *purumbhangsho* (परमहँस), *dundie* (दंडी) and *attithie* (अतिथि), *shunniashie* (संन्यासी) and *oodasheen* (उदासीन) are impossible to be distinguished in a general enumeration of the population'.[2] It was even known that impostors not having the least acquaintance with any of these persuasions freely roamed about, pretending to be devotees.

The problem was compounded by the general ignorance of this subject among the people themselves. The variety of names with which the same caste is called in different places further aggravated the problem. There was also a tendency to confuse caste with occupation. An attempt to seek caste adjustment for upward caste mobility was equally noticeable in some groups, especially those placed at the bottom or near the bottom of the traditional Hindu caste hierarchy. Thus, members of the *nai* (barber) caste took a liking for the term 'Nai Brahman' and pleaded for its recognition as a special caste. The 'chamars' (cobblers) formed an 'All India Shri Jatava Mahasabha' and wanted to be enumerated as Jatavs in the Census of 1941.[3] The 'dushads', also known as Gehlot Rajput, wanted their name removed from the list of depressed castes.

Caste information suffered from yet another limitation — that of vain-glorying on the part of the people at large. A tendency to inflate one's caste and assert tall claims marked the enumeration. In the words of a census report, 'inferior castes' tended 'to extenuate their present status by claiming an origin of fabulous glory, and the conviction is so rooted in the native breast that if the Government asks him what is his sect or otherwise, it is his business to have a sect or otherwise or if he has hitherto been unaware that he possesses one to invent one on the spot for the satisfaction of his superiors'. All this cumulated into a thought in certain circles of the colonial administration that the caste information was not worth the pains involved and deserved deletion. An additional reason for dispensing with the column in caste also was that they had already previously collected a great deal of information on caste and the variation disclosed by a compilation of caste statistics after a short gap of ten years would not be worth the trouble and cost that the operation would involve. W.C. Plowden recommended its total deletion in census taking. He observed:

> On the subject of caste, the results obtained. . . are by no means commensurate with the labour involved, and, unless some better arrangements are made, it would, probably be advisable to omit the column altogether. . . In the eight reports about 200 pages are devoted to a description of the various castes, with some 1,370 pages of tables and though there is in them much interesting matter, it is very doubtful whether the information thus gained has at all repaid the trouble taken in the compilation.[4]

Notwithstanding the criticism, the item on caste was retained in the census. The harsh fact is that the whole social fabric of India rests on caste, and so long as this is so it would be extremely short-sighted to omit it from the census. What is more, once it is dropped it would be very inconvenient to resume it.

Caste being easily a unique social institution among the Hindus, to gain insight into it has been a primary pre-occupation of the census. In the eyes of the census organisers, it has been considered as important as the name of the individual himself. In the first all-India census held in 1881, 207 castes were identified; in addition, there were 65 other castes, making a total of 272 castes in India. Caste, to begin with, was of anthropological interest. Gradually, other uses too were discovered.

Whether caste should be included in the census schedule, thus, came up for discussion many times but never more forcefully than at the time of the 1931 census. The 1930s were a period of political turmoil in India, characterised by Mahatma Gandhi's civil disobedience movement against the British rule. Around this time many social reform associations were also activating themselves to influence census taking as well as the contents of census information. The Arya Samaj, a social reform organisation founded by Swami Dayanand Saraswati in 1875, for instance, wanted the caste column in the census to be made optional. The Punjab had a society called 'Jat-Pat Torak Mandal' (Society for the Breaking of Caste among Hindus, a wing of the Arya Samaj) which called upon the Census Commissioner for India to press its point and later even addressed a memorial to the Viceroy of India requesting him 'not to insist upon the registration of caste in the case of those who do not want to have it recorded in the census returns.'[5] A few other social organisations also took a similar stand. Newspapers like *The Tribune* (Lahore), *The Leader* (Allahabad) and *Hindu Herald* (Lahore) too favoured deletion of the 'caste' column in the census schedule.

The Census Commissioner, Hutton, to whom the Jat-Pat Torak Mandal memorial was sent by the Home Department for 'advice', opined that 'it would harm the census very little if the actual members of the (Jat-Pat Torak) Mandal were permitted to return 'no caste', but figures for the depressed and backward castes are essential.'[6] Hutton did not visualise great harm if the supporters of the Jat-Pat Torak Mandal refused to return their caste at the census. He was, however, apprehensive of the campaign by the movement not to insist on information about caste being taken outside the Mandal with a view to giving an appearance of greater solidarity to the Hindu community than it might otherwise appear to possess. The authorities could not compel people to declare their caste if they refused to do so 'on any large scale'. If the number of dissenters was low, no harm would be done. The enumerators would return the caste of such individuals as 'they will generally know it'. In Hutton's view, 'it is perhaps just this that the Mandal really objects to'.[7] Secondly, even when believing that caste is an 'anti-social' feature of the Hindus the mere fact of not stating it in the census return was hardly to have any effect. Thirdly, Hutton favoured caste return in an obvious recognition of the ground reality: a very large number of people observed caste, whatever their theoretic or sympathetic inclinations.

In January 1931, Gaya Prasad Singh tabled a question in India's Central Legislative Assembly on exclusion of caste:

(a) Has any memorial been received by the Jat-Pat Torak Mandal to issue necessary instructions to the census authorities not to insist upon the registration of caste in the case of those who do not want to have it recorded in the coming census returns ?
(b) Are Government aware that societies like the Arya Samaj, Brahmo Samaj, Dev Samaj, Swami Samaj, etc., do not believe in the caste system ?
(c) It is a fact that the Adi Dharmis of the Punjab, who do not believe in castes, are not compelled to give their castes in the census returns ?

The Home Member, Sir James Crerar, replied:

(a) Yes and the necessary instructions have been issued;
(b) Yes;
(c) There is no compulsion in this matter at all.[8]

Official opinion was gradually building against the inclusion of caste in the census returns, at any rate in minute details. M.W.M. Yeatts ventured to observe in 1939: 'It is my opinion that the census should no longer seek to record individual castes. This table is one of the most expensive and difficult of all and a record of individual castes is, in my opinion, no longer worth the money spent upon it. Certainly in a census threatened with a cost limit, it would in my opinion be unjustified to spend money on this detail.'[9]

In January 1931, twenty-five members of the Central Legislative Assembly, including Sir Hari Singh Gour, submitted a joint resolution asking the Government of India to issue instructions to the census authorities to allow Hindus, who had ceased to believe in the institution of caste and who did not observe its rituals, to describe themselves as non-caste Hindus. 'Hindu reformers feel that time has now come when the census authorities should record the trend of public opinion against caste, and this is only possible if Hindus, who have withdrawn from the observance of caste, are entitled to report that fact in latter form'.[10]

Though the resolution was eventually withdrawn, it was becoming clear that the wind was blowing against the caste column, and the demand did not emanate from North India only. Writing in 1940, one scholar from the University of Madras wrote: 'One of the columns that may be dropped with advantage is that relating to caste. It is one of the most expensive items for tabulation. Further, the best minds in India want to get away from caste.'[11]

Yet the opinion favouring the deletion of the caste column was not unanimous, for it was believed that this information did serve some socially useful purpose. If the caste column was removed, one would not know about the progress made by different castes in society. It is, for instance, universally assumed that the incidence of infant marriage tends to be high in the lower castes and low in the higher ones. If figures for caste are not available, trends of this kind cannot be detected, important as they are.

The 'caste' column always appeared in the census during the British rule, but since 1931, its recording was not insisted upon. Hindus could return themselves as not belonging to a caste and were to be so recorded. But most Hindus did not avail of this option. In the 1931 census, which gave the option of saying 'no caste' in reply to the question on caste, out of 238,622,602 Hindu respondents only 1,883,464 persons gave a return of 'caste nil', proving that leaders are often far ahead of the led on many questions of social reform!

A section of the British bureaucracy read a deeper political meaning in the demand not to insist on information about caste. The Director of Public Instruction, for instance, wrote:

> The attitude taken up by the Jat-Pat Torak Mandal is likely, sooner or later, to receive greater support. If the matter were one of pure social reform it would take time to gain strength because very few social reformers would at present be prepared to ignore caste at social or religious gatherings or for the purpose of marriages. But the motive behind the move is political as liberty to withhold information regarding caste will be of distinct help to the Hindu community.[12]

It was said that the motive behind the proposal of Jat-Pat Torak Mandal, which would no doubt receive support from Arya Samajists generally, was that the 'Untouchables' should be included in the return of Hindus to greatly swell their total in comparison with that of the Muslims.[13] The Director of Public Instruction visualised two other consequences also. He observed:

> I fear that in the present state of Hindu-Muslim feelings the demand of the Mandal (*i.e.* Jat-Pat Torak Mandal) might be made the subject of agitation. Another fear I might mention is that those Arya Samajists and others, who sympathise with the civil disobedience movement, might possibly try to exploit Hindus of certain castes by persuading them to defy Section 7 of the Indian Census Act, and thus bring themselves within the purview of Section 10(c).[14]

Criticisms against the inclusion of 'caste' in the census return were many. In the first place, an accurate return on caste was unobtainable. Secondly, it was doubtful if the return served any statistical or administrative purpose. Thirdly, the return involved a troublesome quantity of irritating propaganda which could be a serious affliction to census officers. J.H. Hutton recommended the abolition of the 'caste' column 'at any rate at the sorting and compiling stages.'[15] Yet 'caste' was retained. The view that was provisionally taken by the Government was that any move to drop the return on caste was surely to provoke outcry from the orthodox sections of the people. This question was, however, to be decided in consultation with the next Census Commissioner. 'Meanwhile we may mark time.'[16] Till 1941 the column on 'caste' was retained in the census but freedom was given to those sections of the Hindus who were averse to recording their caste not to reply to this query. But the caste column was not altogether obliterated, thus favouring that section of the Hindus who were keen on preservation of the caste system or those who wanted to record their numerical strength, say, for the purpose of special franchise or other considerations. The caste return, however, was not tabulated.[17]

Under the impetus provided by the census, caste organisations began to be formed in various parts of the country with the principal object of achieving some gain or advantage for themselves in the census. One is unsure about the extent of mass support behind such bodies. Many of them must have become active only just before the census enumeration. A list of organisations representing different communities about matters of caste or communal interest arising in regard to the census enumeration is given here:

Organisation	Objective
1	2
Akhil Bharatiya Nayee Brahman Mahasabha, Lahore	That Nayee Brahmans should be recorded as such in the census
Akhila Bharata Varshiya Surya Rajput Mahasabha	That members of the community should be recorded as Surya Vamsa Rajputs
All-Bengal Buddhist People's Association	That the Buddhists should be treated as a separate community as in previous censuses
All-Bengal Jamiatul Momineen	That all Muslim weavers following the profession of weaving should be recorded as Momons in the census
All-India Dayanand	Complaint that Ratlam census Salvation Mission authorities returning Hindu Bhils as tribal against their declaration
All-India Hindu League	Complaint that instructions regarding the classification of aboriginal tribes in Bihar is not followed
All-India Hindu Mahasabha	That every Hindu should be registered as Hindu first and in other column as Arya, Jain, Sikhs etc.
All-India Jatav Youth League	That the Jatavs should be recorded under scheduled castes
All-India Kashyap Rajput Mahasabha	That members of the community should be recorded as such
All-India Khangar Kshatriya League	That members of the community should be recorded as Kshatriyas
All-India Koli Rajput Mahasabha	That the Kolis in various provinces should be recorded as Koli Rajput in the census
All-India Kushwaha Kshatriya Mahasabha	That members of the community should be recorded as Kurmi Kshatriyas
All-India Maheshwari Mahasabha	That members of the community should be recorded as Maheshwari Vaisyas
All-India Meo Panchayat	That the member of the community

1	2
	should be recorded as Meos
All-India Panchal Brahman Mahasabha	That the members of the community should be entered as Panchal Brahmans
All-India Shia Conference	Complaint that no instructions have been issued to record the sect of Muslims
All-India Tailik Vaishya Mahasabha	That members of the community should be recorded under the head Teli
All-India Tinsosath Gotra Kshatriya Mahasabha	That members of community should be described as Kshatriyas with their Gotras in the census
All-India Vaishnao Brahman Mahasabha	That community should be recorded as 'Chandravashiya Kshatriya with the title Singh
All-India Yadava Mahasabha	That all sections and sub-sections of the Yadava community should be recorded as Yadavas in the census
Arya Samaj Rohtak	Complaint that Hindu houses have not been enumerated
Bangadeshiya Kayastha Sabha	That members of the community should be recorded as Kshatriya
Bengal-Assam Namabrohma Association	That members of the community should be entered as Namabrohma
Bengal Provincial Hindu League	Complaint against the recording of castes for Hindus in Bengal
Bihar Hindu Provincial Sabha	That the non-Christian aboriginals should be recorded as Hindus in the census
Hindu Backward Classes League	That caste of the backward classes should be recorded
Hindu Sabha, Gotegaon	Complaint that Hindus were disallowed to enter in third column of the census schedule
International Aryan League	Complaint against the instruction in Bihar to record the religion of aboriginals
International Aryan League	Complaint that census officers refuse

1	2
	to enter 'Vedic Dharma' in the census
International Aryan League	Complaint that Aryas are not recorded in the return.
Jain Mahasabha Political Committee	Complaint that Hindu census officers dissuade Jains from returning as Jains
Jain Swetambari Terapanthi Sabha	That Vishwakarmas should be recorded as Vishwakarma Brahmins in the census
Jangid Brahmin Mahasabha	That Jangid Brahmins should be enumerated separately
Kudaleshkar Adyogaud Brahman Mandal	That members of the community should be recorded as Kudaleshkar Brahmans
Marwari Association, Calcutta	That aboriginals should be recorded as Hindus
Perika Mahasangham	That members of the community should be recorded as Perikas
Radhaswami Satsang Sabha	That Radhaswami should be entered as the sect of Hindus who return it
Rohela Tank Kshatriya Mahasabha	That members of the community should be recorded as Rohela Tank Kshatriya
Shiromani Gurdwara Prabandhak Committee, Amritsar	Complaint that Sikhs are not enumerated in Amritsar.
Shree Kimichi Valnad Sanathan Dharam Mandal	Complaint that the names of the community are not properly recorded
Shri Gurusingh Sabha Hardwar	Complaint that Hindu enumerators showing Sikhs as Hindus
Shri Pushpadha Gaur Brahman Mahasabha	That members of the community should be recorded as such
Singh Sabha Bombay	Complaint that Bombay Sikhs wrongly entered as Hindus.
Sri Sayana Association	That members of the community should be recorded as Sri Sayanans
United Provinces Teli Mahasabha	That members of the community should be recorded as Teli Vaishyas

One may thus see that a case against the inclusion of 'caste' column in the census schedule was gradually building up. At first, those who did not wish to have their caste recorded were free to return 'no caste'. In other words, caste became optional. Secondly, statistically minor castes were overlooked at the stage of tabulation; while collecting information, the percentage to qualify for tabulation was raised. Thirdly, the tabulation of 'caste' too became optional and 'caste tables did not appear save where paid for by a provincial government'.[18]

While the census bureaucracy veered round to the view that information on caste was of extremely limited usefulness and the column could be deleted, even the political leadership of the country was demanding its abolition. A question asked in the Central Legislative Assembly on 15 March 1939 confirms how the political wind was blowing. An important political figure, S. Satyamurti asked:

> I think I heard the Honourable Member (Sir Reginald Maxwell) to say that the Government is considering the omission of information about caste. Am I right?
>
> Sir Reginald Maxwell: Yes.
>
> S. Satyamurti: May I know whether Government will consider the general public opinion of the country which is that we must not divide up the country into these castes and decide to drop all information about these castes?
>
> Sir Reginald Maxwell: I understand that that is under consideration of the Commissioner designate.

Caste and Muslims

It was a practice in the earlier census reports to discuss, even if not very comprehensively, caste among the Muslims. In the census of 1921 and earlier ones, all castes among the Muslims were mentioned. In the census of 1931, however, the information sought from Muslims was on whether they were Momins or non-Momins. The Muslim League was ideologically against the mention of 'castes' among the Muslims. As a result of the agitations launched by it, the list of castes mentioned for Muslims was shrinking. But the Muslim League stood for its total abolition in the case of Muslims. Moulvi Mohammad Abdul Ghani, a member of the Central Legislative Assembly belonging to the Muslim League, strongly pleaded that no castes were written against the names of Muslims.[19] Sir Reginald Maxwell, the Home Member, in his reply said:

> The standing instruction to enumerators at this census follows the principle, namely, the answers given by the citizen should be recorded. Consequently it is in each citizen's hands what answer he gives to this question and there is no intention on the part of census officers to pursue a record of caste in the case of Muslims.[20]

Mohammad Ali Jinnah, President of the All-India Muslim League, issued firm instructions to the Muslims at the time of the 1941 census that no castes were to be written against the names of Muslims. In the census, the caste system of Syed, Sheikh etc. had already been abolished.[21] The argument was that there are no castes among Muslims, and even the existing classification of Muslims into Momins and non-Momins should be done away with.

Caste was deleted from the census-schedule in Independent India. As such, the country lacks reliable information on caste-composition of the population. When the Second Backward Classes Commission under B.P. Mandal was set up in 1978 it had to refer to the census of 1931 for obtaining information on backward castes. Today, India has emerged as more caste-conscious than in its recent political history. Information on scheduled castes and scheduled tribes is already collected. With extension of job and seat reservation to backward castes, information on them, too, requires to be collected. One may thus say that India is surely seeing a return of caste in the census, perhaps with reinforced aggressiveness.

REFERENCES

1. *Report of the Punjab Census*, 1881, p. 10.
2. *Home—Public*-A, 28 January 1871, Nos. 38-43.
3. *Home—Public*, F.45/21/36-Public, 1931.
4. *Home—Public*, March 1878, Nos. 76-78, p. 9.
5. The Jat-Pat Torak Mandal's memorandum dated 18 August 1930 submitted to the Viceroy of India. *Home—Public*, File 45/60/30-*Public*.
6. *Ibid.*
7. *Ibid.*
8. *Home—Public*, File 1/9/31-*Public*.
9. Yeatts' note dated 2 February 1939, *Home—Public*, F. 1/1/39-*Public*, 1939.

10. *Home—Public*, 2/3/31-*Public*, 1931.
11. P.J. Thomas: 'The Census as an Agency for Economic Planning', in *K.V. Rangaswami Aiyangar Commemoration*, Volume, January 1940.
12. *Home—Public*, F.2/3/31-*Public*, 1931.
13. *Home—Public*, F.45/46/30-*Public*. The DPI's note dated 16 October 1930.
14. *Home—Public*, F.45/46/30-*Public*.
15. *Home—Public*, F.45/102/33-*Public*, 1933.
16. *Ibid.*
17. Yeatts' note dated 2 February 1939. *Home—Public*, F.1/1/39-*Public*.
18. *Home—Public*, F.45/5/41-*Public*.
19. Central Legislative Assembly Debates, Vol. 5, 1939, p. 347, Pursue a record of caste in the case of Muslims.
20. Maxwell's letter No. 45/5/41-*Public* dated 14 February 1941. Home F. 45/5/41, p. 2.
21. Jinnah's overall strategy was to drive out all potentially divisive elements among Muslims and keep them united and homogeneous.

10

POLITICS OF CENSUS

Democracy is basically a numbers game. In a democracy, therefore, the census may be exploited for public including political uses on a multiplicity of issues—indeed on all issues which agitate people's mind. In all such matters it is the number that decides: in majority lies the legitimacy of decision.

In India, democracy made its regular and formal beginning under the Government of India Act, 1919, which came into enforcement in 1921. It was for the first time in the next census of 1931 that its political uses began to be discovered. The national movement under the leadership of Mahatma Gandhi was touching new heights and mobilising nearly all sections of society. In the 1930s the Congress under his stewardship launched the civil disobedience movement. The Party declared a boycott of the census, which could not but affect the accuracy and completeness of head-counting. The Census Satyagraha did lead to under-enumeration of the Hindus in certain tracts, which certainly included Calcutta and Midnapur.[1] But on the whole, the census was conducted peacefully. In retrospect, the Census Satyagraha of the Congress was an unwise, short-sighted move, more so when the national movement was not equally shared by the two major communities—Hindus and Muslims—in India.

Items like language, caste and religion are highly inflammable, in a vast diversified country of India's continental dimensions, where centrifugal force always threatens to outweigh the centripetal pull. It was inevitable that the census figures on these should be made to serve as fodder to incite politics. These are briefly discussed below.

Language

Census is the only authentic document on statistically true information on items covered in it like language spoken, religion professed, caste, etc. The political importance of the census becomes obvious when, for instance, a province is being bifurcated on the basis of language, or on the basis of any other divisive criterion.

Language became a topic of discussion and debate in Orissa in the census of 1931. The Presidency of Madras at one time was a sprawling one, including within its territory, among others, parts of the present-day Orissa. Orissa emerged as a separate province in 1935 but the demand was of long brewing. The district of Ganjam, which was originally in Madras, had a sizeable mixed population containing both Oriya and Telugu-speaking people and the census results were eventually to determine the limits of the Orissa Province. Ganjam with its Telugu-speaking people was thus a disputed area, being claimed by both Madras and Orissa. Both linguistic groups were consequently quite worked up when the census of 1931 was due. It was in the context of Orissa that the concept of joint enumerators in census was first propounded. The suggestion was that each census block should have a pair of enumerators, one Oriya and the other Telugu. This was firmly opposed by M.W.M. Yeatts, who was then the Census Superintendent of Madras. Yeatts argued that it was in the interest of all concerned that the actual enumeration was carried out without friction or artificial methods; that every census reposed on trust and that the enumerators, if left alone, could be relied on as citizens of the country to do their duty. Commenting on the merit of the proposal for joint enumerators, Yeatts said that this 'would be fatal to the enumerator's position, would destroy public confidence in the census and would produce figures which would command no confidence and would simply serve as a basis for continued dispute.'[2] The proposal was ultimately dropped. Yeatts observed: 'The enumerators had gone ahead and done their job honestly and conscientiously.'[3]

Eventually the district of Ganjam went to Orissa. But the Orissa case carries a larger meaning. The use of numbers for purposes of political decision-making was now discovered. The problem was presented in a much intensified way at the time of next head counting in India.

The Government of India Act, 1935

The Government of India Act, 1935 introduced provincial autonomy in India. This, among others, sharpened communal politics in the country. In the wake of the election held in 1937, the Congress formed ministries in eight provinces—Bombay, Madras, Central Provinces, United Provinces, Orissa, Bihar, Assam and the North-West Frontier Province. The Muslim League, which was not a major party until then, formed the government only in Bengal and that too with the prop of other parties. The Punjab was under the Unionist Party with Sikandar Hayat Khan as its Premier. The Sind United Party under Ghulam Husain Hidayatullah, and later Allah Bakhsh formed a coalition in Sind. It was only after the 1937 election that the influence of the Muslim League began to grow fast, with M.A. Jinnah's popularity among the Muslims showing a steep rise. The League was making ever-expanding communal claims and was fast moving towards the two-nation theory, which it ultimately proclaimed at the Lahore session in April 1940 (known as the Pakistan Resolution). The Muslim League, in other words, was no longer thinking in terms of percentages and weightages, proportion of representation, guarantees and safeguards, shares in services, etc. These were swept aside, being no more than outworn gadgets of a conventional democracy totally inappropriate to the peculiar conditions of India. The Muslim League now stood for an arrangement which gave the Muslims equal power and authority with the majority community. The demand for a separate and independent homeland for Muslims, namely Pakistan, made in 1940, gave them a new plank, a new goal, a new vista, free from the danger of what was described as the Hindu Raj.

This, briefly, is the political background of the census scenario which was unfolding in India. Communal feelings, as already indicated above, began vitiating the census with the introduction of province level democracy, called provincial autonomy, in India. By the time the 1941 census was due, communalism in various forms had acquired a definite force in Indian politics. One may first begin with its manifestation through language (or script).

In the 1941 census, the last before partition and independence, language became the political symbol, particularly at the hands of the Muslim League. In the province of Bihar, to give an example, Maithili, which is virtually the same as Hindi script, is the accepted language, and the census enumerators were, not unnaturally, writing their slips in Maithili. This was the accepted practice despite a recent amendment in the official language of the province. The Congress Party, which formed the ministry in Bihar in 1937, had declared Urdu as an optional court language, but this meant that only petitions could be filled in Urdu. 'No evidence is recorded in it, however, no registers are maintained in it, no record of rights has ever been prepared in it, and the majority of magistrates and clerks do not know it.' So commented the Census Commissioner Yeatts while forwarding his comments on script to the Home Department.[4] At the time of the 1941 census, the Muslim League pressed the case for Urdu with unusual vehemence. In February 1941,

Abdul Sattar Haji Ishaq Seth, a member of the Central Legislative Assembly belonging to the Muslim League, raised the issue in the form of a matter of urgent public importance, namely, the failure of the Government of India to supply census forms in Urdu in Bihar and the compulsion to fill up these forms in English or Hindi only.[5]

The notice of the adjournment motion was naturally sent to the Census Commissioner for comments. The latter favoured rejection of the demand. According to him every Bihar Muslim who was literate could read and write the 'Bihar script' known as Maithili; the same could not be said for Urdu. Urdu literacy was much rarer in Bihar. In the past, the enumeration in Bihar had been, as a rule, carried out only in Maithili by Muslims as well as Hindus without any trouble. In 1941, however, communalism coloured census-taking, as also some other spheres of public life. In Bihar, hardly any Hindu could read Urdu and so the census authorities recommended *status quo* in regard to the use of script in the interest of economy and efficiency. But the Census Commissioner for India was apparently keen not to allow the script quarrel to form the spark which might in mischievous hands travel far farther than was realised. His specific opinion was: 'Where a Muslim enumerator wished to write in Urdu, the general desirability on grounds of efficiency and economy of Maithili record should be put before him but if he still insisted, an Urdu record should be accepted'.[6] This meant a definite provision that preference was to be given to persons acquainted with both the Maithili and Urdu scripts. Was it the classic imperial policy of divide-and-rule? Be that as it may, census did come under political stress.

In the ultimate analysis, however, the quarrel over script died out without serious consequences. In September 1940 the district census officer of Monghyr (Bihar) reported to the census superintendent, Bihar that certain Muslim, Christian and Anglo-Indian enumerators in Jamalpur and Monghyr were experiencing difficulty in filling up the house-list forms in Maithili or Nagari and requested permission to employ Urdu or English forms. The census superintendent replied: 'There is no objection to the enumerators filling up the house-lists in English but it is regretted that Urdu cannot be accepted as owing to financial stringency it will not be possible to employ the special sorters which Urdu entries will involve.'

Subsequently, in November 1940 while checking house-lists in Sheikhpura (Bihar) the district census officer found that certain house-list forms had been filled in Urdu. He had made enquiries in other charges in the district and learnt that nowhere else had Urdu been used. He then wrote to the charge superintendent, who was the sub-registrar of Sheikhpura and a Muslim, that Urdu could not be accepted and instructed him to get the house-lists written in Hindi or English. In the event of the charge superintendent being satisfied that a particular enumerator did not know either Hindi or English, a substitute might be appointed. In reply, the charge superintendent reported that he had called all the enumerators concerned, impressed upon them the difficulties involved in the census forms being filled up in Urdu, and explained that behind the instruction to fill up forms in Hindi or English there was no idea of discouraging the Urdu script. As a result, he was able to persuade those Mohammedan enumerators who knew Hindi and Urdu to use Maithili or Nagari script while in the case of seven enumerators he appointed substitutes. The district census officer reported that there was no other complaint elsewhere and that enumeration proceeded without a hitch.

Tribes and Religion

The question of tribal religion has always been a source of difficulty and the figures obtained had been viewed by the census functionaries themselves as of little value. Hutton's Census Report of 1931 and Yeatts' own for Madras are evidence of this. This ambiguity does not help Islam or Christianity: it does help Hinduism. The frontier between tribal religion and Islam or Christianity is clear, sharp and definite. But with Hinduism there is no sharp boundary. A very wide no-man's-land lies between animism and Hinduism. The accommodative as well as assimilative power of Hinduism is enormous. Traditionally, the Adivasis were classified among Hindus until the census of 1931. But instructions on religion were changed in 1941, particularly in Bihar. Leaders of the Hindu community had particular reason to be agitated about this development, for it was a time when the Muslim League was propagating the two-nation theory and playing the Muslim card and the Christian missionaries, too, were active among the tribes and promoting the Cross.

In 1941, because of the changed instructions, Uraons, Mundas and Kharias were to be recorded as tribals. This was because the Uraons observed the Sarhul festival, the Mundas the Baha festival and the Kharias the Jamkou festival. This was to the disadvantage of the Hindus.[7] M.S. Aney, President of the All-India Hindu League and Bhai Parmanand met the Home Member of the Government of India in November 1940 to discuss the issue. Their complaint was that the special instructions which had been issued to the enumerators for recording the religion of members of the aboriginal tribes of Bihar, Orissa and Central Provinces were wholly unnecessary and unwarranted. It was urged that members of the aboriginal tribes such as Santhals, Mundas, Oraons, Gonds, Bhils, etc., should have the right to name their religion as every other Indian has. The enumerator should not ask any questions regarding the observance of any festivals and be given the option to infer from the replies received what religion was professed. The 'festival' test entailed injustice for the Hindus. It is not a fact that all Hindus in all the provinces observe all the Hindu festivals. Besides, there are special Hindu festivals for special castes. Non-Christian Oraons, Mundas and Kharias were all Hindus, observed all Hindu festivals, believed in Ram and Krishna and observed the Hindu mode of worship. Their manners, customs and observance of ceremonies in marriage were also similar to those of the Hindus. Nor should one forget that Hinduism is such a diverse, heterogeneous religion that seldom is a festival, observed in one part of the country, shared by another. Above all, the religion of a man should be recorded according to his statement, and no supplementary test, whatsoever, be applied. The Government's controversial instruction in 1941 was:

> Question 4: Religion. This question is for individual religion professed by each person. Ask him what his religion is and if he states the name of a particular religion or gives the name of a tribe, record what he says: examples are Uraon, Munda, Kharia, Islam, Christian. If he is baffled by the question ask him if he observes the Sarhul festival (Uraon, Khaddi, Munda, Kharia, Jankore). If he says 'yes' do not ask any other question but write the name of his tribe Uraon, Munda or Kharia as the case may be. If he says 'No' ask him if he observes Mohammedan festival of Bakrid, the Hindu festival of Diwali or the Christian festival of Christmas. If he says he observes Bakrid write 'Mohammedan'. If he says he observes 'Diwali', write 'Hindu'. If he says he observes Christmas write 'Christian'. If none of these festivals is observed put a X. In the case of other aboriginals who are baffled by the question ask if they observe the tribal festivals which their ancestors observed. If the answer is 'yes' do not ask any further question but write the name of the tribe. If the answer is 'No' ask the second question and make any enquiry accordingly.[8]

The Muslim League wanted Adivasis to be shown as tribals, not as Hindus, its motivation was plainly political. It observed:

> The Muslim League as the representative of 90 million Muslims of India do hereby lodge a protest to the Government of India, to the Census Commissioner of India and the Census Superintendents of Bengal, Assam, Bihar, C.P. and Bombay and request them to take steps to rectify this wrong (classification of Santhals and other tribals as Hindus), otherwise the Muslims and the minorities will be forced to challenge the entire census return and demand a new census by a cent per cent paid staff under gazetted officer appointed with fair representation for all communities in the census agency.[9]

In Bihar, there was indeed a popular agitation against the census authorities' decision not to include the Sanatan Adivasis in the census returns. Writing under the caption "Adibasi Hindus and Census", the Patna-based *Indian Nation* (13 November 1940) editorially commented that the decision that 'the Adivasis are not Hindus because they do not observe certain Hindu customs and festivals' had shown 'great ingenuity no doubt' and had played with 'the feelings and the sentiments of the concerned people themselves who show that they consider themselves as much to be Hindus as any other section of that community does.' The paper continued: 'The agitation that these latter (adivasis) have been carrying on for the last few months against that decision must have convinced our unknown anthropologist that he has hit very wide of the mark.' The ultimate fact was that the numerical strength of the Hindus was adversely affected by excluding the Adivasi Hindus from their number.

On 19 November 1940 the *Indian Nation* editorially criticised the attitude of the census authorities for their 'anti-Hindu attitude'. It wrote: 'If an Adivasi says that he is neither a Hindu, nor a Mohammedan nor even a Christian he may be. . . enumerated as 'tribal'. But on the other hand, if he says that he is a Hindu, or a Mohammedan or Christian it will be against all canons of justice and equity to enumerate him as 'tribal'. The paper went on to speak about the on going agitation among non-Christian Adivasis of Chotanagpur against the arbitrary circular of the Government and reports of public meetings which 'give an idea of the intensity of feeling among the non-Christian Adivasis on this question'.

Religion and Census

When caste column lends itself to political manipulation—as we have seen in the last chapter—religion cannot remain immune. Indeed, religion may be subjected to even greater census abuse, considering that India is inhabited by groups and sections characterised by deep religious ambiguities. From the census angle, communal rivalry became conspicuously sharp in the two provinces of Bengal and the Punjab and also to some extent in Assam. Where no community enjoys clear and obvious majority, numbers become important, and the census process comes under political pressure. According to the census bureaucracy, Bengal and the Punjab offered studies in contrast. The Bengal Government was consistently wrong-headed in the matter of census; its actions contributed to the undoubted excesses of communalism. The Punjab retained its cool but soon broke down under the combined influence of Pakistan and anti-Pakistan public meetings all over the province. Census politics in the Punjab, Bengal and Assam is discussed in what follows.

Punjab

At the time of the 1941 census, the Punjab had the Unionist Party in power, with Sikander Hayat Khan as the premier. One-half of the Punjab population was Muslim, the Hindus three-eighths and the Sikhs one-eighth. The communally surcharged position in the province warranted greater discretion in the selection of the superintendent of census operation, which the central census authorities did not get. Fazl-i-Ilahi, a Muslim officer belonging to the provincial civil service was appointed as the census superintendent though Yeatts pleaded for a British officer of the ICS for the post. While writing his report on the work of the superintendents of census operations, Yeatts wrote:

> The Government of Punjab and the Central Government itself made a mistake in disregarding Dr. Hutton's recommendation and my own that, given the obvious possibility of acute communal tension in the Punjab, a British officer should be appointed for this census. In such cases public confidence is of the highest importance and nothing should be omitted which could tend to raise or maintain it. I believe that with a British officer in this post the developments of the last days of February (when enumeration is undertaken) would have been avoided or at any rate been much less pronounced. I should have preferred a British officer and consider it a mistake that one was not appointed.[9]

About Fazl-i-Ilahi, Yeatts had nothing but a string of superlatives in praise, which did not exactly correspond with the ground reality. The census superintendents' performance is thus described by the census chief:

> Khan Bahadur Fazl-i-Ilahi's work and conduct were throughout admirable. His personal probity is beyond question and he has in addition to excellent intelligence and impressive industry, pleasant manners and a faculty for getting on with people of widely different types. He is a good budgeter and a sound administrator and can be relied on to give effect to directions from his superior officers. This faculty showed itself when, after being slightly shaken by the extent to which communal passions rose at the end of February, he rallied at once to the lead I gave and carried out through deputy commissioners a thorough scrutiny of the whole Punjab enumeration. I have found Khan Bahadur Fazl-i-Ilahi better than I ever expected any Muslim deputy collector could be in these circumstances, and I consider myself lucky, if I had to have a deputy collector, to have had one of his calibre.[10]

Around the time of the 1941 census, Jinnah toured the Punjab to revive enthusiasm for the Pakistan movement, primarily among Muslim students who at the time had been drifting towards socialism. Jinnah publicly took the view that Muslims in India were not a minority community but were a nation, and a nation must have its territory. A nation could not live without land and it must be given that land. The communal situation in the Punjab had been far from satisfactory for some time but it began quickly deteriorating as a result of the speeches of Jinnah and other communal leaders. Speeches in the Punjab Assembly too developed on communal lines.

In the census, there were complaints regarding deliberate non-enumeration of Hindus and false returns with regard to language and script. Raja Narendra Nath of the Hindu Mahasabha and a resident of Lahore, for example, telegraphically made one such complaint on 4 March 1941 and demanded a fresh census. His was not an isolated complaint. In Ludhiana, an organisation called Hindu Census Committee was formed and on 7 March 1941 it wrote to the Viceroy recording its 'emphatic protest against the irregular manner in which census operations had been carried out in this town', which had resulted in an abnormal increase in the population of Muslims and decrease in the number of Hindus. This had happened 'on account of the overwhelming preponderance of Mohammedans in the census machinery such as (charge) superintendents, supervisors and enumerators, who deliberately increased the number of Mohammedans by including fictitious names and decreased the number of Hindus by omitting to enumerate several Hindu residential houses'. The Hindu Census Committee asserted that 'in case the allegations made here are found incorrect the Hindu community is prepared to pay the expenses of re-enumeration'.[11]

The All-India Hindu League under the presidentship of M.S. Aney, also complained about the counting in the Punjab being biased against the Hindus. It made two points. First, it protested against the circular of the Punjab Government declaring that the 'Adivasis' were not to be tabulated as Hindus. Secondly, the Hindus were not rightly recorded in the census and deliberate omission on a large scale had taken place. 'In the opinion of the (Hindu) League, the record of the last (*i.e.* 1941) census will not be a reliable one and it will not correctly reflect the Hindu population in Punjab. The Working Committee (of the Hindu League) urges upon the Government to take steps to put things right and bring offenders to book under the Census Act.'

Yeatts described the demand for a fresh census as 'pathetic'. The rural enumeration was sound, he said, being done by the patwari; but in towns, where municipal staff were deputed for this work, faulty and suspicious cases arose. 'I have always stressed the fact that the towns generally were the weaker links of enumeration but unless substantial extra-expenditure is accepted, there is no getting away from the use of municipal staff'.[12] That the Punjab enumeration had tripped was admitted even by the census bureaucracy, though not publicly, the blame for which was ascribed not to the enumerators. The view taken was that 'the root responsibility for what corruption has entered is not with the enumerators but with such bodies as this very (Hindu) League and its parallels in other communities who incited their fellow citizens to cheat and lie.'[13] Yeatts minimised the problem of faulty counting by asserting that no big organisation was without its weaker vessels. He put his faith in the people: 'no census anywhere can rise above the level of the citizens'. 'If a householder is prepared to cheat and lie then there is a limit to the power of correction exercisable by any census staff'. He observed: 'Communalists know only one mood—the superlative; and violent and almost grotesque exaggeration is their daily diet. The majority of these complaints are either exaggerated or absolutely false'. In his view, 'the country, fortunately, is far sounder than the shouters made out'. His advice was to put out as little as possible, and thus to keep off, the contentious topic of these allegations.

Census operations, thus, clearly assumed a political-religious complexion. Every community complained about the unfairness of enumerators. The Hindus alleged that Muslim officers in their anxiety to swell the Muslim population failed to register all the Hindus and made fictitious and exaggerated returns of Muslims; the Muslims accused Hindu enumerators of unfair attempts to reduce the number of Muslims. A report, marked confidential and bearing the title 'Report on the situation in the Punjab for the first half of March 1941', notes:

> Most district officers believe that there has been a great deal of falsification of returns and in many cases enumerators were not sufficiently tactful or educated to fill in all columns of the register correctly. In a village in Gujranwala an attempt to burn down a gurudwara is believed to have been inspired by revenge on the part of Muslims against the Hindus and Sikhs who accused the Muslim patwari of bias in enumeration.

The daily report dated 3 March 1941 of the Central Intelligence Office, Lahore has this to say about the census situation of the time:

> Much has happened within the last few days to aggravate inter-communal tension. First, there is the census and with it the intense keenness of all classes to prove that the respective population of the various communities has increased from previous years. Muslims are determined to see that their majority is upheld and Hindus and Sikhs are equally keen to prove that the strengths of their communities have relatively improved. Innumerable complaints have been heard about the trickery of census enumerators and it is believed that in some larger areas of Lahore city and elsewhere no census figures were recorded at all. On the other hand, some enumerators never troubled to visit their beats and put in purely fictitious returns. Generally speaking, the intelligentsia are laughing at the census operations, whilst the illiterate are disgusted and dejected.[14]

One must not overlook the fact that such census figures became the base for the creation of Pakistan and demarcation of its boundaries.

Bengal

In Bengal the impact of communal politics on census was much wider and deeper. It was alleged that the preceding census of 1931 had favoured the Muslims because of Mahatma Gandhi's call for civil disobedience movement. At the time of the 1941 census both Hindus and Muslims were geared up to secure as favourable an enumeration of their respective communities as possible. The Hindus were disturbed over house-numbering. The Bengal Government under the Muslim League wanted joint enumerators to undertake enumeration of population. There were protests and processions after the enumeration. This is dicussed in what follows.

In Calcutta there used to be a grassroot level functionary called house-numberer whose task was to number off the households in his beat. The standing practice was that the task was entrusted to the elements of population prevailing in a particular area. In other words, Muslim numberers were appointed for Muslim households and Hindus for Hindu households, and so on. This was an innocent census practice, in observance for quite some time in Calcutta. In Bihar, the enumerators did the house-numbering.

In 1941, however, house-numbering became a politically contentious issue. Raja Yuvaraj Dutta Singh put the following interpellation in the Council of State on 19 November 1940:

> Have instructions been issued by the census authorities to the effect that normally Muslim house-numberers should be appointed for Muslims in all areas in Bengal and Calcutta, in the coming census; and have no corresponding instructions been issued to the effect that house-numberers should be appointed for Hindus in all areas?[15]

This question and the underlying fear—arose from a press note issued by the special officer for the census of Calcutta, which said that Muslims should be appointed to number off the houses in exclusively Muslim areas in Calcutta. From this it was inferred, first, that whereas for Muslim areas, only Muslim house-numberers were to be appointed, Hindu houses could be numbered off by house-numberers of any community; secondly, this discriminatory treatment was sure to injure the enumeration of the Hindu community.

The Government of India, in order to quell these fears, clarified as follows. Both communities were to be treated on the same footing. The apprehensions regarding the house-numberers' functions were misplaced. House numbering was a purely executive measure done in as economical a manner as possible. House-numberers were not enumerators: they only affixed house numbers to houses and prepared house lists. House lists were not used for the counting of heads. The census was taken on enumeration slips with which the house-numberer had no concern.

It may be seen from the above how surcharged the political atmosphere was in Bengal, to the extent that even normal administrative practices aroused fear and suspicion. The ruling Fazlul Huq Government itself, rather than maintain a neutral stance, was actively projecting politics in censusing, thus fouling up the atmosphere.

In the communally charged background, it was feared by both the communities that attempts might be made to falsify the enumeration. At the same time, a proposal was made by the Bengal Government to the Government of India in December 1940 for the appointment of 'joint enumerators'. In other words, enumerators were to work in pairs consisting of one Muslim and one Hindu, who would check each other's work. The Government of Bengal explained by way of justification:

> It is the general apprehension in this province (Bengal) that attempts will be made by interested persons of different communities to get exaggerated statements recorded in the forthcoming census operations regarding their numerical strength. All sections of the responsible public and the press appear to be united in their demand that effective steps should be taken to check this tendency. During the last session of the Provincial Legislative Assembly this demand found clear expression from practically all sections of the House. It is, therefore, necessary to devise necessary measures to deal adequately with the problem. One of the measures, that has received the largest amount of support, is the appointment of a Muslim and a Hindu enumerator for the purpose of undertaking jointly the work of enumeration for each household. The Government of Bengal is strongly of opinion that such a measure if given effect to would provide an effective check on exaggerated claims from political motives and would commend it for the serious consideration of the Government of India.[16]

The Bengal Government addressed its letter direct to the Home Department and not to the Census Commissioner. Yeatts, hospitalised at the time, did not like his office being so bypassed by provincial governments but considered it more prudent to keep silent and not to harp on procedural improprieties at such a moment. When the matter was referred to him by the Home Department, he replied that he found the proposal to be full of difficulties and impracticalities. This was his interim reaction; he would send his considered views when he was better. This he did after ten days, on 21 December 1940. In his detailed comments, Yeatts feared awesome consequences if the Bengal proposal was accepted. The demand for joint enumerators, which he called a mutual spy system, directly presented the effects of the census being used as a political stick in the local political controversies so prominent in the province. The Bengal Government should have itself realised that census was a central subject in which it had no tenable interventionist role and so better kept itself out. Even otherwise, the proposal suffered from poor quality: it was not discussed even with the provincial-level census superintendent of Bengal. In bypassing the provincial head of the census, the Bengal Government's behaviour, according to Yeatts, was neither judicious nor courteous. Yeatts emphasised that all functionaries associated with census work should be absolutely detached from any partisan activity or assistance. The enumeration work, particularly, was to be distinctly above reproach—like Caesar's wife. The census functionaries had to treat every citizen as an ally. A high standard of accuracy and detachment was absolutely necessary in the enumerator and supervisor, for on the enumerator falls the mantle of government. Yeatts commented, 'The census in any country anywhere depends on the response of the people and the value of the tabulation is in direct proportion to the degree to which they are generally accepted as the outcome of spontaneous and uninfluenced reply.' Yeatts further wrote:

> On the actual proposal itself, it is difficult to speak with sufficient condemnation. To begin with, it is simply not feasible. In large areas in Bengal sufficient Hindus or Muslims, as the case may be, could not be found for the enormous effort of doubling up enumerators for every block to act as spies on each other. The total number involved would be over 30,000. Local knowledge is an important factor in enumeration, and in East and West Bengal the Hindu and Muslim element, respectively, would not be forthcoming. Is it the Bengal Government's suggestion that they should be imported from outside? One has only to put the question to realise the absurdity of the position—quite apart from the financial aspects. Enumeration is not a matter of a few hours or a single day but of considerable number of days, and the financial implications are obvious.[17]

Yeatts argued that enumerators had to the impartial and detached but under the Bengal proposal they would *ex-hypothesi* be partisan performers: they would lack objectivity regardless of the amount of training imparted to them. Secondly, the census organisation selected the enumerators carefully and trained them to make them fit and suitable. It was not prepared to take enumerators blindly thrown at it by Bengal. The census anywhere reposed faith in the enumerator and trusted him, whether he was a householder as in the UK or an enumerator after the US or Indian fashion.

The Government of India, in a long letter written to the Bengal Government, turned down the proposal of rival escorts for the enumeration, giving reasons, originally advanced by Yeatts. First, the difficulties involved in giving effect to the proposal were insuperable. In large areas in Bengal sufficient members of suitable Hindus or Muslims could not be found locally for the enormous effort of doubling up enumerators for every block. Secondly, local knowledge was an important factor in enumeration and any wholesale importation of outsiders, quite apart from the discredit, it was to throw upon the census, could only lead to trouble and inefficiency. Unless the two enumerators were equally instructed in enumeration technique, the time required for the whole process was to be vastly extended for misunderstanding and dispute. It was, moreover, impossible to provide any machinery for settling a dispute between the communal enumerators and the result might well be to hold up the census altogether apart from the possibility of actual communal clashes if those being enumerated themselves took part in the dispute.

The proposal, moreover, involved difficulties in finding out such large numbers of suitable men and imparting to them adequate training, the Government of India said. The financial implications of the proposal were enormous. Finally, with the abandonment of one-night theory in 1941, the Bengal proposal was to have the effect of making the enumeration stage vastly complex. The communal problem obtruded itself in other provinces also, and thus the proposal for joint enumerators was to be put in practice in other provinces too. This would 'produce difficulties and confusion in nearly every area in India' removing altogether the value of the census. In short, in the opinion of the Central Government, 'the proposal is not in itself practicable and invites condemnation on other grounds. It is not in conformity with the traditions of the Indian census and will in all probability render impossible its continuation on its former lines'.

The communal ill-feeling in Bengal was steadily worsening and its shadow over census was lengthening. The Intelligence Bureau's 'Daily Summary of Information' dated 3 February 1941 observed:

> Communal ill-feeling has been worsened in some places in view of the forthcoming census operations. In Bengal, both Hindus and Muslims are determined to do all they can to insist on the proper recording (and, if possible, inflation) of their population figures. In a secret meeting of the Muslim Central Census Board on 8 February, attended by nearly all the Bengal Muslim ministers it was decided to observe a census week for propaganda purposes. It is believed that at this meeting the chief minister agreed to consider the possibility of (a) Government publishing draft census figures with a view to inviting public comment and (b) the Bengal Government undertaking a parallel census as a check on normal census operations.[18]

The Muslim League, the party in power in Bengal, had little hesitation in taking recourse to all sorts of methods to embarrass the census in a bid to tilt it. It had constituted the Muslim Central Census Board to promote 'consciousness' among the Muslims about the importance of their numbers. It decided to observe a Census Week all over India for propaganda purposes. At its meeting held on 6 February 1941, Fazlul Huq, the Bengal Chief Minister, talked about the Bengal Government publishing draft census figures with a view to inviting public comment and undertaking a parallel census as a check on normal census operations. Also, the Muslim ministers and leaders were asked to devote themselves to supervision of census work in their respective areas of influence.[19] Pressure on Calcutta was particularly severe. Calcutta had a sizeable middle class which was, at the same time, volatile in temperament and politically well organised. Both the major communities, Hindus and Muslims, were keen to show an improvement in their numerical strength over the previous census figures. Even M.A. Jinnah, the President of the All-India Muslim League, had written to Fazlul Huq asking for a report on the situation regarding the Bengal census in view of the disquieting news. On 1 March 1941, soon after the enumeration was over, Fazlul Huq wrote to the census superintendent (of Bengal), pointing out that it had not been possible to stop corrupt practices in the recording to the census and it was certain that there would be an inflation of the numbers of Hindus and a decrease in the numbers of Muslims, especially in Calcutta. He requested the census superintendent to publish draft figures in the first instance after which eight or nine days could be given to examine reported cases of inflation or deflation, special officers being deputed for the purpose.

The Government of India did not accede to the request. Meanwhile, the Central Intelligence Office filed a secret report on the census situation in Bengal dated 10 March 1941:

> On 9 March, a large meeting of Muslims numbering over 10,000 assembled at the Town Hall to support the stand taken by Fazlul Huq in connection with the census and to condemn the criticism of Huq by the Hindus. Processions were taken out and among them were nearly 300 uniformed Khaksars and 200 un-uniformed volunteers of the Muslim National Guard, the Dacca Muslim Club and the Khilafat Committee. Resolutions were passed expressing dissatisfaction with the irregularities committed in connection with the recording of the 1941 census as a result of the machinations of the Hindu Mahasabha and the Congress; urging the cancellation of the census as regards Bengal; requesting the Government of India, in consultation with the Government of Bengal, to appoint an independent enquiry committee and a joint enumeration board on which there should be representatives of both communities and recording the meeting's implicit faith in Huq and his cabinet.

Yeatts, however, did not consider there was much wrong with the Bengal figures.[20] The census bureaucracy in Delhi was not totally unfamiliar with the bluffing nature of the Bengal Chief Minister. In a note, Yeatts observed, 'The Bengal Premier (*i.e.* Fazlul Huq) has made things difficult for every one and is still doing so'.[21] In another note, he said, 'I fear that the only figures which would command Mr. Fazlul Huq's confidence would be something of his own devising'.[22] He further commented, 'If the Bengal figures were to be unsatisfactory, there need be no long search for the main culprit.' Allegations about faulty enumeration or other matters relating to census were being made to the Central Government. The course of action suggesting by him was: 'the less correspondence the better, it only to let hot heads cool down and reflections have a chance'.

Meanwhile, the All-Bengal Hindu Mahasabha Census Board publicly thanked the enumeration agencies 'for having carried out their duties ungrudgingly and by working so hard day and night'.[23] This the Muslim League interpreted as yet another concrete proof of pro-Hindu projections in the enumeration of the population. Indeed, it went further and observed Sunday, 9 March 1941 as a day of protest against what it called 'the large-scale irregularities in the census operations in Bengal under the influence of the Hindu Sabha'.[24]

Heading the census operations in the politically tense province of Bengal was R.A. Dutch, a member of the ICS joining in 1929. As superintendent of census operations Dutch confronted challenging tasks in a province the political leadership of which was bent upon politicising the census. Fazlul Huq and his Muslim League failed to realise that census is a central responsibility and they would do better to steer clear of it. Rather, they were directing all their energy to ensure that the Bengal census was conducted on lines desired by them. Evaluating Dutch's role in these difficult circumstances, Yeatts, his boss in Delhi, had this to say:

> A very good officer in every way and easily the best all-round census superintendent. A cool head, sound judgment and general imperturbability, added to intellectual qualities above the average produce an excellent amalgam. He had much the most difficult job of any superintendent. Quite apart from the size of the province, he had to cope with the extreme difficulties caused by communal tension and the astonishing activities of persons in public position. Although no pusher of himself personally, he is an officer of strong character and in my opinion of outstanding ability. Mr. Dutch spent some time in hospital and was one of the four if not five officers who contracted, as I did myself in the 1931 Census, amoebic dysentery as a consequence of incessant and frequently rough touring.[25]

Assam

Assam had a confusing multiplicity of parties after the 1937 election. First, Sir Muhammad Sa'adullah formed a government but in September 1938, Gopinath Bardoloi of the Congress became the premier. At the time of the 1941 census, Sa'adullah was again in power. In short, Assam was another communally infected province. The census of 1941 created many surprises and problems. The following table shows the fluctuations in the population of various communities in Assam in the period 1931-41.[26]

This happened perhaps because of change in instructions and definitions as also because of a measure of arbitrariness exercised by

		Figures in 1931	Figures in 1941
1.	Hindus	52,64,650	45,40,497
2.	Muslims	27,80,514	34,74,141
3.	Christians	2,49,246	67,184
4.	Buddhists	15,045	8,317
5.	Tribals	9,92,390	28,24,133

the ground level operators. At any rate, this made the 1941 figures suspect in some circles, which demanded 're-sorting and re-counting'. V.D. Savarkar, President of the Hindu Mahasabha issued a protest on 8 July 1941 under the title 'Hindu Assam in Danger'.[27]

The inter-census jump in the Muslim population was made possible by the way the Land Development Scheme of the Assam Government was being operated. It was a colonisation scheme and Muslims in large numbers from outside provinces migrated into Assam, thereby disturbing the demographic balance. In this truly lies the present problem of 'outsiders' in Assam. This must be carefully noted.

In short, the 1941 census was characterised by 'a great deal of political wire-pulling going on about these census returns with the object of increasing the numerical strength of various rival communities'. India appeared to be fast moving towards political polarisation. The Indian Muslim League was adopting a political position from which it was very difficult for it to return. Yeatts was perhaps seeing the writing on the wall. In a three-page note by him, dated 14 June 1940, there occurs an intriguing sentence: 'As I have told Home Department more than once, this census (of 1941) is in some respects critical'.[28] As subsequent events proved, the head-counting of 1941 really proved to be critical in India's history. The boundaries of the newly created independent states of India and Pakistan were determined by what the numbers told.

The foregoing uncovers the potential political uses to which numbers have the potency to lend themselves. India is a land of many religions and many times more castes. Not long back in history, the country suffered a partition which was based on religion. This possibly carries a danger for the future also. Religion may again be invoked to extract political gains. The census figures since Independence have been showing varying growth rates of different religions. In the first census after independence, that for 1951, Hindus constituted 84 per cent of the total population while the Muslims were 9.9. In 1981, the respective percentage of the two major religions became 83.09 and 10.88. The 1991 census further confirms these trends and shows that Hindus constitute 82.00 per cent whereas Muslims claim 12.12 of the total population. The percentage of population accounted for by each of the six major religious communities, namely, Hindus, Muslims, Christians, Sikhs and Buddhists and Jains in the 1991 census are given below:

Religious Community	Percentage to Total Population	Percentage Decadal Growth rate 1981-91
Hindus	82.00	22.78
Muslims	12.12	32.76
Christians	2.34	16.89
Sikhs	1.94	25.48
Buddhists	0.76	35.98
Jains	0.40	4.42

(Excludes figures of Jammu and Kashmir where the 1991 census was not held).

Demographic fluctuations shown above are not entirely harmless or innocent. The contemporary political scenario in India shows an unexpected invigoration of ascriptive idioms like caste, religion, etc. and policy decisions of varying levels of gravity are increasingly made, precisely making these as their base. Emergence of vote banks in the country carries darker forebodings. Democracy inevitably speaks the language of numbers. When different religions grow differently the classic rhythm of politics gets threatened with possibly far-reaching repurcussions for the future of the country, particularly when seen in the background of India's theocratic next door neighbour.

REFERENCES

1. *Home*, F.45/46/30-*Public*.
2. *Home* F.45/40/40-*Public*.
3. *Ibid*.
4. *Home-Public*, 2/1/41-*Public*.
5. *Ibid*.
6. *Ibid*.
7. *Report* dated 7 February 1941 from the Superintendent of Census Operations, Bihar. *Ibid*.
8. *Home-Public*, F.45/39/40-*Public*.
9. Sent by the *Calcutta District Muslim League* on 5 March 1941.

10. *Home-Public*, F.45/11/41-*Public*.
11. *Home-public*, p. 10.
12. *Ibid.*
13. *Ibid.*
14. *Ibid.*
15. Council of State Debates, Vol. II, No. 1, p. 9.
16. *Ibid.*
17. *Home-Public*, F.45/40/40-*Public*.
18. *Home-Public*, F.45/11/41-*Public*.
19. *The Report*, sent by the Central Intelligence Office to the Government of India dated 21 February 1941. *Ibid.*
20. E. Comran Smith, Secretary, Home Department's note to the Home Member, dated 9 April 1941. *Ibid.*
21. Yeatts' note dated 4 March 1941.
22. Yeatts' note dated 6 March 1941 addressed to the Secretary, *Home*, F.45/11/41-*Public*.
23. *Amrita Bazar Patrika*, 5 March 1941.
24. The Calcutta District Muslim League's letter dated 15 March 1942 to Sir Reginald Maxwell (Home Member). F. 45/11/41-*Public*.
25. *Home*-F.45/26/41-*Public*.
26. Sir Reginald Maxwell's letter to Sir Thomas Stewart. *Home-Public*, F.45/39/40-*Public*.
27. See the letter to Assam Provincial Hindu Sabha to the Census Commissioner, dated 23 August 1941, *Home* F.45/11/41-*Public*.
28. *Home*, F.45/40/39-*Public*.

11

LEGAL BASIS OF THE CENSUS

During the entire colonial period, the census in India rested on a temporary piece of legislation. One may thus naturally ask why a statute was considered at all necessary for carrying out the head counting. Theoretically, a legislative enactment was not strictly essential for this action. Yet it was considered so, the chief motivation being to squarely put both the census personnel and the enumerated within a legal framework of enforceable duties and obligations. This was all the more necessary as the census staff, especially of the lower levels, were, as a rule, non-officials and thus not under traditional governmental discipline. The census work was voluntary. A law was also required as rumours of all sorts surrounded the census work when it first began in India. Census, one may note, was viewed as preliminary to fresh taxation in many areas, making people suspicious and uncooperative. It was even believed in some tracts that the census was being taken to forcibly take away Indian women for the British. In the initial stage, thus, the people were not only hesitant but even positively hostile to census taking. Even troops had to be called occasionally to maintain law and order even though, fortunately, such instances were not many. Popular perception to census passed from deep suspicion to indifference to calmness. The point to be noted is that in such a situation a law was considered to be absolutely essential to oblige the people to cooperate.

Because the census organisation was purely temporary the law enacted too was temporary. The Census Act of 1880, for instance, said: 'Whereas it has been determined to take a census of British India during the year 1881 and it is expedient to provide for certain matters in connection with the taking of such census, it is enacted as follows'.

Thus, the time-honoured practice in India in regard to population counting has been to enact a legislation every time a census is taken. The Census Act was a temporary one, relapsing as soon as the census was over. For the first time the question of introducing a permanent

Act was raised by Sir Edward Gait, the Census Commissioner in 1909. The issue was again considered in 1920. It was, however, always decided after some discussion that the practice of basing the census on a decennial Act should be continued. Thus, a permanent legislation remained shelved. A temporary Act has advantages of its own and, besides, was in conformity with the practice obtaining in Great Britain. Hutton, the Census Commissioner for 1931, in his Report on the Census of India, 1931 strongly urged for a permanent legislative provision to back the census. Hutton's recommendation received reinforcement from another report submitted around this time, by Dr. Bowley and Robertson. But a decision on it could not be taken. The question of a permanent legislation was integrated with a decision on the more important question of a quinquennial census with a permanent staff.

The Census Act, which was passed, was a brief one and was silent on many matters. It did not specifically lay down that all counting was to be completed in one night. It also did not specify the mode to be adopted for taking the census. The census was *de facto*, which means, it aimed at a return of all persons actually found in India at a given moment. It was customary to fix a date for the census in consultation with the provincial governments. Dr. J. H. Hutton, the Census Commissioner for 1931, made the suggestion that the census should cease to be *de facto* and that *de jure* census be substituted such as that taken by the USA. Hutton favoured a permanent Census Act mainly with the idea of making possible a permanent Census Department and quinquennial census; while the Bowley-Robertson report advocated permanent census legislation because it was basic to their suggested plan for an economic census.

In his defence of a permanent legislation, Hutton saw the advantage of avoiding political log-rolling in matters of counting. As India was on way to evolve a new constitution (of 1935), Hutton believed that the provision for taking periodic census was better included in the future constitution.

The proposal for a comprehensive economic survey and the setting up of a permanent economic staff and the holding of an interim quinquennial census were turned down by the Government on the score of expenses. The plea for a permanent census legislation was also ultimately voted down by F.H. Puckle, the Secretary in the Home Department. Puckle wrote in his note of 23 November 1938:

> In the ten years which follow 1941, before the next census is due, there may be many constitutional developments which we

> cannot foretell, and I am inclined to prophesy that, if we now put permanent legislation on the statute book, it will require extensive amendments before the census of 1951. Another and a very practical argument against permanent legislation is the dislike which the Assembly has evinced to legislation being put forward in anticipation of and taking for granted the inauguration of Federation.

The Home Secretary concluded: 'My conclusion is that we should stick to a temporary Act'. R.M. Maxwell, who was Member, Home, agreed with the Secretary, and India continued with the temporary Act.[1]

The Census Act made ample provision for delegated legislation by the Central Government. The rule-making powers conferred upon the latter were also exercisable by the provincial governments. The provincial governments were entrusted with the power to frame rules on a wide variety of census matters. But before they were so entrusted, their consent was obtained. To save time the normal practice with the Government of India was to inform provincial governments that unless they intimated any objections by a particular date, the Central Government would issue the formal notification of entrustment. Under this delegation the provincial governments could appoint persons as census officers and make other decisions on census matters.

During the entire period of the British Raj, census rested on a temporary piece of legislation though the census hierarchy was supportive of a permanent statute. It was only after independence that it was firmly underpinned by a permanent legislation.

The Census Act, 1948

One of the earliest tasks of the Government of independent India was to draft a permanent legislation and thus to put census on a statutory basis. Within a year of independence, the Government got ready the necessary legislation on census, which was introduced in the Constituent Assembly of India (Legislative), which was the Parliament of the time. Yeatts was the census chief at the time. The Bill was piloted by Sardar Vallabhbhai Patel, the Home Minister. Patel advanced two main arguments in support of the legislation. First, the proposed Bill would ensure that the census would not only be scientifically organised but also the enumeration figures 'would be accurately prepared, updated and maintained'. This was absolutely necessary as census is made the basis of internal constitutional changes when necessary. He observed:

> There was a time when census was apt to be regarded as a mere formality yielding certain statistics—not very accurately prepared, obtained indifferently but tabulated very carefully. Now, this kind of census has caused immense injury on occasions when very important constitutional changes take place. As the House is aware, in the last constitutional changes we had to rely upon this census which was very imperfectly prepared. Even portions of India were partitioned, relying on the census which was very inaccurate. Experience has shown that occasions arise very often when we have to rely upon census figures, which, if not accurately prepared, lead to a result other than what is desired. As the world is progressing towards a scientific appreciation of an important operation of this nature, we think it is necessary to have a proper census prepared and for that purpose we would not rely upon periodical enumeration or operation of this nature, but we should have some kind of permanent process of enumeration and checks and counter-checks introduced by which a correct census—a more or less accurate census—may be prepared and kept ready. For this purpose this is an attempt to put in a permanent piece of legislation on the statute book.[2]

Patel's second argument was the need for maintenance and updating of house list. This provided the true basis of any census, which was 'very important', Patel said. He continued:

> It is obvious that the census operation must largely centre round the house list. It is proposed to prepare the house lists in advance of the main census operation. The provinces have agreed to cooperate in this business. It is intended to keep these house lists up to date, so that except for the floating population there will be an estimate of population annually available to us. At present, we base such annual estimates on the figures of the vital statistics which on account of their imperfections are not a safe guide. For the maintenance of these house lists alone, it would be necessary to have permanent legislation and I have explained to the House why we consider this and I have legislation necessary.[3]

The Census Bill was passed in one brief session taking less than one and a half hours. In all, eighteen members spoke but the points of intervention were generally procedural though some pertinent observations were also made. Sardar Patel, of course, dominated the debate and never for a moment let the initiative slip out of his hands.

Broadly, the Census Act, 1948 was on the pattern of previous legislation on the subject. The only material change was in the enhancement of the penalty or fine in the making or an abatement of census offence, in the provision relating to the tampering of records and making it mandatory for persons nominated as census officers to serve in that capacity as directed. Enhanced punishment was preferred on the ground that this would check the interplay of sectional, religious or communal rivalries which, unfortunately, came to light in the past censuses. Secondly, the Act made the abetment of census offences punishable to discourage their occurrence. Thirdly, anyone appointed as census officer could not refuse appointment. Such a provision was necessary for the efficiency and orderly progress of the census operations.

Eighteen members spoke on the proposed Bill, the more notable of whom were M. Ananthasayanam Ayyangar, Pattabhi Sitaramayya and P.S. Deshmukh. Ayyangar emphasised the need to keep out religious and communal considerations in the enumeration of the population. He said:

> Though some communities are not able to multiply as quickly as other communities, the census is taken advantage of for bringing into existence a large number of children. That is unfortunately what happened in Bengal and other places some time ago. Very great care is necessary in this respect. All loop-holes must be avoided so that no minority community may get a larger number of seats. Of course, the majority community is already there in divided India. All those who try to increase their number by merely census operations should be punished.[4]

Pattabhi Sitaramayya narrated a case confirming the genuineness of such a fear. 'I remember a case which was narrated to me from East Bengal. 'There was some census and a man gave the names of 27 members. When the police went there and he was compelled to produce ration cards he could produce only four cards. The mistakes are there but how are you going to cover them'?[5]

Complete unanimity prevailed over keeping the census uncontaminated by communal considerations. Physical verification of the enumerated was suggested but the prevalence of the purdah system stood in the way. This problem, however, could be overcome by recruiting female enumerators and ascertaining the names from neighbours.

Whether caste of the person should be ascertained or not came up for brief but animated discussion. P.S. Deshmukh preferred its retention and argued that this would indicate whether all sections and sectors of the population were more or less equally progressing or the progress was lop-sided, benefiting only a few castes. He said:

> In my own province (Bombay) 3 per cent of the people whose population is 5 lakhs have as many as 415 gazetted posts while the scheduled castes who number 30 lakhs have only 3. The Malis are 12 lakhs in population but have only 5 and Marathas and Juabis numbering 20 lakhs have 12 posts only. If such state of affairs still exists, I claim, Sir, that it is too early to expect that people will agree to the abolition of caste. These very people now wish to continue their exploitation in the name of no-caste. Census operations are very important and for all people they serve as an excellent index to ascertain the progress they have made from time to time. If India is to progress the progress must be all-sided. It should be incumbent upon us to see that every section of the Indian population shares the advancement and only then we shall be able to claim that India has advanced. There is no doubt that the advancement of India is lop-sided and those at the top are exploiting the situation.[6]

The general consensus, however, was in favour of deletion of 'caste' from the census schedule altogether, branding it as a barrier to India's cherished dream: lest members of the scheduled castes and scheduled tribes suffer, a column could be inserted in the census schedule to ascertain whether the person belonged to scheduled castes and scheduled tribes.

The Bill was unanimously passed and became a law in September 1948.

The Census Act, 1948 is a brief piece of legislation comprising eighteen sections and running into bare four pages. It empowers the Central Government to take a census whenever it wants. The Central Government may appoint a Census Commissioner and Superintendents of Census Operations in the states. (The latter functionary was renamed in 1974 as the Director of Census Operations: 'superintendent' apparently was not very appealing or glamorous to independent India's mandarins.) The Census Commissioner is 'to supervise the taking of the census throughout the area in which the census is intended to be taken', and 'the Directors of Census Operations to supervise the taking of the census within the several states'. Census being a subject of national importance, consultation with the states is provided for in the Census Act, 1948. State Governments are consulted while finalising the schedule of questions to be put to the population. What is more, the original law provided that the state governments could add additional list of queries considered by them to be necessary; but the Centre's approval was necessary. As the responsibility for taking census falls on the state government, the latter may appoint persons as census officers 'to take, or aid in or supervise the taking of the census within any specified local area'. Such persons cannot refuse their appointment. All census functionaries are conferred the status of 'public servants' and are thus bound by the Indian Penal Code. In case any census officer neglects his duty he is liable to be punished. The Act puts the enumerated also under a set of obligations: they must answer questions put by the census officer (enumerator) and must cooperate with him in his official work. The Act ensures confidentiality to the census information: records of census are not open to inspection nor admissible in evidence. Finally, the Central Government has been authorised to enact subordinate legislation under the Act.

The Census Act, 1948 is reproduced in Appendix II.

REFERENCES

1. *Home*, F.45/12/38-*Public*.
2. The Constituent Assembly of India (Legislative) Debates,. 18 August, 1948, p. 429.
3. *Ibid.*
4. *Ibid.*, p. 430.
5. *Ibid.*, p. 434.
6. *Ibid.*, p. 435.

12

FROM PHOENIX TO PERMANENT ORGANISATION

All these receive their Birth from other things,
But from himself the Phoenix only springs:
Self-Born, begotten by the Parent Flame
In which he burn'd Another and the same.

—**John Dryden**, 'Ovid's Metam'.

Phoenix organisation is not a standard term, because this type of organisation is not a common variety. Most organisations enjoy more or less extended durability. They continue even though their personnel change. Phoenix organisations fall in an altogether different category.

The phoenix is a bird of Greek mythology, of gorgeous plumage, which after living its allotted life burns itself to ashes, and re-emerges later from its ashes, to live through another cycle of years. The word phoenix entered the English language around the year 1591 when it was used to refer to something which rises from the ashes of its predecessor.

A phoenix organisation must not be confused with a terminal organisation. The latter vanishes altogether after achieving its target, which itself is time-bound. An example could be an organisation set up to cope up with an emergency or an unforeseen situation, such as a flood, an earthquake or a cyclone. In practice, terminal organisations are generally region-specific: their jurisdiction being restricted to affected parts, or groups of people, of the country. A phoenix organisation, on the other hand, vanishes after completing its one-item task—only to re-emerge in its former form after an interval. It has, thus, a predictability, a rhythm, a cycle—and, of course, a known terminality and rebirth.

Most organisations in public administration do not accept the category of phoenix. Organisations are durable formations, and are seen in practice to continue even after their original goals have ceased to activate them. They are known to have discovered new goals to keep them going. At any rate, not many organisations are created with a predetermined death calendar.

A phoenix organisation, on the other hand, carries a warrant of its death at the time of its birth itself. It burns up and reduces itself to its ashes. To carry the analogy further, like the phoenix, it is the only bird of its kind. This, in India, was the census organisation, the agency whose task is to count the human heads in the country. India's census, right since its first conception in the later part of the nineteenth century until 1941 observed the phoenix principle in the sense that it came into shape, then burnt itself out completely only to re-emerge to its full form after an interval. In independent India the census has been given a permanent administrative base and existence. During the entire period of the Raj, a Census Commissioner had to build up an entire organisation every ten years, which, after the census was taken, was allowed to break up and vanish. M.W.M. Yeatts, the Census Commissioner for India in 1941, thus, describes the transitoriness of the census organisation:

> When I took over as Census Commissioner the only member of my predecessor's staff still in Delhi was his daftry. The others had been dispersed all over and those whom it would have been advantageous to recall quite naturally declined to come. They were established in permanent positions and what had the census to offer them? Nothing but one or two years of overwork and then the sack. The whole system, by which the census is carried out in this country (India), can without injustice be described as fantastic.[1]

Yeatts further observed, 'the census is regarded, every ten years, like a foundling; it is nobody's child and has to put up with what it can get'. He added: 'I suggest that this attitude is not creditable to the Government of India and most definitely is not in the interests of efficiency'.[2] There was no continuing body of knowledge in the Government of India or elsewhere regarding census, which was—and is—decidedly India's largest single major administrative performance. The Administration Report of 1941 Census observed:

> The root cause of census defects is the fact that the census is

> a temporary make-shift organisation. A frame-work is hurriedly run up. Certain departments are pressed into service and a great deal of 'forced labour' is then extorted from the public. It is not surprising that this rickety and medieval machine should work with friction, and that it should now be on the point of breaking up. If there is to be any radical improvement it can only come through the census being made to some degree permanent, to some degree a part of the ordinary annual administration of the province.[3]

The terminal nature added greatly to the difficulties of the Indian census. The phoenix principle means that a lot of valuable knowledge and experience is wasted.

A difference marks an organisation from human beings, who man it. The latter are recruited and retire. An organisation continues as ever even when the currently working individuals retire, new ones are recruited, and also not all men leave together. But a phoenix organisation is on an altogether different footing. The phoenix organisation itself dies: all its personnel routinely go out. For the 1931 census, the Census Commissioner joined in October 1929 and remained in office until June 1933 when the post was abolished. The post thus lasted less than four years. The provincial census superintendents used to be appointed nearly six months after the appointment of the Census Commissioner.

The point of termination is certainly a traumatic moment in the lives of the census staff. Many Census Commissioners felt emotional when the hour of departure came. J.H. Hutton, the Census Commissioner in 1931, observed regretfully: 'in closing down my office, so many of them (employees) must start again to search for employment in an uncomfortably competitive world.'[4] An organisation is not only a work-place—it is a social system too. Robbing individuals of the social face of an organisation is no less an agonising deprivation.

The phoenix nature of the organisation sees to it—and even ensures—that nothing is remembered. The resultant dependence on temporary men, always unsatisfactory and particularly so in a very specialised office which has to work against time, produces serious consequences. By keeping its organisation phoenix-like, Indian census claimed the merit of being the cheapest. It made the least demand on the tax-payers. The first ever general census undertaken in 1881 cost Rs 24,79,730, 15 annas and 5 pies. This excluded the expenditure incurred in the princely states of Bombay, Central India and Rajputana and in Baroda, Cochin, Hyderabad, Mysore and Travancore. It also did not include the charge of printing the three volumes containing the report. The Census Commissioner maintained an office in England where the expenditure was £482-3s-9d. This came to Rs. 5,786-4 annas according to the then prevalent exchange rate. This was to be added to the total cost for the enumeration of 208,202,050 persons for the whole of India, for the preparation of the reports, and for the printing of all the reports. The total census expenditure was Rs. 2485,517-3 annas and 5 pies, or at the rate of Rs. 11-15 annas per 1,000 persons. The then Census Commissioner wrote, 'The extreme economy with which this great work has been effected will be evident if we take this rate and apply it to the figures for the population of England and Wales, according to the Census of 1881. . .'[5] The census of 1891 cost only Rs. 25,97,161. The scale of expenditure was kept low throughout. The cost of the census of 1921 was Rs. 14 per 1,000 persons enumerated. The cost of the 1931 census worked out at Rs. 48,00,000, which came to Rs. 12 per 1,000 persons enumerated. A phoenix organisation, thus, incurs the least budgetary outlay. The picture underwent a change when a permanent organisation emerged in the 1961 census. The expenditure incurred for the 1981 census was Rs. 54,22,47,000. It is true that the purchasing power of the rupee has suffered serious erosion since the pre-independence days but one cannot deny that a phoenix organisation is economical.

Mechanisms of Memory Retention

Even a phoenix organisation rètains elements, however, imperfect and inadequate, of memory and hence a kind of continuity. Because of the absence of a between-census continuity elaborate written records became a necessity. Preparation of a census volume on administration marked every census and was seriously read and assimilated by the successive census commissioners and other officials. The contents and style of the administrative report were necessarily conditioned by the ten-year hiatus. As Yeatts put it:

> With census commissioners coming in after such a gap possibly without provincial census experience themselves; without any practical census knowledge in any department of the Government of India; and in view of the other peculiar aspects of census functioning in the past, the administration report had to dwell on all sorts of topics, great or small, in order that the new census commissioner, working as always against time, would be able to see at once what to pursue.[6]

The report on administration gives an account of the manner in which the census operations were carried out and of the difficulties that were encountered, with the suggestions made for removing them at subsequent enumerations. The report on administration was comprehensive and was a most valuable reader for the successor. Rightly did one census superintendent write: '. . . my successor in 1931 can safely accept it even in minor details, as a sure basis for his arrangements for the next census.'[7]

Each provincial-level superintendent of census operations routinely prepared a volume on administration in which he laid down comprehensively, for corrective action in future, the administrative problems and issues which he had encountered while organising the census. Based on all such provincial reports as well as his first-hand knowledge and experience, the Census Commissioner prepared his own volume on administration. This report was examined by the administrative department, namely, the Home Department in the Central Government. When the next census became due, the report was carefully gone into. Some suggestions regularly found their entry into the census statute.

Unlike other reports of the Census Commissioner, the volume on administration is not made available to the public: it is meant for official use only. It is not known if administrative volumes were prepared for the first two censuses of 1881 and 1891. For every census held subsequently such a volume was considered an integral part of the Census Commissioner's responsibility and was invariably prepared. The rhythm, however, was not maintained in independent India. Not all state level census heads cared to compile administrative reports and even the Census Commissioners took the time-honoured practice as an optional obligation.

Another powerful device to capture memory and continuity is the census conference, which was first organised in December 1889. The census conference is, as a rule, held before each census and its purpose is to construct a complete scheme for the administration of the provincial operations. One of the earliest actions of a newly appointed Census Commissioner was the convening of this census conference. Soon after his appointment to the post, he carefully studied the provincial census reports and noted the doubtful points and difficulties that arose in the course of the last census. He, thereupon, submitted to the Home Department a note on these difficulties and on other points connected with the census, which needed further elucidation.

The census conference was attended by the provincial census superintendents. It met for a fortnight to discuss thoroughly the questions brought before it. The matured opinions of experts from different provinces facilitated the settlement of important general questions. The conference discussed not only the administrative details of the forthcoming census but also statistical information considered desirable to obtain. It ascertained what information was to be collected and how far it could be obtained consistently with the procedure pursued for the census. It approved the schedule and accompanying instructions. A detailed report including recommendations for the coming census was sent to the Government, which then consulted the provincial governments before finalising its decisions. The Census Commissioner, then, issued the final instructions and standard forms.

A conference of this composition and functions was originally proposed in W.C. Plowden's letter of 24 December 1888 and was viewed as the best method of harvesting the experience gained at the last census. Testifying for the usefulness of such a get-together Baines, the Census Commissioner for 1891 wrote: 'The subsequent labours of the (Census) Commissioner, who attended the conference in his capacity of former superintendent of the Bombay operations were so materially lightened by the help thus rendered to him by his colleagues, that he feels that this opportunity must not be lost of thanking them'.[8]

To capture continuity and retain memory, care was taken to fill census positions with persons who had earlier done census duty. One notable name in this context was D. Natarajan, who had started his career as a lower level functionary in census work in the old Madras Presidency. When M.W.M. Yeatts became the Census Commissioner for the census in 1941, D. Natarajan was traced and brought all the way to Delhi to assist. In the 1931 census, Mirza Sher Muhammad was appointed deputy superintendent of census operations in Baluchistan. He was selected because of his association with the census operations in 1911 and 1921. It was thought that being a local man, he would be very useful for tribal census, especially because he had done this work on two previous occasions.[9] The clerical functionaries at the time really worked hard and with meticulous care, thus constituting a real asset to the organisation. This is especially mentioned here in view of the general fall in standards of work at these levels in independent India.

To promote continuity and preserve memory, some staffing stratagems were also tried or recommended in the phoenix organisation. One was the attachment of a young I.C.S. officer to the Chief Commissioner as his Chief Assistant. M.W.M. Yeatts, who made the proposal in 1938, explained:

> This would be the first step towards that continuity which I

> think is essential and which could no longer be disregarded. After his spell with me, he could join, for example, the Home Department as under or deputy secretary and thereby produce there the necessary continuity of experience and knowledge. If chosen of the right seniority and presuming a high degree of competence he could possibly conduct the next all-India census, or at any rate, could be of the greatest value.[10]

Another device was to pick the supportive census staff from the regular secretariat service recruited in the ordinary way. On the completion of census work, they were absorbed into the Home Department or some other Department.

Also, one may note the advice which in 1931 J.H. Hutton gave on organisation making:

> At the start of operations the Census Commissioner will find two or three things essential. The first is to have a capable financial assistant accustomed to the Government of India Secretariat procedure and the methods of the Finance Department. Statistical knowledge is not required till a later stage. I started by appointing an assistant with statistical knowledge, but his expert knowledge was largely wasted at the earlier stages. I would recommend no appointment of a superintendent till later, and that the staff should at the start consist of a financial assistant, and a tour clerk who is also a steno-typist, to whom should be added a little later a third clerk preferably with a knowledge of enumeration work in one of the major provinces—Madras, the United Provinces or Bengal. The nucleus of the office should be clerks with permanent posts to revert to, as this nucleus is likely to form also the ultimate remainder, and has less motive for unduly prolonging work and less inclination towards scamping it when the final stages are reached.
>
> For the first three months the Census Commissioner's office should not be in the position of an attached office, but should be started as a branch of the main department. This would allow time to make arrangements for an independent supply of stationery, furniture, accommodation, etc. It would obviate the necessity for a third clerk at the beginning as bills would be prepared in the main department, and it would give an opportunity for the Census Commissioner's office to learn its

> work before making an independent start. Much inconvenience was caused in 1931 by the creation of an independent office at the very outset when neither the Census Commissioner nor his office had any experience of Government of India Secretariat procedure and when forms, stamps, stationery and every sort of information had to be lodged or borrowed from permanent departments.[11]

One should also note another point. The staffing requirements of a census organisation, brought into existence every ten years, showed a rapid acceleration. M.W.M. Yeatts wrote: 'I am quite prepared to start small, but it will be necessary to develop the staff appreciably after a few months and, of course, again when the tabulation begins later. It is important that the Finance Department should understand this point.'[12]

Continuity in an otherwise memory-less organisation was promoted fortuitously too. Though the Census Commissioner was a bird of passage, continuity was provided at the bottom. In rural tracts particularly, which form the great bulk of India's surface and hold a great bulk of its population the enumerator was the patwari, who was hereditary during the whole period of the Raj. Patwari was a universal standby in India. As Yeatts observed, 'One may have in a village the whole all-India census series represented in actual experience in the successive generations of the village headman or accountant'.[13] In urban areas, though the hereditary principle was absent and though urban enumeration offered problems and difficulties, an element of continuity was secured through the municipal staff, many of whom were found in practice at any one time to have had earlier census experience.

Nevertheless, such an outfit—or lack of it—was incongruous and irksome. As India entered the 1930s, there was a growing realisation that as in other countries India should also have a continuing, permanent organisation in which the knowledge and experience of one census could be carried forward to the next and thus remain available for gainful use. In a permanent organisation, the system of tabulation is bound to be more continuous and less convulsive. The additional advantage of the proposed standing body was that it could be entrusted with a great many other allied functions when the pressure of census work eased. Also, growing international contacts on matters relating to census sharply brought out the handicaps of the phoenix system. Mention was made of the Chinese visit to India in the mid-1940s. When the Government of India was approached for guidance on census, it had no continuing organisation of any kind available for consultation. Yeatts reminisced and observed: 'It was an accident that I happened to be in Simla (India's summer capital) in another Department which enabled the Chinese representative to get the guidance he sought'.[14]

As census is a decennial activity it necessarily entails peaks with in-between lean periods of activity. Its organisational requirement is thus atypical and unique. The Census Commissioner had to build a new organisation from scratch. It was important, therefore, that an appropriate officer be appointed, much in advance, and left free to apply his mind to the various problems of coordination and planning both for standards and their attainment. Yeatts' practical tip was that the newly appointed Census Commissioner

> could start with, on the administration side, one sound and experienced man like Mr. Natarajan as superintendent, a general clerk, typist and a really good stenographer plus, of course, a jamadar and two or three chaprasis. In addition, he should have a good statistical officer. This could be a young man but must have good statistical qualifications. This officer need not join at once but should be provided for within one or two months.[15]

Attempts Towards Permanence

It was Dr. J.H. Hutton, the Census Commissioner for 1931, who first recommended the creation of a permanent census organisation. The existing method of creating an agency for the taking of a census, destroying it and re-creating it periodically was prodigal of effort and of experience. Continuity depended entirely on an inadequate written record. A great deal was learned at each census which was then forgotten and relearned ten years later. Improvements were, therefore, very difficult to introduce. The whole procedure consisted of organisation and analysis undertaken against time, and it was, therefore, rash as well as difficult to undertake any change that needed to be prepared in advance. A good case in point was the introduction of a mechanical sorting in census. This proposal was examined in 1921 and postponed for re-examination during the census of 1931. The hurried conclusion on that occasion was against it on the ground that it was too late to introduce it on account of the changes in procedure involved. A decision on the matter was postponed again for another decade. Hutton recommended: 'The true solution would appear to be to amalgamate the office of Census

Commissioner with that of the Director-General of Statistics and Commercial Intelligence putting the two under a permanent head, whose permanent office would form the standing nucleus of the periodic census department.'[16] Continuity in censusing was most essential, he asserted.

The suggestion remained unheeded again to be picked up by his successor Yeatts. Yeatts' mind was more or less working along these lines right since his assumption of the office. In his note dated 5 August 1938, he wrote to the Home Department about an appointment which, as he observed, would be the first step towards that continuity 'which I think is essential and which can no longer be disregarded'. He wanted an ICS officer to be appointed as his assistant to gain census experience, who could thus be well equipped to succeed him for the next census.[17] He wrote in May 1939:

> On the matter of permanent existence for a census organisation, the American example has again offered much food for thought. I doubt whether India is developed to the extent of carrying an organisation of the elaboration I find here. I always felt that, of course; but I felt also—and feel—our past practice means a great waste of the most valuable thing in life, experience; and that if we could devise some method, suited to India's needs and situation, of carrying on the knowledge and actual experience gained in census, we should be able to achieve economy of effort and of expense.

He noted further: 'I am still reflecting on this point and shall not reach my final conclusions until I have visited Canada, and have had discussions with the Registrar-General in England'. One specific suggestion Yeatts made was as follows:

> One point, however, I suggest now might be considered, *viz.*, that the ordinary office staff of the Census Commissioner should be taken from men admitted to Government of India Service. These men would always be available later on for census or allied work if necessary. No one can work in a census office without learning a great deal of the way in which things are built up and run, and it would be most valuable to have this kind of knowledge represented in the Home Department.

In July 1939, Yeatts reiterated even more firmly the need for a permanent nucleus for the census staff, 'the existence of which could preserve something of the knowledge and experience acquired during each census'. A note in the Home Department dated 10 July 1939 stated: 'Such a nucleus might perhaps be kept in the Home Department and employed on other work in the period between census activities'. Yeatts spelled out his staff requirements. At the beginning, the Census Commissioner's staff was to consist of an assistant (Natarajan), a stenographer, a general duty clerk and a jamadar. While Natarajan was to be brought from Madras Government others were to be from the ordinary secretariat service of the proper classes. Clerks at the time provided so strong a base for organisations. He did not lay emphasis on either the stenographer or the clerk to be particularly senior or experienced. Natarajan will supply these qualities. He explained:

> My idea is that the men in my office should have entered the secretariat service in the ordinary way and on completion of the census work would pass on into the Home Department or some other Government office. This would mean that the routine administrative experience, which is so useful, particularly at the beginning, would be preserved for the future. Elements of continuity were thus being gradually built and consolidated and much yet awaited doing in this direction.

Population Data Committee

In May 1944, the Government of India appointed the Population Data Committee headed by Yeatts to examine and advise on the available data relating to growth of population. The committee submitted its report in 1945. It was this committee which first made a firm recommendation about the desirability of an organisation at the centre definitely charged with the coordination of all information on population growth and allied matters. It was suggested that this should take the form of a Registrar-General who would have the statutory duty to report each year on the state of India's population. The Registrar-General was in course of time to replace the Census Commissioner and was to operate under the Home Department. It was not necessary that the Registrar-General should be, and in fact was not to be, a mere statistician. He was to be an officer from the top rank of the administrative service.[18] The Committee report said in part:

> It is essential that the Central Government enter the field of

> vital statistics by prescription of standards, establishing a right of inspection of provincial and (princely) states' figures, and by financial or other assistance, at the centre. There should be an officer or organisation at the centre definitely charged with the coordination of all information on population growth, that is covering not only the census but the vital statistics and all allied matters. The provision should take the form of Registrar-General. Whatever the form adopted, the functionary should have a statutory duty to report each year on the state of India's population. This must be an absolutely clear and individual responsibility.

Around this time, another committee, known as the Health Survey and Development Committee, under the chairmanship of Sir Joseph Bhore, also reported favouring a permanent central organisation which would have the duty, among others, of undertaking a periodic census at such intervals as might be laid down by law. The recommendation was examined at various levels of the Government and it was generally agreed that there was justification for the establishment of such an organisation as soon as possible, one of its immediate tasks being to prepare the ground for the next census and to fill the wide gap left in the census of 1941 on account of incomplete tabulation.

The Population Data Committee submitted its report to the Department of Education, Health and Lands (which had appointed it). The report, naturally, came to the Home Department for further processing. For the proposed post, Sir Francis Mudie, Member, Home at this time, preferred the title of Director, already in vogue in Indian administrative hierarchies. He, moreover, wished to entrust the responsibility of the job to Yeatts, who had by then joined the Department of Supply in the Government of India.

Mudie and Yeatts held conflicting views on the christening of the post. Yeatts was then a deputy secretary but had no fear in articulating his views freely and frankly: the traditions of the service had given him that measure of independence, which is in sharp contrast with the present day servility of the administrative hierarchies. Yeatts had recommended the nomenclature of Registrar-General to head the proposed Population and Census Bureau. In his letter to Mudie, dated 10 September 1945, he explained his preference for this nomenclature:

> This (census head's) is a big post and will require, apart from

> particular qualities in the incumbent, a definite and considerable status. He will have to build up from nothing and also to resolve overlaps between Departments of the Government of India. In addition to this, he will have to bring provinces into line, to get them to develop their own organisations, to raise their standards, and so on. Everything will depend in these first years on whether, for example, the more intransigent provinces are prepared to listen. The title of Registrar-General seems to me the best.[19]

Nor was one to forget the challenge thrown up by the Indian princely states. They were jealous about their separateness from British India, but their importance in the head counting could not be ignored, representing, as they did, one-fourth of the entire country in population. But, as Yeatts explained, the princely states were apt to be suspicious of Government of India's interference, and certainly of 'low-level' entry. The officer in this post would have to be able to carry them with him and to get the whole force of the states' administration working on the lines he proposed. This again, quite apart from the qualities of the officer himself, would call for a very definite status. Yeatts told Mudie that the designation that Mudie offered, namely that of Director, was to be fatal. That designation would put the incumbent on a line with, say Directors of Agriculture. He plainly told the top boss: 'I am quite certain that the sort of man you have in mind would not look at the job under this appellation'.

Yeatts, in short, did not consider fit the proposed designation of Director. The least he wanted was that of Director-General, a title which was to put across the absolutely essential all-India point of view. Nor did he like the nomenclature 'Population and Census Bureau': this limited the job far too much. Yeatts had a larger perspective in mind. He wrote:

> The whole idea is to get away from the old limitations on the fundamental approach to population statistics. But this office would ultimately become the focus of much more than just population. For example, if it ran the house list, it would be dealing with a fundamental piece of administrative procedure, the uses and effects of which would go far beyond the plain population data. Incidentally, I do not think it would take long for it to become such a focus ; the field is so chaotic that the mere appearance of a post of this kind, if it were on a proper level, would precipitate on it a great deal of hitherto

uncoordinated effort. And that would be a very good thing.[20]

These reasons induced Yeatts to suggest the title of Registrar-General: 'It has the great merit of being brief, it definitely puts over the all-India range, and it is not tied on to a purely limited concept that would prove ultimately a serious handicap to its operations'.[21]

Mudie remained unconvinced. He described Yeatts' suggestion as 'impossible', saying that the proposed Registrar-General could not stand by itself—he must register something. Under the Government of India Act, 1935, he could not register births and deaths, which was a purely provincial function. Mudie cautioned: 'whatever we may manage to do in practice, we must not infringe the provincial sphere on paper'.[22] To this, Yeatts replied that the Centre was already operating in areas of provincial action. In other words, the Central Government had posts in fields admittedly of theoretically provincial responsibility such as agriculture and animal husbandry. Even the census was basically a provincial phenomenon in the all-important first stage of enumeration, Yeatts maintained. Enumeration was carried out by the provinces and at their expense. 'The cardinal point is to seize on the all-India aspect which in fact is at the root of the whole thing.'

For his demand in favour of the title Registrar-General, Yeatts took inspiration from the British practice where the Registrar-General was entrusted with numerous matters not strictly covered under the technical term 'registration'. The proposed functionary was gradually to take hold of the basic essential of the whole statistical field of India, namely, putting on to a sound all-India system the securing of information about the people of the country and how they lived. In the same letter Yeatts defined the scope and functions of the proposed Registrar-General.

> It will be the duty of the Registrar to deal with all matters bearing on the extractions of data relating to the population of the country including those hitherto associated with the periodical censuses. He will also carry out any other appropriate functions entrusted to him by the Central Government. He will be directly responsible for all registration of vital statistics in the central areas and for the improvement in methods, and cover and accuracy of such statistics. In consultation with provincial and state (*i.e.* princely states) governments he will endeavour to improve the quality of these and other related statistics and work towards uniformity and raising of standards. He will give technical advice to all Departments of the Government of India on statistical matters

> assigned to him and may also be consulted by provincial and state governments. He may correspond direct with provinces and states on matters connected with the above field of operation.[23]

Mudie, thereupon, sought the advice of the Economic Advisor to the Government of India, Sir Theodore Gregory. Gregory emphasised the need for much more serious attention to the census and population statistics than had been given in the past. The person to head such an organisation was to be given a sufficiently high status and sufficiently wide powers to carry out his duties properly. His nomenclature, according to Gregory, was of secondary importance.

R. Tottenham in the Home Department separately took up the recommendation for a central statistical bureau and attached the highest priority to it. He observed on 4 August 1945:

> In view of the fact that several different departments are interested in the census figures and the methods of supplementing and improving them in order to form a basis for many economic inquiries, etc., it seems to me that the most important recommendation of the Committee (Population Data Committee) is that dealing with the organisation of a Central Statistical Bureau with an expert at the head of it who could take over all these questions and the census itself together with all work between census periods connected with it. My own opinion is that this should be pushed forward as quickly as possible.[24]

Ultimately, Yeatts prevailed. The administrative system under the Raj gave full freedom of expression to its functionaries in its internal decision-making, which brought out the best in them. Mudie did not feel small in agreeing with Yeatts in his note of August 1945, he (Mudie) agreed that a post analogous to that of Registrar-General in the United Kingdom be created and attached to the Home Department. Because of his competence in the job, Yeatts was invited to head the proposed organisation. The latter prepared a comprehensive note on planning of census, dated 17 November 1945, a piece which is of classic importance in institution-building. Below is given a summary of this note:

> Statistics do not fall like manna from heaven; they have to be developed and the methods of development are of the utmost importance. It is time that the most serious attention was given to the whole statistical set-up in India and planning for statistics should start along with every kind of planning.

> In fact, the flow of information should be organised before action begins. This is what engineers do where river works are concerned; they make arrangements to measure flow, volume, flood range, etc., long before draining works, bridges, etc., are taken up... In other fields of activity the need is not so apparent or possibly so acute, it is nevertheless present. Great development schemes should start from information, and should embody specific provisions to enable a record of performance to be thrown up automatically as the schemes go on.

The perfect statistics is the meter reading. We switch on the fan or the lights or the heater or the stove and switch off.

As we do so, the recording mechanism sets down every unit we consume and presents it in an immediately comprehensible and usable form whenever we care to look. To provide automatic continuous record of performance should be the ambition.

The information need falls into two aspects where development or extensions are concerned:

(1) What facts at present exist ?
(2) What facts are essential for a continuing study of performance?

There is often more information available than is realised. The trouble is that it is not organised, different packets are locked in different containers all of which have different keys and some of which are not known at all. The first stage, therefore, is simply to comb the ground to discover by the most careful shifting what kinds of information are, in fact, available and where. There follows at once the value of this information *i.e.* the range within which this is accurate. This range itself will frequently, in fact almost certainly, vary, and vary widely according to the production source and an estimate of this range is essential... The census should be the concern of the central statistical direction. The content of the questionnaire and the method of collection, etc. . . . fall in the central direction field.

Vital statistics in India offer an astonishing picture of confusion and misunderstanding. They have tended to be looked on as purely a public health matter. Actually, they are basic and should join the central direction field along with the census.

> instead of being left to the most astonishing range of first, second or even third hand collection and a value zone which often is so wide as to remove significance from the collected figures.
>
> In view of the extreme importance of the population aspect in a country holding one-fifth of the world's people, India should have a Registrar-General with the statutory duty of putting out each year a report on population and with powers of inspection, advice and assistance vis-a-vis provinces and state collection of vital statistics. The population field is so great and so difficult and at present so empty that the Registrar-General should have a definite place for himself but it would be possible ultimately to bring this within the Dominion Statistician's field—a common scientific pool in which methods could be devised, tested and improved. In fact, the setting up of the Registrar-General might be the first step towards a systematic organisation of India's statistical requirements and channels.[25]

When Yeatts was musing on statistical planning for India, the country was witnessing high voltage changes in politics. The Second World War had ended and Indian political leaders, including Mahatma Gandhi were out of jail. Great Britain had initiated a serious dialogue with Indian political leadership on the question of India's political future. Soon, the country was to be partitioned and each newly created country was to emerge independent. Naturally, the proposals on census took a back seat for some time. The office of the Registrar-General, subsuming the responsibility of the Census Commissioner consequently, remained shelved. It was in 1969, twenty-two years after independence, that India passed the Registration of Births and Deaths Act, which, among others, provided for the appointment of Registrar-General. Since then, the Registrar-General functions concurrently as the Census Commissioner of India. Since 1969, thus, the census organisation acquired a standing base and its phoenix nature was finally put to an end.

Census is the most authentic source of information on population, but being a decennial event it does not provide data on annual changes in it, which can be obtained only through compulsory registration of births and deaths. Thus, census and registration of births and deaths, one must note, are mutually integrated. A beginning towards blending the two was made in the middle of the nineteenth century when the registration of deaths first began, even though haltingly. Collection of information on deaths was considered to be essential for the introduction of sanitary reforms at local level in India. Births evoked interest much later. The Indian Famine Commission (1880) was the first official body to point out the need for registration of births and deaths. In 1886, an Act was accordingly passed, but its provision for optional registration made the Act virtually ineffective. Besides, different parts of the country had different legal provisions resulting in an absence of uniform registration practices. It is not the purpose here to recount the slow, even meandering progress towards compulsory registration of births and deaths. Sufficient to say, registration of births and deaths in India was characterised by a multiplicity of Acts and rules.

A growing realisation of the lacuna inherent in the prevalent arrangements led to the enactment in 1969 of a law providing for compulsory registration of both births and deaths. This was the Registration of Births and Deaths Act, 1969. The legislation, among other things, establishes statutory authority at the centre and in each state to undertake registration. The administrative machinery at the central level is headed by the Registrar-General. In view of the close interface between census and vital statistics (data that record the rates of births and deaths) the office of the Census Commissioner was integrated with that of the Registrar-General. The Registrar-General has work all round the yea and to him is entrusted, since 1969, the 'spasmodic' work of censı The demand for merging the office of the Census Commissioner w an existing organisation engaged in a related activity, the reader note, was of long standing. Census itself needed to be made perma but because in itself it was not viable enough it had to be linked some related activity.

REFERENCES

1. *Census of India 1941*, Report I, Vol. II, Administration Report, p
2. *Ibid.*
3. *Bihar Census Administration Report* (Extracts), Census Report f
4. *Census of India*, Vol. I — India, Part V, Administration Report, Si of India Press 1933, Foreword.
5. *1881 Census of India*, London, H.M.S.O. 1883, p. 471.
6. Government of India 1941, *Census Report*, Part II, Administr p.1.
7. *Census of India 1921*, Vol. V, Bengal and Sikkim, Part III, Ac by W.H. Thompson 1923, p. 1.
8. *The Census of India 1891, Part I—General Report*, p. 2'
9. *Home-Public*, 45/19/30-*Public* 1930, p. 27.
10. *Home-Public*, 45/20/38-*Public*.

11. *Census of India 1931—Vol. I, India, Part IV—Administration Report*, pp. 10-11.
12. M.W.M. Yeatts' letter No. 2964/39-*Public*, dated 28 July 1939 to E. Conran Smith in the Home Department.
13. Radio Talk by Yeatts on 9 December 1939.
14. Yeatts note dated 15 September 1945.
15. *Ibid.*
16. *Census of India, 1931: Vol. I, India, Part V—Administration Report*, Simla, Government of India Press, 1933.
17. *Home-Public*, 45/20/38-*Public*, 1938, p. 2.
18. Government of India, Ministry of Education, Health and Lands, *Report of the Population Data Committee*, 1945, p. 20.
19. *Home-Public*, F.45/10/45-*Public*.
20. *Ibid.*
21. *Ibid.*
22. Mudie's letter to M.W.M. Yeatts dated 19 September 1945. *Home*, F.45/10/45-*Public*.
23. *Home*, 45/10/45-*Public*.
24. *Ibid.*
25. *Ibid.*

13

CENSUS AND THE GOVERNMENT OF INDIA ACT, 1935

Census, from the outset, was the responsibility of the Government of India. In 1880, the year before the first general census was held, a separate Census Branch was set up in the Home Department. Census continued to be a central responsibility even under the Government of India Act, 1935, which became the constitution for the time. paving the way for a federation in the country and entailing a division of functions between the two levels of government. The present Constitution, in operation since 1950, continues this arrangement. In all federations, the function of census rests with the national government, it being a subject of national importance requiring country-wide uniformity.

In India the census was a centralised affair but its operational responsibility always rested with the provincial governments. It was they who looked after the actual conduct of head counting. The central control over census was tight and all-pervasive, but the provincial governments were, as a regular practice, consulted on a broad range of matters. The inter-governmental consultative culture was a truly notable feature of the Raj.

Provinces were originally consulted even on holding the census. In 1869, were consulted on the feasibility of holding the census in 1871. Provinces were likewise consulted while finalising the census schedule. Equally regular was the practice with the Central Government of consulting them before enacting the census legislation. Importance was given to their views. for they—and they alone—possessed authentic knowledge of local conditions.This is as it should be. As enumeration of people, the critical input in any census, is virtually provincial responsibility their experience can be made use of in drafting census legislation. When the 1929 Census Act was passed, provincial governments were not consulted in advance, which left certain defects in the census law.[1]

Apart from such consultation, the provinces were otherwise permitted little local initiative in censusing. Whenever they ventured any such move they were firmly reminded about the primacy of command of the Secretary of the State and the Government of India, in that order. 'The views of Her Majesty's Government in regard to the taking of a general census should be borne in mind and the consent of the Government of India should be previously obtained'[2] in case the provincial government contemplated adopting any measures of an active nature in the matter of taking a census. It naturally followed that census being a central function, the entire funds for it came from the central exchequer.

That the operational responsibility of the census falls on the shoulders of the lower level governments is not constitutionally mandated but practice has made it so. Because census is an item of national importance, being vital for socio-economic planning and policy-making, the state governments expect to be, and indeed are, consulted by the centre while finalising the schedule, which forms the basis of obtaining information from the enumerated. According to the stipulations of the 1948 Act, the state governments could insert their own questions in the schedule and obtain information on such additional queries. This was explicitly provided in the Census Act, 1948 itself. Section 8(1) says: 'A census officer may ask all such questions . . . for which he is appointed as, by instructions issued in this behalf by the state government and published in the Official Gazette, he may be directed to ask'. That the lower level government could add to the list of questions prepared by the Census Commissioner was not a new arrangement introduced under the Constitution of 1950; indeed, this had always been the practice. The earliest Census Act, 1881 also contained a similar provision. Section 6 of the Act provided: 'Every census officer may ask all such questions... as, by instructions issued in this behalf by the local government and published in the official gazette, he may be directed to ask.' The state governments at present do not have any such power to add its own questions to the census schedule.

The census arrangement, which as a rule relied heavily on the lower level governments for actual head counting was showing stress and became irksome and difficult even under the Raj, more so with the passage of the Government of India Act, 1935. This Act inaugurated a new pattern of relationship between the Government of India and the provinces, installing as it did a federation in the country for the first time.

Though the census was a central responsibility, the provincial level census superintendents and others were as a rule appointed by the lower level governments. In practice, the central government always advised on these appointments, the provinces listening to it and acting accordingly. But the sailing was not always smooth. Some provinces developed a tendency to spare for the job officers who were 'sparable'. The central government surely resisted such moves, but to little avail. Bombay and the Punjab did not always take their census responsibilities very seriously. A glimpse into Bombay's cavalier attitude is provided by Yeatts:

> Bombay in fact have had it both ways: they push off the man they want and they get the Government of India to take the responsibility of appointing him. All this points to the desirability at future censuses of getting the enumeration responsibility more correctly located *i.e.* on the provinces. Once this is done they will see that a good man is put on to it or will put the whole force of the provincial government behind it or both.

Yeatts concluded, 'I quite realise that the Central Government is in a weak position inasmuch as it cannot compel a province to release a particular individual, and as the Bombay case shows, is in the unfortunate position of having to pay the piper without being able to call the tune'.[3] The Punjab was another province which imposed its own choice on the census despite the centre's opposition.

A mention of census as a central responsibility in the Government of India Act, 1935 gave rise to problems. As enumeration rested with the provinces, they began to show a tendency to regard census work as an imposition. The lower level governments and personnel showed barely disguised reluctance in shouldering census responsibilities and were often passive performers in the game. This compelled the census bureaucracy to search a possible solution. To overcome this reluctance a lasting solution perhaps lay in bifurcating the census into: (i) enumeration and (ii) tabulation. Enumeration should be made a provincial (*i.e.* state) subject. While the provision of the schedules would remain a Central function, physical enumeration should be done by the provinces. Yeatts examined this question and had the following to say: 'I would recommend the division of the subject 'Census' into a federal element which would cover all matters of tabulation and ultimate direction and control, and the provision of the actual paper on which the enumeration is carried out; enumeration being declared a provincial subject.' He concluded: The definition might be afforded compendiously by declaring as a provincial subject 'enumeration' except the actual provision of the schedules or slips on which the enumeration is carried out; and is a central subject, everything except the operation described'.[4] Yeatts wrote elsewhere:

> The present system is profoundly unsatisfactory inasmuch as it is provincial agencies which carry out the enumeration but a central agency, which is responsible, directs the provincial staffs and pays them nothing. In the old days of a unitary government this might work but under a quasi-federation it courts great difficulties.[5]

The propensity in the lower level functionaries to shirk the census responsibility has a long history in India. Yeatts faced the problem of provincial government employees showing aversion to census work and was inundated with requests for exemptions. For some time, Bombay had acquired a level of notoriety for its not very cooperative attitude towards the Centre on census. The Superintendent of Census Operation Bombay, openly referred to 'lack of satisfactory response' on the part of the Bombay Government.[6] Neither did the Central Government Departments take census very seriously. Authorities under the direct control of the Government of India 'did not offer the required cooperation to the Census Department in the matter of loan staff.'[7] The Superintendent of Census Operations, Bombay, complained in a letter in 1941:

> The number of persons required for census work in Bombay during the enumeration process was about 6,000 and municipality could muster about 1,000 employees only. It was, therefore, very very necessary that offices with really large staffs such as those addressed by the executive health officer of the Bombay Municipality should have spared at least 75 per cent of their clerical establishment for the period from 28 February 1941 to 3 March 1941.[8]

But the necessary level of cooperation was not forthcoming, causing considerable tension to the official concerned.

The Central Government was itself to set an example to the provinces in deputing the personnel for census work. Its offices were expected to spare their men liberally for census duties not only as an example to provincial governments and local bodies but also because the more outgoing the response they made the less was to be the cost of the census operations falling on the Government of India.

Here, too, there was reluctance to do census work. Yeatts, who was the superintendent of census in Madras in 1931, narrated the incident of certain Central Government employees posted in Madras securing exemption from census work. This had a demoralising effect on other employees. Yeatts recalled: 'I well remember the effects in Madras in 1930 when some central employees carrying no greater burden of duties or responsibilities secured an exemption in a certain district (secured, I may say without my knowledge); the natural reaction showed itself; hard-driven officers murmured at central officers being freed from what was in their view a central subject; and work suffered in that district.'[9] In his volume on Administration, Yeatts referred to the corrupting influence cast by such wayward central employees who were called 'discreditable shirkers.'

> The tendency was noticeable for Government of India servants to try to dodge census duties in the provinces and the Survey of India in particular showed up rather badly in the U.P. The Calcutta offices of the Government of India were also unsatisfactory and the Reserve Bank (of India) seemed to consider itself over any kind of service in the census, and in general if the Government of India wish this remarkable system to continue they will have to see that their own people give a lead instead of being in most areas away from the Government of India's own headquarters.[10]

Yeatts concluded:

> The main fault is in the heads of the offices whose responsibility it is to see that the Government of India's orders are carried out. In the provinces, we have the whole body of provincial officers working overtime and spare time unpaid on the census, which is a central subject. When they see central government employees dodging their plain duty as census they feel quite naturally that they have not been fairly treated. The principle is simple enough. There should be no general exemptions of any kind except for serving soldiers and police.[11]

But a bigger problem was yet to confront the census authorities. In June 1940 the Legal Remembrancer, Bombay had held that no person could be appointed as a census officer under section (2) of the Census Act, 1939 without his consent. This interpretation came painly as a bombshell, leading Yeatts to comment, 'It is perhaps characteristic that this particular bombshell should come from Bombay'.[12] The Legislative Department of the Central Government, which was consulted on the matter, concurred with the Bombay Legal Remembrancer's interpretation. It observed:

> The opinion given by the Legal Remembrancer, Bombay is unexceptionable. Section 2 of the India Census Act, 1939 has not the effect of empowering the Central, or the provincial government to press into service for the purpose of census any person they like. It merely empowers them to appoint any person who is willing to serve as census officer. The opinion of the Legal Remembrancer is expressly confined to persons not in the service of the Crown. Persons in the whole-time service of the Crown are subject to their conditions of service—bound to discharge such functions as the appropriate government may assign to them. Such persons can, therefore, be appointed as census officers irrespective of their consent.[13]

Such an interpretation was unnerving and at once put the census hierarchy in a dilemma. Yeatts, thereupon, hit on an ingenious way to overcome the problem. He simply did not wish to over-publicise the 'consent' part. For the Legal Remembrancer's interpretation certainly handicapped the Central Government in effectively discharging its census responsibilities. He wrote:

> If we are careful not to draw undue prominence to it, it may well remain so. I must say that this seems to me a case in which a dog that has slept for decades might well be left to slumber a little longer. There is no reason in the world why we should throw stones at it. . . If we avoid drawing the attention of the entire country to this hole in the Act, then we may escape substantial demand for remuneration which otherwise it will be difficult to avoid.

Yeatts summed up:

> Final action which I myself contemplate taking, if Government approves of this note and the course proposed in it, is to communicate personally confidentially to superintendents (of census in the provinces) the substance of the present ruling,

> telling them, however, to keep the matter to themselves unless cases of refusal to serve occur in which cases they should do their utmost to solve the difficulty either by persuasion or substitute appointment, with as little fuss as possible. I do not contemplate the communication of this to collectors etc., etc., for the present at any rate.[14]

In the end Yeatts again emphasised the 'undesirability of pursuing this hare in full cry'.[15]

The Government took the decision: 'Let sleeping dogs lie. As the matter is one of policy which we may accept with advantage and for which no criticism can be levelled against Government—because unnecessarily publicising this legal position may substantially put an end to the vast Indian census made possible largely on account of public cooperation free of cost—the course proposed by the Census Commissioner may be approved.' To summarise, the Central Government could not press into census everyone in the country without his willingness. Only Central and state government employees were bound by central directives. Employees of the local government, both rural and urban, could not, for instance, be forced into accepting census responsibility.

In India, the census has been substantially unpaid, which has kept it economical also. In view of the 1941 ruling, the voluntary basis of census stood virtually knocked out. To obviate the problem, the Central Government decided not to give publicity to the Legal Remembrancer's ruling.

The constitutional arrangement made for census under the Government of India Act, 1935 has been continued under the Constitution of Independent India. Census figures as item 69 in its Union List. In Independent India, the director of census operations functions under the direct control of the Central Government, being on deputation to it, though he is drawn from the service cadre of the state of his posting. But the enumerating personnel belong to the state government and come under its control. There are signs of their resistance and unwillingness to take up census work, which causes not a little worry to the census bureaucracy. Yet a perfectly sound solution does not yet appear to be in sight. Mention has already been made of bifurcating census into: (i) enumeration and (ii) tabulation in the interest of eliciting greater willingness among state government workers to do census duty. It also began to be felt that it was wrong to put all census expenditure on the Central Government alone. The arrangement that makes the latter pay for head counting is wrong in theory and inexpedient in practice. There must be, according to this view, cost-sharing between the Centre and the constituent units. The latter under the Constitution spend funds on education, public health and other developmental activities. Naturally, it is of the utmost importance to them to know objectively and incisively to what purposes such funds are spent. The demand for sharing census expenditure between the Centre and the provinces began to be particularly made after the enactment of the Government of India Act, 1935. The municipal and local self-government laws already in force contain provisions empowering the local authority to spend money out of the local fund for the purpose of census.

REFERENCES

1. *Home-Public*, F.45/12/38-*Public*.
2. *Home-Public A*, 28 November 1864, Nos. 53-54.
3. Yeatts' note dated 27 January 1940. *Home-Public*, F.45/17/31-*Public*, Part II, p. 158.
4. *Census of India 1941, Part II—Administration Report*, 1942, p. 1.
5. *Ibid*., p. 3.
6. *Home-Public*, 45/2/40-*Public*, 1940.
7. *Ibid*.
8. *Home-Public*, Letter No. ASU PT-33 dated 14 December 1940 from the Superintendent of Census Operation, Bombay Province.
9. *Home-Public*, 45/40/39-*Public*.
10. *Census of India 1941, Part II—Administration Report*, 1942, p. 3.
11. *Ibid*., p. 7.
12. *Ibid*.
13. *Ibid*.
14. *Ibid*.
15. *Ibid*.

14

RECAPITULATING AND BEYOND

Census is one of the oldest activities of the Government of India, having begun in a regular way in 1881, if not earlier. Also, it is India's single largest exercise though it is undertaken decennially. From the outset, the census operation followed a broad plan. There was first a preliminary enumeration of the population made carefully and at leisure, some time before the actual date of the census. Secondly, there was on one night—the same for the entire country—the final correction of the entries. On this night each enumerator visited every house in his (census) block, taking with him the book of schedules prepared during the preliminary enumeration and on the spot corrected and completed it, striking out the entries for those persons who had left the house, and entering the particulars of those persons who had come to the house since the preliminary counting.

While uniformity of census arrangements was a general policy, a measure of flexibility was also permitted to respond to local variations. This was done for certain difficult tracts in the country. Mention may here be made of Baluchistan. The circumstances and the organisation of the census in this province were peculiar. In Baluchistan, census was organised independently of the district and political officers so that they remained free of all responsibility for the inspection and superintendence of local work, which was done by the superintendent and the assistant superintendent of census operations. One of whom worked in the tribal and one in the administered area. The population in Baluchistan was highly scattered and enumerating one household could take even as much as half a day.

Though India was a colony under the Raj, its census had aroused international interest, even admiration. The country won the appreciation, particularly, of the United States of America for two of its administrative achievements. One was the census and the other was the Survey of India. That country consistently showed interest in India's census reports.[1] Other countries were China, the Philippines, South Africa, Ceylon (now Sri Lanka), Burma (now Mayanmar), Malaya etc. Talking about the census, M.W.M. Yeatts observed in 1941:

> There is here a population of 390 millions—a fifth of the world. Your census from A to Z costs you under Rs. 50 lakhs. This is only made possible by the people of the country coming forward and taking their unpaid share. In America they pay their men four cents a head. The American census for a third of our population costs Rs. 12 crores, that is 24 times the cost of the Indian census. The English cost of census is Rs. 150 per thousand. The Indian figure comes to under Rs. 15. If you paid your enumerator one anna per head you would add Rs. 2.5 crores to the cost of the census. If you paid them one pie per head you would add Rs. 62.50 lakhs to the whole cost. You had nearly 3 million enumerators in 1931. In 1941 you have a million and a half at least. You are able to conduct this so cheaply because the people of this country take this enquiry on their shoulders. That is an enormously creditable thing and one that our people should realise. It is a very advanced position for this great country—that this big social enquiry should be carried on by the people and within their financial resources. It is a much more advanced position than is the case in some countries that are considered to be ahead of us . . . Strictly speaking . . . the census is the most truly all-India effort . . . Take the ordinary basis of enumeration in a village. Really half the village may take part because things like determining age will often be settled after consultation with the older grown-up people, the stand-by in the village who remember what happened fifty years ago.[2]

In censusing, the year 1941 is another landmark, the first being the year 1881. Yeatts broke new ground in many directions and as a result, the census of 1941, the last under the Raj, was very different from that of previous decades. The one-night theory was abandoned in favour of a 'spread-over' or 'period system' to give full scope for the economical and efficient use of the widely differing provincial systems. One must remember that India's census is unpaid. The number of enumerators, as a consequence of the change, was in 1941 more than halved in British India and was approximately half for the whole country. The schedule of former days was abandoned and the enumeration carried out directly on to the slips which were later sorted to produce the tables.

These slips themselves represented another radical departure since they carried no words in any language and could, therefore, be run off by the hundred millions at a single printing press. A location code was devised which enabled district and other identifying detail to be printed on the slip in the course of its preparation.

For the first time in the history of head-counting in India, direct enumeration was undertaken beyond the north-west frontier—in Dir, Chitral, Swat and Kurram by applying to these areas the full conventional census system. Separate scrutiny was conducted of certain sections of population in the north-west. But the most interesting innovation was the taking of 1/50 random samples of the entire population of the country. These samples were kept at the headquarters of each province, or census unit, and could be used for ascertaining, for instance, as to what proportion of the population was supported by agriculture and make other deductions.

For reasons of economy, the Government of India did not sanction the full grant of expenses, with the result that although the census of 1941 had been carried out on an elaborate scale the results were not tabulated except for variation of population. Tables giving such important information as age, or means of livelihood, or literacy by age were not prepared. Thus insurance companies and local bodies interested in social services were, consequently, not able to get the help they used to receive from the census report.

Census and the Princely States

Great Britain directly ruled over a major part of India, which was called British India. But the concept of India is much larger: it included the princely states which, nonetheless, were under the remote control of the British. Besides, there were the French and Portuguese settlements in India. One has also to keep in mind Nepal and Bhutan which came within the sphere of the imperial influence.

India, thus, evoked three levels of interest of the British Government as regards census. Organisationally, this concern was shared between the three departments of the Government of India. The Home Department administered the census so far as British India was concerned. The Political Department dealt with census in the case of the Indian states while the External Affairs Department was concerned with Sikkim, Nepal, Bhutan, French and Portuguese settlements.

Broadly speaking, the bigger princely states carried out their census separately but all the same closely adopted British India's rules, practices and arrangements. In other words, they administered head-counting by their own personnel but observed all the British rules and instructions. Such states were Hyderabad, Mysore, Travancore, Cochin, Baroda, Kashmir and Gwalior. The Home Department of the Government of India made arrangements for Rajputana, Central India, Western India, Punjab, Gujarat States, Kolhapur, Madras, Eastern States, Rampur, Benares, Manipur, Khasi States and the Frontier States. The census figures for these territories were included in the provincial reports. The smaller states were linked to the neighbouring province for this purpose and the provincial census chief was responsible for census in them also. Assam, for instance, was responsible for Manipur and the North-Western Frontier Province (NWFP) for Chitral, Dir, Swat and trans-Indus Amb. The Indian census did not cover Nepal and Bhutan. The French and Portuguese settlements fell in line with India in this respect—as also in some others.

The Government of India Act, 1935 was a constitutional landmark in the country, articulating far-reaching changes in the arrangements of governance; but mention here needs be made only of the change visualised in the relationship between the Government of India and princely states. Under it, India was to be a federation comprising the princely states and the British Indian provinces but the latter two being on different levels of relationship with the centre. Census—entry 16 in List I of the Seventh Schedule—was directly affected as the precise pattern of relationship rested on the specific terms on which the Indian states were to federate.

The Act of 1935 could not become fully operative, and the princely states remained on the old track. After some initial debate, even hesitation, the view which ultimately prevailed was that

> Neither the enactment of the Government of India Act 1935, nor the possible advent of Federation will materially affect the census arrangements in 1941. It was further clarified that the census was to be conducted under a Census Commissioner and a group of census superintendents appointed and paid by the central government. The superintendents were to collate the figures and prepare the reports for the provincial areas for which they were to be appointed while the Census Commissioner was to publish the combined report on the whole of India including the Indian states, Frontier states and foreign possessions in India.[3]

In furtherance of the above policy, two practices were reaffirmed for the 1941 census also even though only the provincial part of the Government of India Act, 1935 came into force. The first was the linking of states which did not carry out their own census operations as closely as possible with the adjoining province most similar to them in natural conditions. The second was conferring complete freedom on the census superintendent of the province in visiting and directing the census within the princely states.

For census purpose of 1941, the princely states were put into the following clusters:

1. Hyderabad
2. Mysore
3. Central India
4. Rajputana
5. Western India States
6. Punjab States (including the Simla Hill States and the Tehri-Garhwal)
7. Baroda and the Gujarat States
8. Madras States
9. Kolhapur and the Deccan States
10. Eastern Estates
11. Kashmir
12. Gwalior, Rampur and Benares

Up to the census of 1931, arrangements for princely states—which in 1941 were included in the Gujarat and Kolhapur Agencies, Simla Hill States Tehri-Garhwal, Rampur and Benares States—were entrusted to the adjoining provinces, namely Bombay, the Punjab and U.P. Similarly, Bengal looked after Cooch Behar and Tripura.

ICS Probationers' Training

Census has always been an important activity of the Government even though it activates itself after every ten years. (Preparations for the census began two-to-three years before and continue for two-to-three years after enumeration.) In view of the importance of the census, J.H. Hutton, the Census Commissioner for 1931, suggested that the Indian Civil Service probationers should be required to study the Indian census in their initial training.

The suggestion was examined by the Government in 1934. The latter sought the advice of the Public Service Commission, which in turn did not find the proposal acceptable. The reasons adduced were mainly three. The probationers had just emerged from a gruelling ordeal of several years' intensive study, culminating in a long and searching examination. Equally weighty, the probationers' syllabus was already fully crowded and included heavy and important subjects 'which, if done justice to, will keep them fully occupied'. Even if this was not fully true, there was no harm if the probationers were allowed to get their breath back during their probationary period. The view taken was that the census was no doubt one of the many things which might be studied with advantage by the probationers. The same was true of many other activities. The probationers could not, for obvious reasons, study everything. In the words of the Public Service Commission,

> it is entirely wrong to expect that a young man can ever come out to India having studied all that he should study about the country and the people. On the contrary. . . a probationer's education in these matters is really only beginning after he has arrived in the country. There are obviously many things that he will assimilate with far greater ease by virtue of the most favourable environment in which he finds himself in India, and one of these is the Census Report.[4]

The Government went along with the view of the Public Service Commission and rejected Hutton's proposal. Nevertheless, 'census' was included in the departmental examination not only for the Indian Civil Service probationers but also for the Indian Police Service.

The validity of the suggestion to prescribe the study of 'census' in the probationary training of the successor service, Indian Administrative Service (IAS), and the Indian Police Service has not diminished, at least for the former service. Training to the newly recruited members of the IAS is imparted in India after independence. If it is true that the career of an IAS officer is barren if he has not done collectoring, it is equally true that 'collectoring' is agonisingly incomplete without censusing. The latter provides to a district officer a rare administrative experience of head counting and a total view of the entire population within his district. Equally necessary is this study for the members of the provincial civil service. 'Census', in other words, deserves to be included in the syllabus of institutional training of the IAS and the IPS after their recruitment by the Union Public Service Commission. 'Census' should be included in the training of the newly recruited PCS officers also.

The post-1947 census scenario marks four important developments in India. First, the temporary legislation on which the census rested has now been replaced by a permanent Act. Secondly, the phoenix nature of the census organisation, created verily out of nothing every ten years, was put an end to; and a permanent organisation for census has been created. Thirdly, information on caste, which used to be collected in the past, was discontinued, and the caste item was altogether deleted from the census schedule. But information on scheduled castes and scheduled tribes is collected in Independent India. Finally, the census chief executive was given the *ex-officio* rank of Joint Secretary to the Government of India.

On all these four matters, wheels were set moving in the 1930s and 1940s. What is more, relevant decisions had virtually been taken by the colonial rulers. Before the time for action came, India attained independence. In a real sense, Hutton and Yeatts pre-empted the future.

Along with the permanence of the census organisation began another administrative practice which must be taken note of. The office of the Census Commissioner was combined with that of the newly appointed Registrar-General and the new functionary bore the designation of Registrar-General-cum-Census Commissioner. With this began the practice of the appointment of what is colloquially called 'In-between Census Commissioner', that is, a Census Commissioner who is appointed to fill the gap between the two censuses. Census is taken decennially but the Census Commissioner is as a rule appointed for a term of five years. As the person is appointed two-to-three years before the head-counting he continues for two-to-three years after the event. Inevitably, another person is appointed to the post but he does not stay long enough to see through the next census. Also, census reports generally continue to flow but—this may be noted—under the name of the previous Census Commissioner who had conducted the census. But there are instances of reports appearing under the name of the in-between incumbent.

The grass-roots enumeration agency claimed close and detailed attention of the rulers in the past. What was known from the beginning was that for a vast country possessing topographic variations inhabited by a large population with cultural and social diversity a large army of enumerators was necessary. Locating such large number was all the more difficult as the rate of literacy was very low—the enumerators must at least know the three Rs. They had to visit every household; necessarily they had to be inducted from the vicinity. An important question was whether the enumeration agency should be paid or unpaid. The unpaid agency could be zamindars, village headmen, the regular police and the chowkidars. All these agencies were tried in one or other of the districts but the result was not very satisfactory. This led some to think in favour of a special and paid agency. But the cost estimated was very considerable and the proposal was dropped. Ultimately, the choice fell on the patwari. The enumeration agency has undergone change since independence. The ubiquitous patwari has been replaced by the school master. During the colonial rule the patwari held his office through the hereditary process, which gave the functionary a rare social position and status in his locality. Usually, his was the richest family in the village. The *patwari*, in independent India, is, on the other hand, a low level (though powerful) functionary appointed by the state government and subject to normal terms and conditions of service including transfers. The house-list continues to be prepared by the patwari but the counting is made the responsibility of the school masters.

Census could lend itself to other uses also. In 1941, when India was in the midst of the Second World War and was passing through scarcities, the Government of Bombay sought the permission of the Government of India to use the census record for the purpose of issuing ration cards in Bombay City.[5] Nearer our own times, census is also used for policy-making on many matters. Since the advent of the Janata Government of V.P. Singh in 1989, politics of numbers abruptly swung into prominence in the policy-making processes of public administration. The Second Backward Class Commission under the chairmanship of B.P. Mandal (1978-80) had made the castes listed in the Census Report of 1931 as its base for purposes of recommendation of reservation in the civil service, thereby lending political meaning to the decennial exercise. But it was the V.P. Singh Janata Government which in a determined bid to create vote banks in the country stirred up social mobilisation on the basis of caste and even religion and announced reservation for other backward castes. In the not too distant past, India, one must note, was practising separate electorate—only to reap the bitter harvest in the form of a separatist demand ultimately culminating in the creation of Pakistan. *De facto* separate 'electorate' is already in practice in India for some time and even a stray demand is sometimes heard of institutionalising the separateness. In that kind of situation, the meaning of numbers gets enormously enhanced, for every caste and religion cluster strives to expand its numerical base.

Major Features of the Census Administration Since 1947

In what follows an attempt is made to recapitulate what has already been discussed, and to discuss some additional aspects.

The census in independent India is consciously addressed to realise the objectives of the Constitution of 1950. The opening paragraph of the Census Report of 1951 emphatically points out that the census from now on is 'to achieve the high purposes enshrined in our Constitution.'[6] It is thus to the philosophy of the Constitution that the census in independent India has got committed. This implied, among other things, wider and deeper social and economic prongs on the part of the census. This point would be taken up in some detail later.

Census organisation, perhaps everywhere, is conservative by nature. As comparison with earlier census data is a necessary part of censusing, not many changes in the schedule are either mooted or accepted. The emphasis is on continuity. Census, moreover, is a non-Plan item, which too inhibits large-scale changes. As a result, the census organisation bears strong resemblance to the past.

Putting an end to the system of phoenix organisation by according permanence to the office of the Census Commissioner has been the single most significant change since Independence. The new functionary, let this be repeated, combined in himself the functions of the Census Commissioner and the Registrar-General of Births and Deaths. The permanent organisation has brought all the advantages and no drawbacks. The earlier problems involved in creating an organisation virtually out of the ashes of its predecessor are no longer there. One should also remember that the idle period between the two censuses is now becoming ever shorter and shorter. Thus, the work relating to the 1991 census is likely to take more than six years and thus would easily spill over to 1997. As is known, the ball for the next 2001 census is set rolling three years earlier. There is, thus, hardly one year's idle time. A permanent organisation became unavoidable in view of the increasing workload generated by the census. One, of course, sometimes comes across a criticism that the census chief executive, coming as he does with previous census experience, tends to equate his new job only with censusing, and in the process, registration work gets neglected to some extent.

The focus of information gathering in the census underwent considerable change and enlargement after independence. The imperial interests were necessarily limited and were, as a rule, restricted to items like caste, religion and tribes. Independent India's concerns are different; they have become more socio-economic. Independent India is primarily concerned with the social and economic development of the country, which require, among other things, collection of data of socio-economic nature. There is, thus, a major shift of emphasis in information gathering. The column on 'caste' was deleted from the census schedule from 1951 onwards. The 'religion' column is retained but is of routine interest. Not only are data of socio-economic nature collected but these are subjected to multiple treatment. The number of tables have increased enormously. Equally, the census organisation brings out a much larger number of reports covering a large variety of subjects. One must note that data collection is much larger than reflected in the census reports. Data on quite a few items, one may note, never ultimately finds its way in published reports; some at least of it remains stored in the census organisation, and may be supplied to the Government on request. The First Backward Classes Commission (1953) under Kaka Kalelkar used the data on castes compiled by the census though the latter did not publish a separate report on caste.

The demand for increased information gathering has been facilitated by the induction of computers in census work. Computerisation of data abstraction is another striking feature of the census since Independence. In India, as in many other countries, the census data was earlier handled manually. Mechanical devices in sorting census data began to be used in a limited way from 1931 onwards. Mention may here be made of the Hollerith machines first procured in 1941 for data sorting. In independent India, computers made their visible entry in 1971. Data abstraction has been computerised in a big way since 1981. Yet it needs to be said that parts of the census are still manually handled. As a result of computerisation, the number of tables prepared in 1981 and 1991 were many more than those of earlier censuses. The following table shows the number of tables in different censuses.

Number of Tables in Different Censuses

Level	Census			
	1961	1971	1981	1991
State Level	53	73	137	142
District Level	53	40	40	93
Tehsil Level	9	4	27	10
Town Level	8	10	24	12

The census, today, collects a massive amount of statistical information relating to demographic and socio-economic conditions of the people of the country. Some of the information published relates to the country as a whole and is known as the All-India Census Report. In 1951, the All-India Census Report was divided into the following five parts: Part I-A, Report, Part I-B, Appendices to the Report, Part II-A, Demographic Tables Part II-B (General Population), and Part II-C (Rural and Urban Population). Other types of data were published separately in a series of brochures. They were self-contained papers which presented the relevant statistics with brief introductory information necessary for their proper understanding. In addition, 'State Census Reports' (compiled by state-level Directors of Census Operations) were also published in different states. Besides, there were District Census Handbooks for each district. In the 1961 census the publication scheme underwent a change. The new classification, which has been observed by all subsequent censuses, categorised census publications under as many as ten heads, each called 'series'. Series A dealt with all-India population data while economic activities of the population were clustered under Series B. Reports relating to social and cultural matters were put in Series C and migration data under Series D. Series E, which dealt with establishments, was later transferred to another organisation, namely, the Central Statistical Organisation and thus remains in disuse. Series F and H covered fertility and housing, respectively. In addition, there were the Scheduled Castes Series, the Scheduled Tribes Series and the Village and Town Directories. This classification, adopted in 1961, has not been changed and has become a stable classificatory arrangement though the number of tables under each series may be changing. Tables under the economic activities of the population were 22 in 1981 but rose to 24 in 1991. 'Migration' Series has become suddenly important, occupying as many as 17 tables at present. Series F, focussing on fertility, covers 18 tables. It needs to be mentioned that some series are published by the states but data for all are centrally collected and compiled. In other words, the census organisation, central and state, churns out a large number of reports relating to the population. But whether the public organisations fully use this statistical information is doubtful, to put it mildly.

Mention also needs to be made of the freedom which the provinces always enjoyed in respect of collecting information of their choice as part of the regular census. This is remarkable, for the country was under a unitary constitution, entailing complete control over the lower level governments. The Constitution of 1950 has enacted a federal system in the country, thereby making the provinces autonomous. The Central Government does not, however, confer the right of choice of questions on the lower level governments, though requests to this effect are continually made by the latter. No state, in other words, can insert a question of its choice in the census schedule without the Centre's prior approval and consent.

The Census Commissioner currently enjoys the *ex-officio* status of a joint secretary. Demand for an *ex-officio* secretariat status was originally made to make the functionary effective, particularly when he was to function within a tight time-frame. The joint secretary's status was conferred on him in the earlier years of the Republic when the secretariat was small in size and the post of joint secretary carried sufficient weight and status. Moreover, at that time, the chief secretaries in the states were themselves of the rank of the Centre's joint secretary. The Census Commissioner, as we know, carries onerous responsibilities, which make it necessary for him to directly deal with the chief secretaries in the states and other high level functionaries. Chief secretaries, today, are ranked much higher and are equivalent to the secretaries to the Government at the Centre. The present *ex-officio* secretariat status is low and needs to be suitably upgraded in order to make the Census Commissioner effective.

Equally deserving of examination is the fixed tenure stipulation of this functionary. At present, the Census Commissioner has a term of five years, on the completion of which he is routinely reverted to his cadre state. As has been made clear, the census operations exceed the five-year span and extend up to eight or even nine years. But the functionary leaves in the middle and thus his successor has to complete the unfinished part of the work. His term thus needs to be suitably extended. Also, it should be considered whether this post really needs to be kept strictly under the tenure system of staffing. Census Commissioner is a functionary whose work content is of common interest and concern to both the levels of government, central and state. This post imparts to its functionary very valuable first hand experience of national range, which is directly and immediately relevant for central-level planning and policy-making. What is argued is that the theatre of next posting of the Census Commissioner should be the centre, preferably the Home Ministry or the Planning Commission, where the experience gathered by him would be in urgent and direct demand.

Caste, one may note, was denounced by the nationalist leadership during the colonial period, the demand being to have the item on it deleted from the census schedule. The first census of independent India, held in 1951, did not have this item. This has been the case until now though the census does collect data on scheduled castes and scheduled tribes. Since the 1980s Indian politics has witnessed a revival and rejuvenation of caste lobbies. Reservation in public service has already been made for 'other backward castes'. Panchayati Raj legislation provides for caste-based reservation of seats in the local bodies. The reservation policy calls for collection of data about the 'other backward castes'. People would try to be included in the category of backward castes, and to this extent pressure on the enumerating personnel would intensify. Castes having become the base of policy-making, information on them has got to be collected. What is conveyed here is that caste, deleted since 1951, is coming back into the census and with full vengeance and the census of 2001 is most likely to contain an item on caste, entailing also the likelihood of caste lobbies becoming vocal.

The census is the Central Government's direct responsibility though enumeration is undertaken by the state level functionaries. This has been the arrangement since the earliest days, but at that time this did not pose any serious problem. When, however, the provinces acquired an autonomous status under the Government of India Act, 1935 problems of centre-state relations in the field of census began to be felt. In 1941 Yeatts even suggested a constitutional bifurcation of census responsibilities, enumeration being made the responsibility of the lower level government while planning and tabulation to remain with the Centre. In independent India, census does not have a smooth run as it has been experiencing reluctant cooperation from the state governments. A long-range solution may seem to lie in a constitutional amendment more or less along Yeatts' line. But in such a case, New Delhi will be left with no control over enumeration, with all the danger that it implies. Caste lobbies, already aggressive in some states and having their sympathisers in the local administrative hierarchies, may get further energised, threatening to vitiate the enumeration process, which is a critical input in the census. It may be prudent to continue the present practice to steer clear of such dangers.

REFERENCES

1. *Home*-F 45/32/38-*Public*.
2. Quoted in *The Indian Year Book and Who's Who*, 1947, Bombay, *The Times of India*, p. 32.
3. Notes on Political Department File No. 69-1, A/37. See *Home* F45/21/37.
4. Public Service Commission's letter addressed to M.G. Hallett, Secretary to the Government of India, Home Department dated 2 April 1934. See *Home* F.116/34-Ests.
5. *Home* 45/13/42-*Public*.
6. *Census of India, Vol. 1-A Report*, New Delhi; Manager of Publications, 1953, p. 1.

APPENDIX I

REPORT BY THE OFFICERS APPOINTED TO CONSIDER THE SUGGESTIONS FOR A GENERAL CENSUS IN INDIA IN 1881

To

The Secretary to the Govt. of India,

Department of Revenue, Agriculture and Commerce.

Sir,

In accordance with Resolution No. 289, dated 6th July 1877, we have considered the various points dealt with in the papers there referred to, and we now have the honour to report, for the information of His Excellency in Council, the result of our deliberations.

2. The papers to which our attention has been directed are a note by Mr. Henry Waterfield, of the India Office, dated the 26th January 1876; observations on the same by the Registrar-General of England; and a brief memorandum from the Secretary of the Statistical Society of England; the two letters dated severally the 10th January 1877 and the 28th February 1877.

3. Mr. Waterfield has summarised the result of his observations as follows:

'A census should be taken in 1881, throughout India, as nearly as possible on the same day.

'A preliminary census should be taken shortly before the final one. The agency employed should be voluntary as far as possible, payment being only made, as a rule, for extra work or very good service. Special legislation should be resorted to where the want of it is likely to be felt.

'The area and boundaries of the census divisions should be distinctly marked.

'The enumeration should be by houses, with permission to reckon enclosures also, if desired. The distinction between superior and inferior houses need not be maintained, but houses uninhabited at night should be so recorded.

'The names of all males should be inserted, females being recorded by a number, if the head of the house objects to give the name. Particulars about relationship may be asked if the Local Government wish it.

'The exact age stated should be recorded, the compilation being effected according to fixed periods. The column of religion should be filled up, as Hindu, Mahomedan, Christian, Buddhist, or other, and be supplemented by a column of sect.

'Caste and nationality should be thrown into one column, the former applying to the four main divisions of Hindus, and the latter to persons of other religions. Specified castes, to be inserted, where needed for inquiries respecting infanticide or any similar custom.

'The occupation should be required in detail, as far as possible, for men, but not for women and children, unless they add to the income of the household. A carefully-classified list of occupations should be adopted in the compilation in all provinces. The education column should be filled up as educated, under instruction, or uneducated.

'Infirmities should be entered as blind, deaf, mutes, cripples, unsound mind, or lepers.

'No inquiries should be made for the census respecting the civil condition of the people, the amount of land revenue, or the number of cattle.

'The forms should be translated, printed and distributed in ample time.

The compilation should be undertaken by the district officers or the central office, as may seem best, in each province, but should, in all cases, be under the supervision of a controlling officer; and each provincial report should, before final publication, be submitted for the general approval of an officer appointed by the Government of India to supervise the whole work. Care should be taken to make all statements in any province work up to the same total number of inhabitants'.

Major Graham's suggestions are given below:

'1. I have always maintained that the census of England, the Colonies and the Indian Empire should be taken in the same year in the present instance in 1881; if the census could be taken on the same day, that would no doubt be in many respects an advantage, and should be aimed at; but looking at the great difference of climate, and the varying habits of migration that prevail, some latitude must be allowed.

2. The preliminary census may be left open; it will no doubt prepare the unaccustomed enumerators for their novel duties. In principle, I think it better to pay the agents moderate sums for their work, as is done in England, as it gives you in general more control over them, and may be so arranged as to secure greater accuracy.

The necessary legislation is indispensable; I may add that in England accurate returns were enforced in the Census Act by fines. This strengthened my hands, but the fines had not to be inflicted in a single instance.

5. It is necessary to lay down the boundaries of the census divisions on maps, to be within the reach, at least, of the superintending census officers. The boundaries and the places should be fully described on each enumerator's book.

6. Houses should be enumerated, and the houses uninhabited distinguished. For the definition of house in the English census I refer to the report.

The enumeration by name of each person has been insisted on at all the Statistical Congresses by the official statists, of Europe, and it is probable that if this were extended in India to females, the return of their numbers would be less imperfect than it now unquestionably is. Some prejudices look more formidable than they really are, as has been found to be the case in respect to suttee.

The relation of the inmates of the house to the head of the family is of importance, distinguishing them as wife, son, daughter, visitor, servant, etc.

7. The question of population in connection with the land is now of vital importance in India, and the recurrent families alone have awakened the attention of this country to it. The population, it has been shown in England, is regulated by the marriage, the conjugal condition of the people, and I know of no information more important than that given in the column headed Conjugal Condition in the English schedule. Such a column in the Indian census schedule would furnish invaluable information. The record of such facts could do no one any real injury, and the objection to it would probably prove to be as futile in India as in the other States of the world.

8. I am quite of accord with the proposal that the exact age or the nearest age known should be recorded; in the transcripts it will be desirable to give the number of children living at each year of age under five, then in quinquennial periods to the end of life.

9 and 10. On the question of religion and caste, I will not pretend to give an opinion, but the suggestions on these heads appear to be

judicious. The census need not recognise all the distinctions of caste which are of no statistical importance.

11. Occupation is of the greatest social importance, and I was pleased to see that so much useful and curious information was collected under this head at the last census. Instructions should be carefully issued under this head for the enumerators suitable to each province, but on the same plan as those issued in England.

I append (1) and English schedule, and (2) a book which was used at the Central office in England, and I would recommend that a suitable book, extended so as to give the synonyms in the principal languages of India, should be prepared for the use of the Central Commissions.

There is a classification which, however, open to criticism it may be in some places, is found to work well, and if altered essentially would destroy the means of comparison which uniformity all over the Empire secures. The alphabetical list affords the abstractors ready means of reference.

In regard to occupation, I think it preferable to return, in the case of both males and females, their actual occupations, and not the occupations of the parents or others on whom they depend. The ages of the persons of various occupations were abstracted in England.

12. Education — This head is not dealt with in England, but the number of children receiving instruction at home or in school was indicated by the work scholar. In the case of adults 'able to read and write' and 'not able to read and write' would probably be as much as could be asked.

13. The deaf and dumb, blind, imbeciles or idiots, and lunatics, were distinguished in England, and 'from birth' was added in the congenital cases. 'Lepers' might be added for India. Indeed, statists who have studied the subjects in connection with public health and productive industry, hold that each particular disease and infirmity that disables men from work should be recorded in the same column of the census schedule. That was done in Ireland, and was found very interesting.

14. It is very undesirable to mix up any inquiry into the land revenue with the census enumeration. The agriculture and the industry of the country should form a separate inquiry; it would embarrass the enumeration of the people in one day.

15. That the forms should be translated, printed and distributed in ample time, is certainly of great importance.

16. The abstracts of the facts should probably be made at the head office of each province; but after conference with the provincial officers measures should be adopted, under the immediate sanction of the

Governor-General and of the Secretary of State for India, to secure uniformity in all the fundamental tables. In one grand set of tables the whole of the subjects of Her Majesty's Indian Empire may be classified. And this set of tables should admit, being on the same general plan, of ready comparison with those of the United Kingdom?

4. In the case of India it is necessary to make all the arrangements in time, and to so contrive that, in the event of any officers failing on the census day, other officers may be ready to step into their places, and to discharge their duties.'

5. It will be seen that the Registrar-General is at one with Mr. Waterfield in his suggestion that the next Indian census shall be taken on one fixed day, if possible, throughout India. He would also have that day the same both for India and England if that can be done. He leaves open the question of there being any preliminary census, but is not averse to it.

He is in favour of paying the enumerators moderate sums for their work as is done in England, as in general more control is thus obtained over them, and greater accuracy can be secured.

Where legislation is necessary he would have it, and he is so far in accord with Mr. Waterfield, who proposes special legislation where the want of it is likely to be felt. He agrees with Mr. Waterfield in regard to all the remaining suggestions made by that gentleman with the following exceptions.

He is of opinion that the names of the females may probably be got. He considers the information contained in the column conjugal condition of the English census most important, and adds that such a column in the Indian census schedule would furnish statesmen, political students and the educated people of India themselves with invaluable information. The record of such facts could do no one any injury, and the objection to it would probably prove as futile in India as in other States of the world. Thus he is entirely in opposition to the suggestion of Mr. Waterfield that no enquiries should be made for the census regarding the civil condition of the people.

He further states the census need not recognise all the distinctions of caste which are of no statistical importance.

6. The Statistical Society, through its Council, recommend that the enumeration of the people of India should be based, as nearly as local circumstances will permit, on the plan adopted in Great Britain, and contain the same or similar information, in as much detail as may be found practicable. The returns should be as simple as possible, and require nothing which may be opposed to native feeling or prejudice. The whole

of the returns should be constituted on the basis of a careful enumeration and definition. In each locality all matters relating to caste, the conjugal relations, occupations, ages, should be dealt with by the local authorities as may be found most expedient and practical, certain leading facts being carefully noted, such as the two great sects of Mussulmans, the great leading castes of Hindus, the chief occupations of the urban and rural populations, etc. Outside this as much may be collected in each district (province?) as the local officers may be able to details and sub-divisions, which cannot be relied on, and which would increase the difficulty without adding to the efficiency of the census operations.

7. We have taken up these suggestions in the following order:

(i) The propriety of taking the census on one and the same day, and at the same time as in England.

(ii) The necessity for a preliminary census, by which is meant the recording of the numbers in the census schedules on a day or days previous to that fixed for the actual enumeration. On the latter date the schedules would be merely checked and corrected to bring them into agreement with the actual facts existing on that day.

(iii) The form of the schedule to be used.

(iv) The agency to be employed in the enumeration and in the compilation of the returns.

(v) The mode of tabulating the returns so as to bring out most satisfactorily the facts recorded.

(vi) The printing and preparation of the forms for enumeration and for compiling the results, together with the preliminary instructions to be issued.

(vii) The necessity for legislation.

8. These we now proceed to deal with seriatim.

I. The Time when the Census should be Taken

In regard to this matter the Committee are unanimous. We consider that one identical time should be fixed for the whole of British India, and on that date the census should be effected. We are of opinion also, that, as a rule, the enumeration should take place on one and the same day. It is no doubt the case that there are some parts of the several provinces where it may not be possible to enumerate the inhabitants on one fixed day, such for instance, as Chota Nagpur, Assam, the Hill Tracts of Orissa and of Chittagong in Bengal, the Hill Tracts of Ganjam and Vizagapatam in Madras, and other similarly situated localities in other provinces. But there is nothing to prevent the great mass of the population throughout Bengal, the North-Western Provinces, and Oudh, Madras, the Punjab, Bombay and the Central Provinces being enumerated on a given day, and the exceptional areas are so thinly populated that their exceptional requirements need not be considered when fixing the time for enumerating the great bulk of the population. In fact, the greater part of the population of British India has already been enumerated in one day, though not on one synchronous day; and it is obvious that where this has been done once, it can be done again, probably, too, over a much more extended area than before.

The census of the North-Western Provinces, Oudh, the Punjab, the Central Provinces, Bombay, Mysore, Coorg, and British Burma was taken on a single day. So, too, in by far the larger portion of the Madras Presidency, and so also in a very large part of Bengal.

The population thus dealt with is in round numbers (160,000,000) one hundred and sixty millions.

	Population	Date of Census	
North-Western Provinces	30,781,204	On	Jan. 18, 1872
Oudh	11,198,095	"	Feb. 1, 1861
Central Provinces	9,251,229	"	Jan. 25, 1872
British Burma	2,747,148	"	Nov. 14, 1871
Bombay	16,228,774	"	Feb. 21, 1872
Punjab	17,611,498	"	Jan. 10, 1868
Mysore	5,055,412	"	Nov. 14, 1871
Coorg	168,312	"	Nov. 14, 1871
Total	93,041,672		
Madras, exclusive of Tanjore District and the town of Palghaut	29,593,389	On	Nov. 15, 1871
Four Divisions of Bengal	36,577,519	"	Jan. 1872
Grand Total	159,212,580		

There does not appear to be any difficulty, therefore, in enumerating the great majority of the people in the British India provinces on one and the same day. In the exceptional parts already referred to, and in any other where the Local Government may find it necessary to do so, it may be left to the Local Government to extend the time during which the enumeration is to be effected, so long as it covers the day fixed for the census in th rest of the country and does not exceed a fortnight at the very outside. But in no case should it be left to the discretion of any local authority to postpone the date of enumeration, as occurred in Tanjore, on account of any local feast or other gathering together of the people. The reason for this prohibition is obvious. If not counted everywhere on one fixed date, a portion of the population may escape enumeration.

9. The question then arises, it being admitted that the next enumeration throughout the Indian Empire should be synchronous what will be the date most convenient to fix? The Committee agree with the Registrar-General of England and Mr. Waterfield that, if it can be done, the enumeration in England and in India should be taken on the same day as well as in the same year. But after giving very careful consideration to this subject, they are notable to see their way to such an alteration in the dates hitherto prevailing as would permit of the Indian Census being taken on the 1st April 1881. The difficulties in the way of fixing so late a date are those relating to season. To secure accuracy and careful testing of the entries in the schedules, it is absolutely necessary that the supervising establishment, including the district officials, should be out and about the best part of the day immediately succeeding the enumeration, as well as the night or day of the census, to say nothing of the exposure necessitated during the time when the schedules are being filled up, which will cover nearly a month. It is only by a careful personal scrutiny of a certain number of entries in the schedules that these can be properly tested. The intense heat in the day-time so late as April would make such a scrutiny attended as it must be by rapid movement from one village to another, and probably involving a ride of 20 to 30 miles in a broiling sun, a most laborious undertaking. Putting out of sight all ideas of exposure, the mere fact that it would not be possible to get through so much work in March and April as in a cooler season of the year, particularly in the more Southerly provinces, makes it desirable to adhere to time which, in practice, throughout the country has been found best adapted for the work. This, as a rule, is the middle of the cold weather, or rather past the mid-cold weather season. Without, therefore, fixing any definite date, and having in view the advantages accruing from the use of a moonlight night for such a purpose as an enumeration, the Committee recommend the early part of February 1881, within two or three days of the full moon, as the date best suited for a synchronous census of British India.

10. We note that these difficulties anticipated in British Burma which led the Local Government to recommend a postponement of the

date for the census of that province from November 1871 to June or July 1872. It was said that the greater part of the population is away from the villages (in the month of November) trading, fishing and timber-cutting, and the country also is full of a temporary population. These difficulties may or may not be insuperable. On this point we are unable to express an opinion; but, the population in British Burma, being so small, it is of little moment if the census in that province is effected in a manner similar to the enumeration in the hill tracts and other exceptional localities. We do not recommend that, in British Burma, the enumeration of the people should be postponed in 1881 to a date later than that fixed for the rest of the Indian Empire, if for no other reason, for the very important consideration that the immigrant population, if not counted on the one day fixed for the general census, will escape enumeration altogether.

The fact noted at page 2 of the British Burma report of a yearly counting of the people being the custom there, removes any inconvenience which might otherwise arise from taking the census of 1881 at an unusual season in that province.

II. Necessity for a Preliminary Census

11. This synchronous enumeration ot the population of British India cannot, however, be effected in the manner customary in European countries. The population being in the main uneducated; and it being quite impossible to rely on the inhabitants to fill up their own returns as in England and elsewhere, it will be necessary to continue the system which has hitherto prevailed, that is to say, to fill up the schedules by other than the householders agency, and to do this prior to the census, so that on the day fixed for the enumeration, the entries recorded a few days previously may be examined and corrected so as to correspond with the facts on the day of enumeration. This, which has hitherto been termed the preliminary census, is accepted as necessary both by Mr. Waterfield and Major Graham.

It has been found in practice that complications and misunderstandings have arisen from use of the term above-mentioned. It is not likely that such misapprehensions will occur again. But, in order to avoid them, we consider it as well to abandon the use of the expression preliminary census, substituting for it preliminary record of entries in the Enumerators Schedules.

It is not possible to lay down any hard and fast line as to the term over which this preliminary record of entries should extend. But it is obvious that the shorter this term the fewer in number will be the final alterations to be made in the schedules on the day of the enumeration. It must be left to those who are acquainted with the local circumstances of the various tracts which the census will cover to determine this point: we merely throw out the suggestion that where the number of enumerators employed is at all on a level with the standard to be subsequently recommended by us, this preliminary record of entries in the schedules need not extend over a month at the outside, and the term may with advantage be curtailed.

III. Form of Schedule to be Used

12. We come now to the most essential point to be looked to in connection with the census, *viz.*, the information to be collected in the Enumerators Schedules.

On the headings of the enumerators form and the instructions upon which he acts in filling up these columns depends the entire fabric of the census.

We proceed, then, to consider what information it is desirable and practicable to collect, and what is the most convenient and simple form in which to record it at the census.

Enumerations in different provinces—in some provinces repeated at longer or shorter intervals—have thrown much light on the feelings of the people in regard to these enquiries, and illusions have been dissipated which, at earlier periods, prevented the Governmet from asking for information on particular points under the apprehension that such enquiries would irritate and offend.

At one time, for instance, it was deemed impracticable to seek for information in detail as to age. At another, any enquiry as to the civil condition of the people was deprecated. Those who took up these positions lost sight of the fact that in the very country where it seemed objectionable to ask for such information, the first questions put to a witness in the box involved one of these enquiries and sometimes both.

It is hardly necessary for us to state that we cordially agree with the Statistical Society's remark that the returns should be as simple as possible, and require nothing which may be opposed to Native feeling or prejudice. We also are of opinion that so far as local circumstances will permit, we should obtain the same information as is sought for in the English enumeration, or information of a similar nature.

In considering the form of schedule to be used by the enumerators, or by the householders who may fill up their own returns, few in number as the latter class will be, we have kept these principles before us.

13. The following, then, are the recommendations we have to make on this part of our subject.

In the first place, we would follow the English plan of showing the details of each family in a separate schedule. It may be objected that this method will involve a waste of paper and add unnecessarily to the bulkiness of the records. But we consider that the increased accuracy to be obtained by compelling the enumerator to fill up a separate form for each family is an advantage which sufficiently out-weighs these objections. We propose, moreover, to show the details regarding males and females in the same columns, having an additional column for sex as in the English schedule, and we thus hope to diminish the number of columns which appear in the standard form prescribed for the last census, and consequently also the size of the form.

The heading of the schedule should, we think, contain the following particulars:

(1) Name of the district
(2) Name of the taluq (tehsil, pergunnah, thannah, or whatever territorial sub-division may be adopted)
(3) Name of the village and its number in the district list
(4) Number of the enclosure
(5) Number of the house
(6) Name of the head of the house or family.

A mojority of the Committee are in favour of exhibiting the number of enclosure as well as of the house, as in the last census. Mr. Beverley, on the other hand, would do away with the term enclosure altogether. He contends that in itself it is not a term which conveys any very accurate impression to English minds; and that on the last occasion in some provinces (*e.g.*, Madras and Bengal) its use was not found practicable, while in others (*e.g.* Bombay) its use is said to have only resulted in confusion.

The Committee believe that the difficulties referred to arise from the want of a sufficiently complete definition of the term; but although they have carefully compared the definitions used in different provinces, they must confess themselves unable to suggest any to which objection in some form or other may not be taken. While dispensing altogether with the term enclosure, Mr. Beverley would adopt the commonly received idea of an enclosure as comprise the several dwelling-rooms which go to make up the home-stead, whether such rooms are occupied by one or more families. This was practically the definition of a house in Bengal and Madras at the last census; and as it is proposed on the next occasion to take the census by families, Mr. Beverley thinks that there is nothing to be gained by taking a separate account of the separate dwellings (whether the whole or part of the homestead) occupied by them. The definition of a house in the North-Western Provinces was essentially that of a family, and the number of families will, therefore, be the number of houses, under that definition.

We are not in favour of attempting any distinction between houses of superior and of an inferior class. The Government orders on which this distinction was based at the last census, arose out of a proposal of the Statistical Committee in 1869 to distinguish houses that were constructed of masonry. A Sub-Committee, consisting of Messrs. H. Bell and Gay, at that time remarked that:

> In Bengal, and we imagine in other parts of India, there is no surer test by which to measure the prosperity of the people than the number of pucka houses that are being built, and we consider it of the first importance that this information should be given at the forthcoming census. The increase in the number of pucka houses is the surest sign of the growing wealth of the people, and our successors who take the census in 1881 will have very just grounds of complaint if we now fail to give this information, and so deprive them of one of the surest means of estimating the increase or decrease of the national wealth during the intervening decade.

The Statistical Committee adopted this view, and proposed to distinguish between houses built of masonry and others. The Committee said:

> It is thought that in this country such a classification will give a most useful indication of the prosperity of the people, and hereafter allow of comparisons between the progress in wealth of different districts.

It will be seen that so far all that was proposed was to distinguish the pucka, or masonry, house in each province; but, after consulting Local Governments and Administrations, the following instructions were laid down by the Government of India (Resolution No. 4800, dated 20th October 1896).

It seems desirable to ascertain roughly how many houses belong to the better class. The dwelling-houses in each enclosure should, therefore, be entered under the headings of the better sort, of inferior sort, the Local Government in each province determining for the guidance of the enumerators what description of house should come under either class. The definitions of pucka and kutcha vary so much in different parts of India, that the adoption of these terms would not yield uniform results. It will be understood that the object is to distinguish substantial houses, whatever the material, from huts, hovels and houses of unsubstantial construction.

We agree with Mr. Waterfield that the results of these enquiries are not always satisfactory. But we are inclined to go further and to question the trustworthiness of these results as a means of gauging the prosperity of the country. As regards pucka house, *i.e.*, houses built of masonry, our experience would certainly lead us to doubt the truth of the proposition laid down by the Statistical Committee of 1869. Not only are there whole provinces, like Burma, where pucka houses are almost unknown, but even in Bengal and the North-Western Provinces such pucka houses as are to be found outside the few large towns and cities are for the most part in the hands of old families who are often anything but well-to-do in the world. The fact would seem to be that in this country where life is for the most part spent in the open air, and where the people have not yet learned to surround themselves with domestic comforts; the nature of a person's dwelling is by no means a sure index to his wealth or prosperity. The proposed test, therefore, however, applicable it may be in the colder and more civilised countries of Europe, is, in our opinion, of little or no value in India; and, considering also the difficulty pointed out by Mr. Waterfield of adhering at each successive census to the many varying definitions of houses of the better sort adopted in different parts of the country, we would recommend that no such distinction be attempted.

Very similar difficulties attend, the collection in this country of statistics as to the number of uninhabited houses. The materials of which the great majority of houses are constructed in some parts of this country are of so unsubstantial a character, that, unless occupied and kept in constant repair, a single rainy season will often suffice to effect their ruin. We do not propose to collect statistics of such ruined houses or deserted sites. We would merely prepare a record of all houses found in existence at the time when arrangements are being made for the census. If subsequently on the night fixed for the census any of these dwellings were found to be uninhabited, the fact would be noted in the schedule.

Shops, etc. which are occupied during the day, but not at night, would have no householders schedule provided for them at all. The details regarding such shops, as well as churches, temples, mosques, and other buildings not used for human habitation, can, we think, be sufficiently ascertained from the Lists of Buildings which we have provided for in a subsequent part of our recommendations.

14. In the Enumerators Schedules we propose that names of all male members of the family shall be given at length. As regards females, we would ask for the same information, but it should be explained that, if the head of the family objects to give the names of the female members, they may be distinguished by numbers. For this purpose we have provided a column giving a serial number for each member of the family, and also a column showing the relationship of each member to the head of the House. The information afforded by the latter column may not, perhaps, be of any great value in itself*, but we attach great importance to it as affording an additional security for testing the accuracy of the return; and from the experience gained in the North-Western Provinces and elsewhere, we anticipate no difficulty whatever in procuring this additional information.

15. The next column which we propose to insert in the Enumerators Schedule is also a new one, and is intended to show the civil or conjugal condition of each member of the family, *i.e.* whether married, unmarried or widowed. This information was on the last occasion collected in the Bombay** Presidency and elsewhere without difficulty, and we have no reason to suppose that it could not be collected for the whole of India with equal facility. In considering this subject in 1869, the Statistical Committee were of opinion that enquiry might lead to suspicion and induce the people to make false returns. But we do not find that this anticipation has been justified by the result. The collection of information on the subject is strongly advocated by the Registrar-General of England, General Strachey, and others, and has been specially insisted on in the North-Western Provinces; and there can be no doubt that it would help to illustrate many questions connected with vital and social statistics in this country on which our information is at present very imperfect. It

* *Note*: In making this statement we do not lose sight of the flood of light which such information, if carefully collated, would throw upon Native social life. The extent of polygamy, the relative ages of husband and wife, the average number of children to a family, and the strength of the Hindu family system in binding the members of the family together, are some of the points which such information would help to illustrate. But on account of the expense which it would involve, we are not prepared to recommend that such information should at present be collated.

** The results, however, do not appear to have been compiled.

should, of course, be laid down that the enumerator is simply to record the answers made to him on the subject without instituting any enquiries as to the legality of the marriage in any case. All that we can hope to ascertain is whether a person considers himself or herself to be married. It is impossible to define in any other way what shall be considered a marriage for our purpose, and any attempt at such a definition would probably only and in defeating the object in view.

16. As regards age, we are of opinion that the exact age on the last preceding birthday should, as far as possible, be given in each case. This was the conclusion arrived at by the Government on the last occasion, and we see no reason why anyother course should be adopted in 1881. It should be distinctly laid down that the age to be given is that on the last, not the next, birthday, and in the case of infants under one year, the age should be stated in months.

17. As regards religion we propose to have two columns, one showing the main religious divisions of the people and the other their caste in the case of Hindus, and the sect in the case of other religions. Any enquiry into the religious sects among Hindus we consider unnecessary and fruitless. The Hindu sects are not very sharply defined, and we imagine that most Hindus would have some difficulty in specifying the particular sect to which they belong. Even as regards the broad divisions of Saivite and Vaishnavite, there were many erroneous entries at the last census. Instead of showing the religious sects of Hindus, therefore, we propose in their case to devote this column to the record of their castes. The records of information under this head is not generally a matter of difficulty, whatever may be the obstacles to a correct and exhaustive compilation of such information when obtained; and though in some parts its collection has been less easy than would have been anticipated from experience in other provinces, we consider information in regard to caste can be obtained with facility. There are unquestionably certain ranges of enquiry where it is of interest, if not important, to secure such data. The Enumerators Schedule at the last census contained a column for caste, and we do not propose to make any material change in this matter further than that involved in showing caste under the head of religion. We have done this as we consider a mistake was made at the last census in showing the castes of Hindus in the statement of nationality, and in introducing into that statement of nationality, and in introducing into that statement the religious terms Hindu and Muhammadan, which have nothing in common with nationality.

18. The table of races and nationalities should, we think, be restricted to an exposition of the actual ethnical elements that go to make up the

population of the country. In this view we consider that the information may be of great practical value. It would not only illustrate, as in the last census, the strength of the foreign element to be found in India, but it would further throw light upon the distribution of the Natives themselves according to provincial and linguistic distinctions. In the specimen form of schedule circulated with the Resolution of 20th October 1869, the column headed Race or Nationality contains the entry Bengali, but in the statements appended to the resolution dated 30th September 1871there was no form or column in which Bengalis or other provincial nationalities could be shown. We think that a table of such nationalities would be useful. It seems important, for instance, that the Government should know the number of persons who speak each of the many languages spoken throughout India, and such a table would also throw light on the migrations of the people from one province to another, and even from one part to another of the same province. It might be desirable that the Chief Commissioner of Assam should be able to test, at each successive census, the growth of the immigrant cooly population that is attracted to the tea-producing districts of that province; and similar information as regards the immigrant population of British Burma would possibly remove the chief objection which seems to attach to the proposal to take the census of that province in the cold weather.

19. An important question, however, is the definition of the term nationality. As regards foreigners, whose nationality is for the most part sufficiently pronounced, there is no difficulty; but it is not easy in the case of the various native races which inhabit the different provinces of India.

Two tests instinctively suggest themselves, *viz.*, those of language and birth-place; but it is clear that either of them is insufficient without the other. Moreover, a column for birth-place seems desirable, in order to ascertain the particulars regarding British-born persons required for the English census without the trouble and expense of a separate census.

We propose, therefore, in the Enumerators Return to give two sub-columns under nationality, so as to show both the language of birth and the place of birth. At the same time, we do not conceal from ourselves that even this arrangement will not in all cases suffice, to convey a correct idea of a person's race or nationality. We, therefore, propose to add a note to the heading Place of Birth for the instruction of the enumerators to secure the insertion in that column of correct particulars regarding British-born subjects, foreigners, and persons of mixed parentage. In regard, however, to persons of mixed parentage, such as Eurasians, Indo-Portuguese, or whatever other term may be applied to designate them, we think there are difficulties to which it is right we should call attention. Past experience has proved, we consider beyond a doubt, that this portion of the community has not been accurately ascertained in the enumeration of the people. Nor is it likely that this defect will be remedied. It is not unnatural that a large number of persons of mixed birth should elect to return themselves under a nationality to which they trace back one of their ancestors, and instances have occurred to our knowledge of persons recorded as of Scotch, English, Spanish or other European nationality, who, from their colour, must have been indubitably persons of mixed race, and yet have returned themselves under the race of a remote ancestor whose language they with difficulty understand. According to the last enumeration the mixed races compose a very minute element of the Indian population. In Bengal, Madras, the North-Western Provinces and Bombay, including the three great centres where Eurasians are found in greatest numbers, the number of persons who have returned themselves either as Eurasian or Indo-Portuguese is 83,335 or one in every 1,700 of the people. It is, therefore, a question whether for so small a class it is worthwhile to attempt any distinction.

20. We have retained the column for occupation, for, although the information hitherto collected on this subject may not have proved of any great practical value, we are of opinion that such information tends to become more accurate and more valuable at each succeeding census. The main reason why it is not of greater value is that people will not describe their occupations with sufficient minuteness, and this is just the sort of defect which we may expect to see diminishing with every successive enumeration.

21. We see no objection to the suggestion made by Mr. Waterfield to prescribe three classes of answer to the enquiry on the subject of education, *viz.* 1. Under instruction; 2. Not under instruction, but able to read and write; and 3. Not under instruction, but unable to read and write; and we have amended the heading of the column accordingly.

22. In regard to the information to be sought on the subject of infirmities, we are of opinion that the number of the blind may usefully be ascertained. Considering, however, that persons who are said to be born blind are generally not so born, but lose their sight in early infancy, we would make no distinction between congenital and other blindness. In order to procure tolerably corrrect figures for deaf-mutes, we could exclude all but congenital cases. In the last census it is believed that many persons were returned as deaf-mutes who were deaf only from old age, and the restriction we now propose will preclude the possibility of such a mistake in future. We are not in favour of procuring information

regarding cripples, as proposed by Mr. Waterfield; we think there would be difficulty in defining the term, and we are not aware of any object for which information on this head would be useful. It is well known that many persons who are permanently lame can, nevertheless, support themselves by the labour of their hands. Nor do we think it either desirable or useful to ascertain particulars regarding eunuchs as was done at the last census in Bombay. Their number is probably very small, but, whatever it is, we could never depend upon its being returned with any accuracy. Further, in some parts of India, registers of persons of this class are kept up by the police, and in such provinces there can be no object in asking for this information; while, if wanted in other parts, the same Act by which registration of such persons is compulsory would, if applied, secure the requisite information, and we consider the fact of the law not having been extended to these provinces is an indication that there is no necessity for collecting data under this head. In ascertaining the number of persons of unsoundmind, no distinction should, in our opinion, be made between lunacy and idiocy. It is very doubtful whether the distinction is fully understood by the majority of natives, and it seems quite certain that it was not preserved in the returns of the last census. We would retain the entry for lepers, but we would restrict the disease to be noted in the returns to the true or black leprosy (*juzam*), as it seems of no great importance to ascertain the number of those who suffer from a mere discoloration of the skin. We have also added an entry for those afflicted with elephantiasis, as we consider that it is desirable to obtain particulars regarding this disease as one of limited geographical distribution.

23. A specimen of the Enumerators Schedule, as approved by us, is appended to this report.

IV. Agency to be Employed

24. In dealing with this portion of the suggestions referred to us for consideration, we have thought most convenient to dispose of all questions relating to the two cognate subjects. A. The agency through which the actual enumeration should be taken, and under this head we class supervision during the enumeration and subsequent scrutiny; B. The agency to be employed in the compilation of the returns containing the information abstracted from the Enumerators Schedules.

25. We are of opinion that it is impossible to employ a paid agency. The objection of expense is alone insurmountable, if, as we believe, results which are accurate can be obtained with an unpaid enumerating staff.

Supposing that each enumerator records the particulars regarding 300 persons and allowing him a fee of Rs. 10 for the job, the paid enumerating staff, exclusive of supervisors, would, taking one province with another, cost at least £630,000. Nor is a paid agency necessary. The village revenue officials under the subordinate Government officers in the northern parts of India, in Oudh, in the Punjab in the North-Western Provinces, in the Central Provinces, Madras in Bombay, and in Burma, are quite able to deal, at all events, with the agricultural population, that is, with by far the greater portion of the people. In other parts of India the headmen of the villages and other local agencies can be trusted to enumerate the people in the localities in which they reside. Where it is necessary, these can be supplemented by the landowners agents and servants, or by the better educated class of villagers themselves.

It may be accepted, we believe, that a fairly efficient unpaid agency can be secured in all provinces to undertake willingly the counting of the inhabitants, and, as has been pointed out in more than one of the reports we have had under-consideration, while such an agency is popular, the introduction of paid and temporary officers, appointed for the purpose, is likely to lead to suspicion on the part of the people, and thus defeat the object we have in view, *viz.*, the acquisition of accurate information as the condition and numbers of the inhabitants.

In towns, unquestionably, there will be instances when paid enumerators must be employed. But it is probable that even in these cases the number will be small.

26. We deprecate the general employment of the police, considering that such action is open to misconception, and may result in some cases in oppression or extortion.

27. It will be necessary to employ a large number of supervisors, whose duty it will be to instruct the enumerators and to test the entries made in the Enumerators Schedules, both previous to the day of census and on that day itself. These men should be taken from the same classes which supplied the supervising staff on former occasions.

28. As a general rule, we are of opinion that not more than 300 persons, or 60 houses, should be allotted to one enumerator, and if possible, we recommend there should be not less than one supervisor to every ten enumerators during the time devoted to recording the entries prior to the census, while on the day of enumeration the supervising staff should be increased in strength.

These, however, are matters which can only be decided satisfactorily by the several local authorities; and we, therefore; simply throw out suggestions on this head. Briefly, we consider that the agency to be employed in the enumeration, and supervision should, as a rule, be unpaid, though, as it will consist largely, if our recommendations are agreed to, of Government officials and village accountants, we can hardly designate it as voluntary.

29. It remains to suggest by what agency the enumerators, returns should finally be compiled, so as to extract the results of the enumeration. We shall deal with the mode in which the results should be exhibited in a later part of our recommendations.

30. It appears to us that two courses are open either a separate officer of some standing should be appointed to conduct the census operations and to compile the returns derived from the Enumerators Schedules for each province, acting under orders from the Secretariat, Government of India. Statistical Department; or one Census Commissioner should be nominated for the whole of British India, who should undertake this onerous charge.

31. It has been suggested (and Mr. Cornish still adheres to this view) that it would be advisable to appoint a Commission consisting of two or more officers for this work, as has been done in England. But if one officer can undertake the duty, we think there are many reasons which make it expedient to retain the work in the hands of one person, rather than to hand it over to a Commission. There is likely to be less danger of uniformity of precept and practice being occasionally lost sight of, and there will be greater economy.

There are, doubtless, considerable advantages to be looked for if the provincial returns are made over to provincial officers who are necessarily well acquainted with many features of the country and its inhabitants, with which an official deputed from a distance would not probably be cognizant. But we consider the same advantages may be anticipated if provincial officers are employed as deputies to the controlling authority for the whole empire. We believe it is in this manner only that uniformity of precept and practice can be secured throughout the vast area to be dealt with at the enumeration of 1881. But the appointment and employment of local officers should, we recommend, be left entirely to the provincial authorities, who must be responsible for the actual enumeration.

32. We recommend, then, that there should be one controlling officer who should supervise and direct the enumeration in the different provinces, it being clearly understood that the responsibility of the Local Governments as regards the enumeration of the people shall not thereby be weakened. This officer should, in fact, be the adviser of each Local Administration in this matter, and should be responsible for the

compilation of the tables in which is exhibited the information collected at the census. Under this officer, who might be designated the Census Commissioner, a deputy should be employed in each province, under whose supervision the census would be taken, and who would manage the provincial office where the abstracts for each province would be compiled. It might in some few cases be necessary, and undoubtedly would be so in Bengal, to have branch offices for compilation where there is any difficulty in procuring, at the headquarters of the province, clerks who could work up the returns given in characters other than those in general use at the headquarters. Both the Census Commissioner and his deputies should be employed some time previous to the date of the census. The chief controlling officer would have to see that the instructions preliminary to the enumeration were uniform and explicit, and would have to make such modifications in them as might be required to meet the necessities of particular provinces. He would be responsible for exactitude of definition in regard to the terms to be employed, and, in those cases where indentical definitions could not be made use of, would have to arrange that the information obtained, if not the same absolutely throughout the empire, should at all event be sufficiently akin in the different provinces to lead to no confusion in the compilation and subsequent comparisons.

He would have to visit each province and there consult with the local authorities as to the measures to be adopted preliminary to the census, and in concert with them formulate the instructions most applicable for the purpose of the enumeration and best suited to the circumstances of the locality, explaining the directions issued for the guidance of the district officers in the several provinces, so as to maintain uniformity in the system of enumeration and identity of information in the compilation of the tables.

33. It is not possible in a great continent like India, with a population of 189,000,000 of people, to frame identical instructions which shall be practically applicable to each separate portion of the vast whole; and yet it is absolutely essential that the information obtained and the mode of dealing with it, so as to exhibit it in the most simple and comprehensive form, should be, if not the same, at all events, of a really similar character.

For instance, we may note the great difficulty in obtaining one definition which shall accurately describe the House of Bengal, of Madras and the North-Western Provinces, or Bombay, or of defining by one formula the village of Malabar and the village of the North-Western Provinces. The Madras report notes that:

The number of villages with populations from 3,000 to 10,000 is much swelled by the inclusion of those peculiar divisions of the Malabar country called amshoms, which properly speaking, are not villages at all.

The amshom is really the smallest revenue division there is in Malabar, and is generally a tract of country some square miles in extent, in which there is no such thing as a village, but a series of scattered homesteads and farms where the owner of the land and his servants reside, not in one hamlet, but separate and apart, the owner on his farm, the different castes of cultivators living apart, in single separate huts or in scattered collections of huts. A village in the North-Western Provinces, the Punjab and Oudh, is a distinct and well-defined collection of houses, sometimes with an outlying hamlet known by a distinctive name. Similar difficulties in the way of uniformity of terms might be pointed to in other directions. But we do not consider it necessary to dwell on this subject longer.

34. In connection with it, however, the Committee would draw attention to the necessity for extreme care in the laying down of boundaries and areas. We have been compelled to consider this matter by the remarkable difficulties which were experienced in Bengal by the officers charged with the conduct of the census at the late enumeration. Thus, it was found in one district that while the register which formed the basis of the enumeratioin numbered 4,999 villages local enquiry elicited the existence of nearly another thousand. In another district, it is observed by the Joint Magistrate.

About a year before (the census) the chowkidari registers had been throughly revised and the population roughly counted without any anticipation of a census. Now the police at each thannah were furnished with the cataglogue of map, villages agreeing with the map and with the traced map, and told to re-write their chowkidari registers according to them, reporting where they could not find the villages, or where they had villages not shown in the new catalogues. This may seem a very simple matter, but in practice we found it very difficult. For instance, I found at Patneetollah Police station there were six villages named Chuk Gobind. Moreover, the real names differed frequently from those given in the map. How the officers who made the survey and maps settled the boundaries, I know not; but although, as far as regards Purneah and Rungpur and most of our thannahs as among themselves, I found the boundaries correct, yet when we came to the borders of Maldah and Bogra, which originally formed part of this district, and also the borders of Rajshahye, the number of villages we had to take over or to make over was found to be very great. In the case of Patneetollah, an originally large thannah, the number of villages taken over from Bogra has been so great that it will be necessary to divide the thannah in two. A long time was taken up in the necessary correspondence with other districts, and it is possible that blunders may still remain to be discovered hereafter.

Again, in the district referred to above—Bogra—the Collector wrote:

> As the officers of the surrounding districts as well as myself were working on the basis of the survey maps, no questions as to the theoretical boundaries arose; but practically, it was found that a very considerable number of villages had hitherto been treated as within the jurisdiction of police stations other than those within which according to the map they should be included, and similarly, that some villages near the boundary had been treated as belonging to districts other than those to which the map assigned them.

These are not the only instances of the confusion which existed in the Province of Bengal in regard to the territorial divisions of area and the number of villages really contained therein. It is obvious that with no real datum line to which to refer either areas or lists of villages it is quite impossible to make sure that all the inhabitants, of a district are enumerated, or, on the other hand, that they are not enumerated in some cases twice over, though this latter error is not likely to occur often. We are not aware how in districts where survey operations are said to have been completed such confusion as has been reported could have occurred. But the fact remains that it arose, and it is by no means clear that errors do not still exist undiscovered.

In Mysore an instance occurred of an entire village escaping enumeration. But with the better administrative system in force there, this error was detected when the lists of villages were compared with the lists of census schedules sent it. In Bengal it seems probable that such errors may have escaped unnoticed.

We would strongly urge the propriety of making such arrangements at once in Bengal as will render impossible the recurrence of such a state of things as has been reported by some of the district officers.

V. Mode of Compiling the Census Tables

35. We now pass to the mode of tabulating the returns so as to bring out in the most simple and exhaustive method the information acquired.

In dealing with this question we have laid down the principle that our Indian tables should, as much as possible conform in shape to English models, at the same time that they permit of comparison with the figures of former enumerations where the forms have not been based on English exemplars.

36. In regard to the tabulation of the census schedules, we think it advisable that the scheme of compilation should be so arranged as to show the following results:

(a) Density of population, giving the number of persons per house and per square mile.

(b) Increase or decrease of population compared with previous enumerations. Similar information should be tabulated for the various sub-divisions of districts which form the circles for the registration of births and deaths in the several provinces. We propose to show the distribution of the population.

(c) by religion,

(d) by civil condition,

(e) by age,

(f) by birth-place and language,

(g) by occupation, and

(h) by education.

In regard to the above heads, we think it desirable to arrange the tables so as to combine information in regard to sex, age and civil condition for each main religious division. We also propose to show the civil condition of the people in quinquennial periods of age except in the first ten years of life.

37. We do not propose any specific table for the distribution of the people by castes.

In the numerations of previous year, at all events from 1865 in the North-Western Provinces, an attempt has been made, while the work of compilation was being carried on, to classify the people according to caste and sect. This has, in every instance, added very largely to the labour of the census compilation, and has not, we consider, been attended with results adequate to the labour involved.

Previous to 1865 it was considered sufficient to tabulate the population according to religion only. Following the precedent of later enumerations, we have provided in the schedule the means of collecting information in regard to the castes and sects prevailing among the inhabitants of the British Indian empire. But we hesitate to recommend that the information so recorded should be brought together in more than major detail in the tables to be used much practical experience in this direction, we have no hesitation in saying that there is no part of the work of compilation which presents so many difficulties, involves so much labour, and at the same time is so unsatisfactory when completed, as the working up of the caste tables. They add enormously, and we think needlessly, to the bulk of the reports, and the frequent occurrence of unknown or illegible subdivisions of caste in the Enumerators Schedules involves the census office in endless correspondence, and encourages the fudging of the abstracts by the clerks employed in compilation.

We are inclined to think that the statistics on this head, if it be thought desirable to group them together, should form the subject of a special compilation to be undertaken by an antiquarian rather than a statistical authority, and entirely independent of, and apart from the establishment or officer employed in tabulating the census figures.

There are doubtless lines of enquiry in connection with caste which, if carefully followed up, might add much interesting information to our knowledge of native life.

The proportion of the sexes in the various castes:

> the distribution of occupations throughout the several castes;
> the fertility of the people in relation to caste distinctions in regard to marriage, or as influenced by caste restrictions as to food;
> the prevalence of infanticide in particular clans;
> the civil condition of the castes;
> the increase or decrease of the free-thinking or independent sects;
> the breakup or spread of caste divisions and other subjects which are referable to caste peculiarities;
>
> are all matters pregnant to the social philosopher and the philanthropist. But we do not consider it advisable that they should find a place in the tables or reports relating properly to the enumeration of the people.

These are all objects of special enquiry, and can be treated best by specialists. If they were all, or any of them included in the scope of enquiry to which the census officer is restricted, the task assigned to him would be far more than could accomplish. In one province alone—Madras—it was found at the last enumeration that the inhabitants were returned under no less than 3,208 different designations of caste and sect. By very careful grouping these varied classes were reduced to 309. But even this diminished number gave separate details for castes embracing as few individuals as the following:

Kayats	65
Marvadi	181
Karttiam	262
Kulatopan	106
Tolikotan	478
Asavan	412
Turayan	237
Tryambadi	358

and there are no less than 78 classes, each containing less than 10,000 persons in addition to those already mentioned as containing less than 500. It is unnecessary to point out how largely the difficulty of classification by caste is increased when we come to deal with the several provincial populations grouped together in tables dealing with the entire people of the empire. If, then, it is thought necessary that the result of the enquiries as to castes and sects should find a place in the final compilation, we suggest that a numerical standard be taken by which to determine whether a caste or sect shall be separately shown, or shall be included without specification among others. It might be laid down, we think, that no caste or sect less in number than 1,00,000 should be separately in the Caste tables.

We do not consider Mr. Waterfields suggestion to recognise only the four main divisions of Manu is satisfactory. Without pretending to express an opinion on the vexed question whether this fourfold divisions ever really existed in practice, we think we may safely say that nearly all trace of it has disappeared in the present day, and that, with the exception of Brahmans, and, perhaps, a few Rajputs, it would be quite impossible to refer any of the existing castes to the fourfold division. We are, moreover, unable to perceive any practical use in such a classification, supposing that it could be carried out. It is found in practice that it is not possible to draw any line separating Vaisyas and Sudras. Indeed, there is difficulty in drawing the line which distinguishes Kshatriyas and Vaisyas. The Shanans (palm cultivators) in Madras, and the Kayeths in other parts, have set up claims to be recorded as Kshatriyas, and have, in some instances, so entered themselves in census returns. so, also, others of the lower castes have recorded themselves as belonging to a caste of a higher rank; for instance, a fisherman (Sembadavam) was found to have entered himself as a Vaisya. We propose, then, if caste classification is considered to be necessary as a part of the census classification is considered to be necessary as a part of the census compilation, that it shall be effected in a far simpler manner than has hitherto been followed. We would suggest that the castes and sects should be arranged alphabetically, details being given for each group that exceeds 100,000 in number, these being further classed under the following major heads:

I. Hindus:

(a) Brahmans	Details arranged alphabetically for each class exceeding 100,000
(b) Kshatriyas	Ditto Ditto
(c) Other Hindus, including Sikhs	

II. Muhammedan:

(d) Sunnis
(e) Shiahs
(f) Wahabis
(g) Others without detail

III. Christians:

(h) Church of England
(i) Roman Catholics
(j) Presbyterians
(k) Baptists
(l) Wesleyans
(m) Armenians
(n) Greeks
(o) Syrians
(p) Others

IV. Buddhists:

(q) Buddhists
(r) Jains
(s) Chinese

V. Others:

(t) Jews
(u) Parsees
(v) Others in similar details

It is to be understood that where particular circumstances may make it desirable to secure detailed information in regard to any special sect or class, whatever its number, the Local Administration will arrange for this as may appear most convenient at the time of the census. We do not, however, recommend indeed we are completely opposed to any classification by castes of the Hindu population of British India.

38. In regard to the classification of the people according to occupation, we are of opinion that the census tabulation should show the industrial pursuits of the people in detail, and that the classification of Dr. Farr, as adopted in the English census of 1871, should be followed. It will be necessary to have prepared in each province, in vernacular and English, lists of the occupations prevailing in the several provinces, arranged according to the classes and orders followed in Dr. Farr's method, which will be used by the supervising and compiling officers employed in connection with the census. We have arranged for the preparation of such lists in that part of our remarks which relates to the issue of preliminary instructions. A majority of the committee is opposed to the detailed classification of the occupations of the people according to age, as productive of a great amount of labour for very inadequate results. In England it was thought advisable to classify each occupation by age, in order to show the proportion of young children engaged in manufacturing industries, or other spheres of child-labour; but in India the information is needed in regard to the ages of people employed in the few cotton or jute mills at present working, a more correct return would be obtained by a special enquiry. The President of the Committee, however, is in favour of tabulating the occupations of the people by age.

39. In regard to the classification of the people as educated or uneducated, we accept the principle laid down in Mr. Waterfield's memorandum, that the tabulation of the census results should show:

(1) persons of either sex under instruction;
(2) persons of either sex not under instruction, and able to read and write;
(3) persons of either sex not under instruction, and unable to read and write.

We think this arrangement dispenses with the necessity for any classification by age similar to that adopted at the former census.

40. We have next to consider the modifications which, in our opinion, are necessary to make the statistical forms laid down by the Government of India in the Resolution dated 30th September 1871 useful in showing the information secured in the revised form of house schedule.

The general results of the Indian census of 1871 were directed to be shown in fourteen tables or statements, the forms for which accompany the Resolution referred to.

As it is proposed to include much new matter in regard to the civil condition, occupations, birth-places and languages of the people, we propose that the number of standard forms shall be increased from fourteen to twenty-eight.

A list of the proposed forms will be found in the appendix, and we have now briefly to explain why the changes in, and additions to, the standard forms of 1871 are suggested.

41. The forms used in 1871 were distinguished by letters and numbers, as No. 1, A, No. 2, B, but we think it more convenient to adopt consecutive numbers for all the standard forms.

We consider that in tables which are intended to show proportions these should be given not by percentages, which frequently involve the use of a number of decimal points, but by showing the proportion in every 10,000 of the population.

We have omitted percentages or proportions in the age statements; and where tables give the proportions of males per 10,000 we have not thought it necessary to add columns showing similar information for females, as being an unnecessary reduplication of columns, attended with no advantage.

We have throughout the tables omitted to enter any column for remarks. If remarks are necessary, they should be noted at the foot of the tables.

We agree with Mr. Waterfield that where, owing to a defect of specification in the enumerators return, information in any class not given for every individual in the population, the totals should be made to correspond with the total for the province or district by the addition of the numbers not specified.

42. The statement No. IV. of the Government of India forms, relating to land and land revenue in reference to populations, we have not included in the proposed list of standard forms. In those provinces in which the necessary details can be furnished by revenue authorities, the table should be given as heretofore; but the details are of such a nature that they cannot readily be obtained in connection with the ordinary operations of a census.

We may note, however, with reference to the Registrar-General's remarks on this head, that in previous enumerations there has been no attempt, as he implies, to mix up any enquiry into the land revenue with the census. When the information was accessible in the revenue offices and this is very largely the case care was taken that it should find a place in the final statements appended to the report, just as extracts from the agricultural returns of England are incorporated with certain tables in the English census report.

43. The first four forms, Nos. 1 to 4, according to our proposals, will contain abstract and general statements, relating to the population, and will deal with the subjects included in the old forms 1A and 1B.

Tables 5, 6, 7, 8, and 9 will include all the information it is thought desirable to tabulate in regard to the civil condition of the people.

The tables 10 to 15 inclusive will deal with the ages of the people. It is proposed to classify by quinquennial periods, and by each year of infant-life upto the age of 5. Special arrangements are provided in the tabulation columns for comparing the results of the last Indian census in which the ages 6 and 12 were specially given. This is done by showing each year of age up to 6 separately, and by sub-dividing the quinquennial period 10 to 15 into two columns 10 to 12, 12 to 15.

For Birth-place and Language two tables Nos. 16 and 17 are suggested. It is not proposed that birth-place for less minute territorial divisions than provinces shall be separately distinguished.

The Occupations of the people we propose to show in two tables modelled on the English system, Nos. 18 and 19.

The information desired under the head of Education will be tabulated in form No. 20.

For infirmities the results will be given in a separate table for each class of infirmity, as is done in England.

Thus, table No. 21 refers to sex and ages of persons of unsound mind in each district.

No. 22 gives the same information in regard to deaf-mutes.

No. 23 - Blind

No. 24 - Lepers

No. 25 Persons affected with elephantiasis.

Table No. 26 is intended for the classification of towns and villages according to the number of their population and is identical with table No. VII. of the standard form of 1871.

Table No. 27 is nearly the same as No. VIII of the standard forms, and has been altered mereiy to show the numbers of each sex in towns with over 5,000 inhabitants; and by increasing slightly the number of columns, a comparison between the last and the present census is effected.

Table No. 28 also is a modification of Table No. IX of the standard forms, and is identical with that adopted in the North-West Provinces at the 1871 census, which permits of the density of the population being exhibited.

It may be observed in regard to all these proposed forms that they are suited for the compilation of the results in any description of territorial sub-division, as well as for a province; and that they can be used with equal facility for collating the census results of the whole of the Indian Empire.

VI. The Printing and Preparation of the Forms and Preliminary Instructions

44. Having now recommended the shape to be given to the forms used for enumeration and compilation, we have to deal with their printing and preparation, previous to the enumeration, and also with the preliminary instructions to be issued and arrangements to be made prior to the census.

For enumerating so large a population, the printing and preparation of the forms will be a serious undertaking. But if put in hand early, the provincial Government presses will not, we believe, have any difficulty in working off the requisite number. From enquiries we have made, we have ascertained that no economy will be secured by letting the printing be done in England. But it is otherwise in obtaining the paper required. A good durable straw paper, which can be purchased in London cheaply, might, with advantage, be used for the house schedules, and should be ordered through the Superintendent of Stationery in sufficient time to allow of the printing of the tendent of stationery in sufficient time to allow of the printing of the forms being completed, by the 1st September 1880. The requisite supply of this paper should be furnished to the Local Governments, with the exception noted subsequently, and they should print the necessary forms required for distribution.

It would probably save expense if the schedules for the North-Western Provinces, the Punjab and Oudh were issued in print from the Calcutta Government Press, where steam permits more economical printing than is possible in the hand-printing offices in Allahabad and Lahore.

45. The forms should be in the several local offices, whether tehsils or thannahs or taluqs, at least two months before the date of the final census.

We consider that the chief revenue authority in each province, *e.g.*, the Boards of Revenue in Bengal, Madras, and the North-Western Provinces, the Financial Commissioner in the Punjab, and the Revenue Commissioners elsewhere, should undertake the requisite arrangement preliminary to the enumeration, such as the preparation of lists of areas and villages, of houses, shops, mosques, temples, etc., which will be the first step to take in setting for the division of the country into convenient enumerators circles that together will cover and embrace every part of the provincial area. This should be done in concert with the officer who may be deputed to control the census throughout India. These arrangements and preparatory measures should be completed by the close of the cold season, 1879-80. By the 1st September 1880 all the country should have been parcelled out into enumerators blocks, and the lists of villages and of enumerators, blocks should be with the census officer appointed for each province by that date at latest. By the 1st December the whole of the enumerators and supervisors should have been selected and appointed, this being done by the several district officers ample allowance being made for casualties so as to supply extra men in such cases; and by that date the necessary instructions for enumerators, both in English and vernacular, should be in the district officers hands. The latter officer and his subordinates must arrange that these instructions are carefully explained to, and understood by, the enumerators and supervisors before the 1st January 1881. These instructions with explanations, where necessary, should issue from the Census Office through the chief revenue authorities.

46. There are some matters to which our attention has been drawn in connection with the preliminary instructions which we deem advisable to refer to in our report.

Special measures should be adopted by the officer in charge of the census for securing the enumeration of the floating population and travellers by land and water. There is reason to believe that this was not in all cases arranged for at the last enumeration.

We recommend that a series of simple questions should be drawn up and circulated in character and languages with which the enumerators are familiar, framed so as to secure a correct record of the facts which the enumerator has to record in the schedule. Experience has shown that without some such aid there will be instances where the enumerators are puzzled by the headings of the columns they have to fill in.

We think that attempts should be made at an early date through the local authorities to compile the lists of occupation prevalent in the several districts in the different provinces, to which we have already alluded.

A similar list of castes and sects should be drawn up by the local authorities as soon as possible, if it is eventually decided that our recommendation to omit any compilation of castes is not to be accepted. These lists, if carefully translated and transliterated, will be of great use to the officer entrusted with the duty of managing the enumeration when he commences his preliminary work. The enumerators should be directed to adhere as closely as possible to the nomenclature in these lists, and not to use English terms which they may consider equivalent to the vernacular designation in the list.

In correcting the schedules on the day of the actual enumeration, persons absent at the original record of the entries in the schedule, but present on the day of the census, should be entered in a supplemental sheet, to which the number borne by the original schedule should be given. A line drawn below this figure and the addition of a fractional mark will prevent any confusion, and it is of the utmost importance that no interpolation should be made in the original schedules. Thus, for example, the original schedule No.24, if it had to be supplemented as described above, would be supplemented by a separate schedule marked No. 24/½.

For persons absent on the day of the enumeration, it will suffice to run a line in red ink through the entries relating to them in the original schedule.

It may not be unadvisable to extend the plan followed in the city of Bombay, where the public offices were closed for a certain number of days to permit of the clerks and other officials employed being utilised for the enumeration and supervision.

We do not touch on any of the arrangements to be made subsequent to the census, as these are much better left to the officer in charge of the entire enumeration.

VII. Necessity for Legislation

47. There remains but one other subject to which our attention has been directed, the question of special legislation in view of the next enumeration. Special legislation is said to be appropriate as securing more control to the administration over both enumerators and the enumerated; and in one instance, at least, the want of special legal powers has been felt. The Town Magistrate of Rangoon writes, speaking in regard to the supervision of the enumerators exercised by himself on the night of the census.

We then witnessed the great want of legal authority in the work, for in some of these barracks the people pretended to be asleep, and not to hear the order of police to open their door and bring lights. All was darkness, and the police dare not resort to force.

In Bengal a short Act was passed, and under its authority the census was effected. But its provisions do not seem to have been resorted to, nor were any penalties inflicted under its sections. In Madras the municipal towns, which include a population of less than two millions, have statutory powers for the enumerating of the people within their jurisdiction. But it was not found necessary to have any recourse to the law. In the North-Western Provinces, in Oudh, and the Punjab no legislation was thought necessary on former enumerations. But legislation has been suggested in the Oudh Census Report as not undesirable, and was recommended formerly in Bombay. Thus, though not seeming necessary in every province, as it is apparently required in some parts of the country, we think it would be advisable to pass a short general Act for the whole of India, which, in cases where opposition or apathy put difficulties in the way of the enumeration, would greatly strengthen the hands of the executive. Such an Act should make provision:

(a) for the appointment by Local Government of a person or persons to take an account of the population;
(b) for empowering the chief executive officer of the district to appoint enumerators and supervisors;
(c) for imposing on landholders, tenure-holders and farmers or their agents the duty of rendering such assistance as the local authority may direct;
(d) for empowering enumerators to put questions in accordance with their instructions, and to enter enclosures for the purpose of enumeration;
(e) for imposing penalties for default to give information;
(f) for imposing penalties for misconduct of enumerators;
(g) for defining by whom and before whom prosecutions under the Act should be instituted.

But the President of the Committee does not consider it advisable to legislate generally where the cases in which legislation may be desirable are exceptional. He considers it would be wisest to leave the question of legislation to be dealt with as the local authorities find it desirable, and that if a general Act be passed of the nature indicated above, a clause should be inserted reserving it to the Local Governments to extend the Act to the territories or such portion of those territories they administer, as they think proper.

48. In conclusion, we summarise the results of our deliberations as leading us to the following recommendations:

I. A synchronous census should be taken throughout British India at an early date in February 1881.
II. The enumeration should be effected by a preliminary record

in the householders schedule of the information required, the entries so made being afterwards tested and corrected to agree with the facts on the date of the census.

III. The enumerators or householders schedule should take the shape of the form we have given for it in the Appendix A.

IV. The census should be taken, as far as is possible by an unpaid agency.

V. The information thus secured should be abstracted and worked up by one central census officer, assisted by deputies at the headquarters of the several provinces or elsewhere as may be necessary.

VI. In abstracting this information, it should be thrown into a series of tables which we have appended to this report, Appendix B.

VII. We consider that the local revenue authorities should arrange for the demarcation of boundaries and areas in concert with the Imperial Census Commissioner, and that the Local Governments and Administrations should be responsible for the enumeration, but not for the compilation of the results.

VIII. We think the Imperial Census Commissioner should be responsible for the issue of instructions for the enumeration, as the only practical mode of securing uniformity and identity of information.

IX. We think legislation is advisable to facilitate census operations throughout the country.

There is also one point to which we would draw attention, though it has not been referred to in the papers with which we have had to deal. We think it would be advantageous if the Government would use its influence to secure a contemporaneous enumeration of the residents in Native States or other foreign territories within the Indian Continent.

It is probable that if only a mere numbering of the people by sex were suggested, no opposition would be experienced, and if this were acceded to, our information would be as complete as it could be made of the actual numbers of the people throughout British and Foreign India.

We have the honour to be,
Sir
Your most obedient Servants,
W.C. Plowden, President
H. Beverley,
W.R. Cornish,

The 29th January 1878.

APPENDIX II

THE CENSUS ACT, 1948, (Act No. XXXVII of 1948)

An Act to provide for certain matters in connection with the taking of Census

3rd September, 1948

WHEREAS it is expedient to provide for the taking of census in India or any part thereof whenever necessary or desirable and to provide for certain matters in connection with the taking of such census;

It is hereby enacted as follows:

Short Title and Extent

1. (i) This Act may be called the Census Act, 1948.

(ii) It extends to the whole of India

Rule of Construction Respecting Enactments not Extending to J & K

2. Any reference to the Indian Penal Code or the Indian Evidence Act, 1872, shall, in relation to Jammu and Kashmir, be construed as a reference to the corresponding enactment in force in that State.

Central Government to take Census

3. The Central Government may, by notification in the Official Gazette, declare its intention of taking a census in the whole or any part of the territories to which this Act extends, whenever it may consider it necessary or desirable so to do, and thereupon the census shall be taken.

Appointment of Census Staff

4. (i) The Central Government may appoint a Census Commissioner to supervise the taking of the census throughout the area in which the census is intended to be taken, and Superintendents of Census Operations to supervise the taking of the census within the several States.

(ii) The State Government may appoint persons as census-officers to take, or aid in, or supervise the taking of the census within any specified local area and such persons, when so appointed, shall be bound to serve accordingly.

(iii) A declaration in writing signed by any authority authorised by the State Government in this behalf, that any person has been duly appointed a census officer for any local area shall be conclusive proof of such appointment.

(iv) The State Government may delegate to such authority as it thinks fit the power of appointing census officers conferred by sub-section (2).

Status of Census authorities as Public servants

5. The Census Commissioner, all Superintendents of Census Operations and all census officers shall be deemed to be public servants within the meaning of the Indian Penal Code.

Discharge of duties of Census officers in certain cases

6. (1) Where the District Magistrate or such authority as the State Government may appoint in this behalf, by a written order so directs:

(a) every officer in command of any body of men belonging to the naval, military or air forces, or of any vessel of war, of India,
(b) every person (except a pilot or harbour-master) having charge or control of a vessel,
(c) every person in charge of a lunatic asylum, hospital, workhouse, prison, reformatory or lock-up or of any public, charitable, religious or educational institution,
(d) every keeper, secretary or manager of any sarai, hotel, boarding-house, lodging-house, emigration depot or club,
(e) every manager or officer of a railway or any commercial or industrial establishment, and
(f) every occupant of immovable property wherein at the time of the taking of the census, persons are living,

shall perform such of the duties of a census officer in relation to the persons who at the time of the taking of the census are under his command or charge, or are inmates of his house, or are present on or in such immovable property or are employed under him as may be specified in the order.

45 of 1860

(2) All the provisions of this Act relating to census officers shall apply so far as may be, to all persons while performing such duties under this section and any person refusing or neglecting to perform any duty which under this section he is directed to perform shall be deemed to have committed an offence under section 187 of the Indian Penal Code.

Power to Call Upon Certain Persons to Give Assistance

7. The District Magistrate, or such authority as the State Government may appoint in this behalf for any local area, may by a written order which shall have effect throughout the extent of his district or of such local area, as the case may be, call upon:

(a) all owners and occupiers of land, tenure-holders, and farmers and assignees of land revenue, or their agents,
(b) all members of the district, municipal, panchayat and other local authorities and officers and servants of such authorities, and
(c) all officers and members of staff of any factory, firm or establishment.

to give such assistance as shall be specified in the order towards the taking of a census of the persons who are, at the time of the taking of the census, on the lands of such owners, occupiers, tenure-holders, farmers and assignees, or in the premises of factories, firms and other establishments, or within the areas for which such local authorities are established, as the case may be, and the persons to whom an order under this section is directed shall be bound to obey it and shall, while acting in pursuance of such order, be deemed to be public servants within the meaning of the Indian Penal Code.

Asking of Questions and obligation to answer

8. (1) A census officer may ask all such questions of all persons within the limits of the local area for which he is appointed as, by instructions issued in this behalf by the State Government and published in the Official Gazette, he may be directed to ask.

(2) Every person of whom any question is asked under sub-section (1) shall be legally bound to answer such questions to the best of his knowledge or belief:

Provided that no person shall be bound to state the name of any female member of his household, and no woman shall be bound to state the name of her husband or deceased husband or of any other person whose name she is forbidden by custom to mention.

Occupier to permit access and affixing of numbers

9. Every person occupying any house, enclosure, vessel or other place shall allow census officers such access thereto as they may require for the purposes of the census and as, having regard to the customs of the country may be reasonable and shall allow them to paint on, or affix to the place such letters, marks or numbers as may be necessary for the purposes of the census.

Occupier or Manager to Fill Up Schedule

10. (1) Subject to such orders as the State Government may issue in this behalf, a census officer may, within the local area for which he is appointed, leave or cause to be left as a schedule at any dwelling-house or with the manager or any officer of any commercial or industrial establishment, for the purpose of its being filled up by the occupier of such house or of any specified part thereof or by such manager or officer with such particulars as the State Government may direct regarding the inmates of such house or part thereof, or the persons employed under such manager or officer, as the case may be, at the time of the taking of the census.

(2) When such schedule has been so left, the said occupier, manager or officer, as the case may be, shall fill it up or cause it to be filled up to the best of his knowledge or belief so far as regards the inmates of such house or part thereof or the persons employed under him, as the case may be, at the time aforesaid, and shall sign his name thereto and, when so required, shall deliver the schedule so filled up and signed to the census officer or to such person as the census-officer

may direct.

Penalties

11. (1) (a) Any census-officer or any person lawfully required to give assistance towards the taking of a census who refuses or neglects to use reasonable diligence in performing any duty imposed upon him or in obeying any order issued to him in accordance with this Act or any rule made thereunder, or any person who hinders or obstructs another person in performing any such duty or in obeying any such order, or

(b) any census officer who intentionally puts any offensive or improper question or knowingly makes any false return or, without the previous sanction of the Central Government or the State Government, discloses any information which he has received by means of, or for the purposes of, a census return, or

(c) any sorter, compiler or other member of the census staff who removes secrets, damages or destroys any census document or deals with any census documents in a manner likely to falsify or impair the tabulations of census results, or

(d) any person who intentionally gives a false answer to, or refuses to answer to the best of his knowledge or belief, any question asked of him by a census officer which he is legally bound by section 8 to answer, or

(e) any person occupying any house, enclosure, vessel or other place who refuses to allow a census officer such reasonable access thereto as he is required by section 9 to allow, or

(f) any person who removes, obliterates, alters, or damages any letters,marks or numbers which have been painted or affixed for the purposes of the census, or

(g) any person who, having been required under section 10 to fill up a schedule, knowingly and without sufficient cause fails to comply with the provisions of that section, or makes any false return thereunder, or

(h) any person who trespasses into a census office, shall be punishable with fine which may extend to one thousand rupees and in case of a conviction under part (b) or (c) shall also be punishable with imprisonment which may extend to six months.

(2) Whoever abets any offence under sub-section (1) shall be

punishable with fine which may extend to one thousand rupees.

Sanction Required for Prosecutions

12. No prosecution under this Act shall be instituted except with the previous sanction of the State Government or of an authority authorised in this behalf by the State Government.

Operation of Other Laws Not Barred

13. Nothing in this Act shall be deemed to prevent any person from being prosecuted under any other law for any act or omission which constitutes an offence under this Act:

Provided that no such prosecution shall be instituted except with the previous sanction referred to in section 12.

Jurisdiction

14. No Court inferior to that of a Presidency Magistrate or a Magistrate of the second class, shall try, whether under this Act or under any other law, any act or omission which constitutes an offence under this Act.

Records of Census Not Open to Inspection Nor Admissible in Evidence

15. No person shall have a right to inspect any book, register or record made by a census officer in the discharge of his duty as such, or any schedule delivered under section 10, and notwithstanding anything to the contrary in the Indian Evidence Act, 1872, no entry in any such book, register, record or schedule shall be admissible as evidence in any civil proceeding whatsoever or in any criminal proceeding other than a prosecution under this Act or any other law for any act or omission which constitutes an offence under this Act.

Temporary Suspension of Other Laws as to Mode of Taking Census in Municipalities

16. Notwithstanding anything in any enactment or rule with respect to the mode in which a census is to be taken in any municipality, the municipal authority, in consultation with the Superintendent of Census Operations or with such other authority as the State Government may authorise in this behalf, shall, at the time appointed for the taking of any census cause the census of the municipality to be taken wholly or in part by any method authorised by or under this Act.

Grant of Statistical Abstract

17. The Census Commissioner or any Superintendent of Census Operations or such person as the State Government may authorise in this behalf may, if he so thinks fit, at the request and cost (to be determined by him) of any local authority or person, cause abstracts to be prepared and supplied containing any such statistical information as can be derived from the census returns for India or any State, as the case may be, being information which is not contained in any published report and which in his opinion it is reasonable for that authority or person to require.

Power to Make Rule

18. (1) The Central Government may make rules for carrying out the purposes of this Act.

(2) In particular, and without prejudice to the generality of the foregoing power, the Central Government may make rules providing for the appointment of census officers and of persons to perform any of the duties of census officers or to give assistance towards the taking of a census, and for the general instructions to be issued to such officers and persons.

INDEX